Roads & Kingdoms Presents

RICE, NOODLE, FISH

RICE, NOODLE, FISH

Deep Travels Through Japan's Food Culture

—

MATT GOULDING
EDITED BY NATHAN THORNBURGH

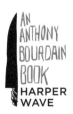

AN ANTHONY BOURDAIN BOOK
HARPER WAVE

HarperCollins books may be purchased for educational, business, or sales promotional use.
For information, please e-mail the Special Markets Department at spsales@harpercollins.com.

FIRST EDITION

Designed by Doug Hughmanick

Library of Congress Cataloging-in-Publication Data

Goulding, Matt.
Rice, noodle, fish : deep travels through Japan's food culture / Matt Goulding ; edited by
Nathan Thornburgh. — First Edition.
pages cm
ISBN 978-0-06-239403-3
1. Food habits—Japan. 2. Food tourism—Japan. 3. Goulding, Matt—Travel—Japan. I. Title.
GT2853.J3G68 2015
394.1'2—dc23   2015005013

15 16 17 18 19   ID/RRD   10 9 8 7 6 5 4 3 2 1

To the shokunin *of Japan, pursuers of perfection,*
for showing us the true meaning of devotion

CONTENTS

IN CORRESPONDENCE WITH BOURDAIN:
How this book was born

Dear Tony,

I'm writing you from a laundromat attached to an old teahouse down a dark alley in Kyoto. I've spent the past month eating my way south from Hokkaido—from the *uni* shrines of Hakodate to the *okonomiyaki* dens of Osaka. I've been invited to dine with the Sugimoto clan tonight, the oldest family in Kyoto, in their 300-year-old home with their 600-year-old recipes, and I need something decent to wear. So while five weeks' worth of memories dissolve in the spin cycle, let me tell you about this idea I have.

If *Parts Unknown* and its many imitators have taught us anything, it's that we're living in the Golden Age of Gastrotourism. The same people who once traveled to Rome to stare at statues now go to twirl bucatini on their forks and filter balls of burrata onto their Instagram accounts. You've helped inspire a generation of food-obsessed pilgrims, the same people we try to reach every day at Roads & Kingdoms: the ones who want to be smarter, eat better, travel deeper. We've given them ice cream crawls in Mogadishu, the chili sauce wars of the Caucasus, the burger kings of Karachi.

But it feels like there's something even bigger out there to tap into, a more complete way to capture the seismic shift that takes place inside of us as we first eat our way through a country. And Japan, where a tangle of undressed noodles can feel like a seminal life moment, is the perfect place to start. I'm imagining a book that attempts to make sense of the many wondrous, beautiful, confounding things the outsider experiences here—both at the table and beyond.

I don't have any clear answers yet, but I know you share my affection for this country and I thought this might be something you'd want to be a part of. Give it some thought and let me know what you think. I'll be here, watching the laundry spin.

Cheers,
Matt

* * *

Dear Matt,

That's pretty much where I'd like to be right now, preparing to go out to dinner in a 300-year-old home—in Kyoto. I stayed in a magnificent old *ryokan* there once, so old there were sword slashes in the ceiling beams. Evidence, I was told, of samurai-related violence.

As you know, Japan hooked me. It was the first Asian country I ever visited. I was alone, clueless, horribly, cripplingly jet-lagged (back when I still suffered from such things), and on an ill-fated mission to consult on a French restaurant project. I'd wake up in Roppongi early in the morning to the shrieks of those giant crows and wander the streets, trying to summon the courage to enter a noodle shop. I will never forget the sense of deep satisfaction I felt when I finally managed to order breakfast for myself.

Tokyo was so dense, so crowded with . . . stuff, so complicated, tempting, delicious, and seemingly unknowable: layer upon layer of maddeningly interesting izakayas in one building alone. One city block a life's work of exploration. It was a glorious and lasting derangement of the senses that first trip, and I've never been the same since.

I became selfish that first time in Tokyo in ways I had never been. Previously, when viewing something incredible, impressive, strikingly beautiful, or interesting, my first instinct was to share. Who might I share this with? How might I best relate this experience?

In Tokyo, alone and traumatized in the best possible ways by this new universe of possibilities, I just said "fuck it" to that voice. This was for me. There was no sharing. I wanted more—whatever it took—and I resolved, consciously or not, I think, to burn down the whole world if necessary to get more of this.

In Japan you are confronted constantly, almost violently, with how much you don't know. I liked that feeling. I liked that steep, virtually impossible learning curve. I liked, it turned out, that feeling of being a stranger in a strange yet wonderful land, not understanding the language, lost. Every little thing was a discovery.

Things kind of worked out. I found a way to ensure many more trips to Japan, television being a small price to pay for the privilege. I know now exactly what you mean when you speak of the joys of undressed noodles. I yearn for the smoke and sizzle of many parts of pampered chickens in an old-school yakitori joint, the clean smell of the fish market at four in the morning (cigarettes and seawater), *chankonabe*, grilled fish collars in Golden Gai, the glory of the Japanese bathroom. They may work punishingly, insanely hard in Japan. But they have relaxation down to a science. To spend a weekend at a traditional *ryokan*, marinating in an outdoor *onsen*, is a life-changing thing. There's no going back. Not all the way back anyway.

I don't know if you know this but I've found that if you sat at a table with eight or nine of the worlds best chefs—from France, Brazil, America, wherever—and you asked them where they'd choose if they had to eat in one, and only one country, for the rest of their lives, they would ALL of them pick Japan without hesitation. We both know why.

I have no doubt that you would make that case brilliantly in the book to come, but I'm going to need more details if I want to convince my cruel masters at HarperCollins. How do you see this playing out on the page?

Best,

Tony

* * *

Hi Tony,

I know what you mean when you say you've never been the same. I'm supposed to be on a honeymoon with my Catalan wife, but every time a piece of *uni* nigiri or *shirako* tempura is placed before me, I feel like I'm cheating on her. I try to shift the focus back to my bride, but then I look over and see her eyes glazed with that same new Japan sheen, and I know that there will forever be a line in our lives: Before Japan, After Japan.

I could see how you would want to keep this to yourself. Something so intense and intimate— it's hard to share without feeling like you're somehow butchering the translation. Judging by the episodes you've logged from Japan, though, you got over that feeling, no doubt for much the same reason that I'm getting over it: we tell stories for a living, and these stories are the best I've found anywhere.

I'm in Noto now, a windswept peninsula on the west coast known as the Kingdom of Fermentation. Breakfast this morning was a piece of mackerel cured in salt and chilies for 12 years (my body is still buzzing from the umami). Chikako Fukushita is the daughter of Noto's preeminent pickle masters: her father has been honored by the governor for his fish sauce, her mother is the sole keeper of over 300 recipes that represent the family's—and Noto's—legacy. They never had a son, so it has fallen to Chikako to catalog every last recipe before they pass away.

The plan is to stay here as long as it takes to find stories like these—deep, experiential narratives that tell us something about this country that only the food and its creators can. On the horizon: a Guatemalan immigrant turned *okonomiyaki* master in Hiroshima, a rebel band of sea urchin fishermen in Hokkaido, and a ramen blogger from Fukuoka who eats 400 bowls of *tonkotsu* a year.

I've talked with my Roads & Kingdoms partners about this idea and they're all in. Beyond the high-protein narratives, we see a series of lighter side stories, photo essays, and illustrated decoders illuminating the most interesting corners of Japanese culture. Doug Hughmanick built our website and would be perfect for designing big, beautiful spreads about the glories of the Japanese convenience store or how to navigate a love hotel. Nathan Thornburgh, whom you already know from his days at *Time* magazine, is an intense and uncompromising editor, ready to make whatever I write stronger.

Good thing, because despite the beauty of these stories, there is infinite potential to make an ass of myself. I'm a novice here. I speak no Japanese. I claim no special understanding of this dense culture and hold no key to unlock the country's many closed doors. I went to a very famous sushi restaurant in Tokyo last week, a place that destroyed me the first time I ate there. I came back with a translator and a suit jacket, waited for two hours until the last guests trickled out, then asked the chef if I might arrange an interview. His jaw dropped, his face contorted. "Why would you come here?" he said. "Next time, please go through the embassy."

I spent the next 24 hours steaming, appalled by the suggestion of involving diplomats to talk about rice and fish and somehow offended that he didn't want to share his story. But deep down there's something almost noble about his reaction: with only six seats and a loyal local clientele, his only objective now is to protect what he has.

There is no escaping my place as the most outside of outsiders here, so I might as well embrace it. There will be plenty of expertise proffered along the way, just not from me—from the chefs and artisans and families who have this cuisine in their DNA, and who have opened up many doors as I've begun to eat my way through this country.

So the big question is, just who is this book for? People already on their way to Japan? People parked in the armchair with no immediate plans to hit the road? The burrata Instagrammers? You're the book guy these days, and no doubt the suits at HarperCollins will want to know. Any guidance you might have will be rewarded with a fugu sake (a blowfish tail set alight and dropped into a glass of rice wine—a group of salarymen hazed me with this hellbroth last night) next time we cross paths.

Cheers,
Matt

* * *

Matt,

Thinking about the smell of hinoki wood. You know the smell. One of those deep water tubs that comes up to your chin. Scaldingly hot water, washcloth on head. Maybe a bottle of sake close at hand.

Do you have any tattoos? This is one of the peculiarities of Japan I find both charming and annoying at the same time. Every time I hit a public *onsen*—or a hotel pool for that matter— as soon as the shirt comes off, some very uncomfortable-looking attendant comes running over with a rash guard to cover me up. Apparently, it's a non-insulting way to keep yakuza out. I wish they would just go with a sign saying "NO GANGSTERS" instead of busting my balls but what can you do? I put the damn rash guard on.

What do you read when in Japan? In Vietnam, it's *The Quiet American* every time. Often, I find it's fiction that better describes a place—the atmospherics, the soul. Graham Greene, being such a terrific traveling companion, it's too bad he never set a novel in Japan. Lowry in Mexico. Orwell in Myanmar. Theroux in Singapore. But Japan? I'm at a loss.

I usually end up watching DVDs that capture better (or more easily) the hallucinatory aspects of Tokyo or Osaka. I've described experiencing Japanese nightlife as like living inside a pinball machine—or dropping acid for the first time—inside yet always outside.

Making an ass of yourself in Japan is an inevitability. Fortunately, we gaijin seem to get cut a lot of slack. I recall with embarrassment being treated to an elaborate kaiseki meal and the elderly geishas who were there to entertain bursting into peals of laughter as I tucked unknowingly into a bowl with my chopsticks, blissfully unaware that it was the condiment not the entree. It's a minefield of potential offense. I'm quite certain that at all times that every single thing about me is somehow "wrong," from my posture, the way I hold my chopsticks, bow, pour my drink, sit, cross my legs—and so on. But I don't care. Japan is just too awesome to not just forge on.

I don't know why you would call that delightful burning fugu tail drink a hellbroth. I love that shit.

And as I sit here and reflect on "who this book is for and what its appeal might be" I no longer care. The more layers you can peel back, the better. The deeper you dive into all those things that make Japan so fascinating and so pleasurable to us, the better for humanity.

Roads & Kingdoms has for some time now been doing the best travel journalism out there. It's not just WHAT it is—but what it is NOT. You're cutting right to the good shit. A person could easily miss what you had the good sense to celebrate. There is enormous value in that.

This is, after all, the beginning of what I fully expect to be a long and fruitful relationship. An unholy alliance between you—Roads & Kingdoms—and whatever it is that I do for a living.

Readers will either read the book and immediately book tickets to Japan to explore for themselves. They will return changed. Unable to look at the world in the same way ever again. Or . . . they might refine and adjust whatever sadly misguided plans they might have had in favor of destinations described here.

Or they might sit in their chairs and dream of a faraway place where the culture is very old, the food extraordinary and refined beyond imagining, and where there are many beautiful things that feel good.

And someday, if given the opportunity to see this place for themselves, hopefully, they will leap.

The world needs Roads & Kingdoms. It needs this book. Let's give it to them.

Best,
Tony

Chapter One
TOKYO

—

If you listen carefully, you will hear the sounds of Japan cooking. But these are not the sounds of a typical kitchen, even a great one, at work—at least not the ones you may be used to hearing. It's not an expediter on a line asking when his rib steak will be ready. It's not the gurgle of a deep fryer violently crisping a thatch of potatoes. It's not the sound of a sauce being scraped across the plate with the back of a spoon, or the pinch of tweezers art-directing another foraged herb into position.

It is the sound of a terry-cloth towel rubbed against the grain of hardwood, scrubbing for hours each night to re-move the gentle stain of fish oils accumulated on the hinoki counter over the course of a sushi service. It is the gentle rustle of fingers gliding over green coffee beans, like wind in the trees, in search of imperfections before roasting. It is the whoosh of a handmade fan used to tame a *binchotan* fire. The dull thump of polished wood against the soft flesh of tomato. The muted cadence of a long, thin knife working its way across the flesh of a conger eel.

These are the sounds of Japan cooking. And everything that you will put in your mouth begins with one of these sounds, barely audible, that rises up and amplifies and takes on a force of its own. In the most perfect moment, when you least expect it, these little whispers will build into a great sonic boom, and all you can do is close your eyes and let it wash over you.

If all of this feels precious, that's because it is. One of your first revelations in Japan, especially while eating, will be just how much the details matter: the angle of the maple leaf garnishing your plate, the mood of the chef when frying your asparagus, the bloodline of the farmer who grew that radish. The fact that you—and everyone else, including experienced Japanese diners—will miss most of these details doesn't matter; there is the underlying belief that nearly imperceptible improvements are made in the quality of the food by the most subtle actions of its creators. The tempura batter tastes better when stirred with chopsticks from the Meiji era; the dashi is purer when simmered by a cook with a clear mind and a light heart.

But not everything is so subtle. There are succulent loins of fatty pork fried in scales of thin bread crumbs and served with bowls of thickened Worcestershire and dabs of fiery mustard. Giant pots of curry, dark and brooding as a sudden summer storm, where apples and onions and huge hunks of meat are simmered into submission over hours. Or days. There is *okonomiyaki*, the great geologic mass of carbs and cabbage and pork fat that would feel more at home on a stoner's coffee table than a Japanese tatami mat.

And, of course, there is ramen, the loudest of all Japanese foods, a soundtrack of thwacks, sizzles, drips, and slurps that undermines everything you thought you knew about this country and its culture. Is that cook chopping leeks to the bass of a hip-hop track? Why yes, yes he is.

No country on this planet inspires wonder like Japan does. Everywhere you turn, you will find a reason to be astounded.

It starts on the airplane, twenty

thousand feet above Tokyo. I remember my first approach to Narita, when the plane knifed through the clouds and suddenly there it was, the biggest city in the history of the earth, pixilated in a billion yellow dots below me. In the early 1600s, when the shogun Tokugawa Ieyasu decided to build his castle here, Tokyo was nothing but a tiny fishing village. By 1800 it was already the largest city in the world, with more than a million people calling Japan's new capital home. Over the years, it would shake, shatter, splinter, and burn again and again. And still it stands and stretches on to infinity.

I first came to Tokyo in the fall of 2008 with no plans, no reservations, not the slightest clue about the transformation that awaited me. With six thousand miles separating me from sleep, I stumbled down into the subway at dawn and emerged on the outskirts of the Tsukiji market just as the sun broke across Tokyo Bay. Inside the market, I saw the entire ocean on display: swollen-bellied salmon, dark disks of abalone, vast armies of exotic crustaceans, conger eels so shiny and new they looked to be napping in their Styrofoam boxes. I stumbled onward to a tuna auction, where a man in a trader's cap worked his way through a hundred silver carcasses scattered across the cement floor, using a system of rapid hand motions and guttural noises unintelligible to all but a select group of tuna savants. When the auction ended, I followed one of the bodies back to its buyer's stall, where a man and his son used band saw, katana blade, cleaver, and fillet knife to work the massive fish down into sellable components: sinewy tail meat for the cheap izakaya, ruby loins for hotel restaurants, blocks of marbled belly for the high-end sushi temples.

By 8:00 a.m. I was starving. First, a sushi feast, a twelve-piece procession of Tsukiji's finest—fat-frizzled bluefin, chewy surf clam, a custardy slab of Hokkaido *uni*—washed down with frosty glasses of Kirin. Then a bowl of warm

The largest city on earth, as seen from Roppongi Hills

soba from the outer market, crowned at the last second with a golden nest of vegetable tempura. By the time the sun had climbed directly above me, I stood before a wall of skyscrapers, smiling stupidly, uncomfortably full but hungrier than ever.

If you've never been before, you will do what we all do when we first come to Japan: you will blink and rub your eyes like a cartoon character, you will lose yourself in the human churn of Shibuya and Shinjuku, you will bear witness to the fantastic collision of past and future as you move from neon jungle to ancient temple and back into Tomorrowland. You will marvel at the plastic food, the bullet trains, the omnipresent vending machines. You will take pictures of toilets. Your e-mails back home will be filthy with exclamation points.

You will feel completely and wonderfully overwhelmed by the stimuli, and there will be moments when you don't know what to do. Which way to turn. Which person to ask. Which dish to eat.

It's the last one that gets me every time. What to eat? You've crossed a dozen time zones to get here and you want to make every meal count. Do you start at an izakaya, a Japanese pub, and eat raw fish and grilled chicken parts and fried tofu, all washed down with a river of cold sake? Do you seek out the familiar nourishment of noodles—ramen, udon, soba—and let the warmth and beauty of this cuisine slip gloriously past your lips? Or maybe you wade into the vast unknown, throw yourself entirely into the world of unfamiliar flavors: a bowl of salt-roasted eel, a mound of sticky fermented soybeans, a nine-course kaiseki feast.

You would be ill-advised to take this decision lightly. Make no mistake about it: Tokyo is the greatest feast on earth. Not New York. Not Paris. Not Bangkok. All of these cities offer sprawling, beautiful food cultures worthy of a lifetime of exploration, but none can compare with the depth and breadth of deliciousness proffered by Tokyo's culinary legions.

First of all, it's the size. New York City has some 30,000 restaurants; Tokyo, 300,000. (Take a moment to let that sink in, please.) Whereas most of the world confines their restaurants to street level, a ten-story building in Japan might have two or three restaurants on every floor, towers of deliciousness stretched toward the heavens like Babel.

But Tokyo's preeminence as the world's most exciting dining destination isn't a quantity thing: it's a quality one. There are a dozen factors that make Japanese food so special—ingredient obsession, technical precision, thousands of years of meticulous refinement—but chief among them is one simple concept: specialization. In the Western world, where miso-braised short ribs share menu space with white truffle pizza and sea bass ceviche, restaurants cast massive nets to try to catch as many fish as possible, but in Japan, the secret to success is choosing one thing and doing it really fucking well. Forever. There are people who dedicate their entire lives to

grilling beef intestines, slicing blowfish, kneading buckwheat into tangles of chewy noodles—microdisciplines with infinite room for improvement.

The concept of *shokunin*, an artisan deeply and singularly dedicated to his or her craft, is at the core of Japanese culture. Japan's most famous *shokunin* these days is Jiro Ono, immortalized in the documentary *Jiro Dreams of Sushi*, but you will encounter his level of relentless focus across the entire food industry. Behind closed doors. Down dark alleyways. Up small stairwells. Hiding in every corner of this city and country: the eighty-year-old tempura man who has spent the past six decades discovering the subtle differences yielded by temperature and motion. The twelfth-generation *unagi* sage who uses metal skewers like an acupuncturist uses needles, teasing the muscles of wild eel into new territories. The young man who has grown old at his father's side, measuring his age in kitchen lessons. Any moment now, it will be his turn to be the master, and when he does, he'll know exactly what to do.

"The *shokunin* has a social obligation to work his or her best for the general welfare of the people," says Japanese sculptor Tasio Odate. "This obligation is both spiritual and material, in that no matter what it is, the *shokunin*'s responsibility is to fulfill the requirement."

Tokyo is the city of ten thousand *shokunin*. If you come to Japan to eat, you come for them.

At first I didn't get this. I ate nothing but ramen and udon and tempura from any place that looked legit—and I was deeply satisfied doing it. But then a friend, Shinji Nohara, a culinary guide who makes a living out of turning first-timers into lifelong Japanophiles, took me to a small coffee shop where an old man named Katsuji Daibo had spent four decades converting muddy water into a religious experience: sifting bean-by-bean through pounds of coffee every morning, hand-roasting each batch for

thirty minutes over a low flame, executing a drip-by-drip pour-over that felt like watching life move backward—a painstaking process that produced the city's richest, most expensive, most labor-intensive cup of coffee.

By the time I emerged from Daibo, Tokyo and Japan and the entire food world had changed for me. I had a new lens through which to view this country and a new reason to keep coming back: to eat the noodles and conveyor sushi and pork-belly pancakes, yes, but also to take the time to experience the true masters of Tokyo, the *shokunin*, the ones who bless this city with their quiet pursuit of perfection.

米 麺 魚

Ginza is the heart of Tokyo's sushi culture, making it the center of Japan's sushi culture, making it the greatest neighborhood in the world for eating fish. Walk these gilded streets for a few blocks and you'll soon figure out why: this is one of Japan's wealthiest zip

"THE ONES WHO BLESS THIS CITY WITH THEIR QUIET PURSUIT OF PERFECTION."

codes, home to extravagant department stores and a battery of international luxury brands housed in beautiful buildings created by famous architects. A perfect fit for the world's most expensive cuisine.

Sushi as we know it today was bred in these blocks. Japanese cooks had been cycling through various permutations of *narezushi*, fish fermented with cooked rice, since the eighth century, but it wasn't until the early 1800s, as Edo (Tokyo's original name) was taking shape as Japan's new capital, that the familiar nigiri formulation emerged. Wooden *yatai*, street food stands, dotted this area, serving urban dwellers the best of the day's catch from Tokyo Bay. Cooks shaped warm mounds of rice by hand, covered them with a slice of fresh fish, and served individual pieces directly to hungry customers. To mimic the puckering flavor of the fermented fish of yore, sidewalk chefs added vinegar to the rice; to kill off potential toxins, they rubbed the fish with a dab of grated horseradish; to season it, a few drops of soy. Modern sushi—*edomaezushi*—was born.

Today, in an eight-block radius you will find the finest sushi bars on earth, a concentrated cluster of polished countertops with claim to sixteen Michelin stars among them. The mighty Jiro Ono operates here, Zeus among the sushi gods of Japan, serving his twenty-minute, $350 feast to a rotating cast of curious foreigners and Japanese heavyweights. So too does Takashi Saito, the young Jedi master with the longest waiting list in town, along with many, many others.

On the third floor of an unassuming office building, one of these *shokunin*, the one whom some have dubbed the soul of Tokyo sushi culture, stands behind a beautiful two-tiered hickory countertop, rubbing a mint-green root of fresh wasabi against a sharkskin grater, preparing for his first guests. He's young by sushi standards, forty or so, and built like a defensive back, with thick arms, shaved head, and heavy eyes that do most of the talking.

I first met Koji Sawada in 2011, when I took a seat at his counter and slowly felt the walls of my food world crumble. To call it a revelation would be to undersell the experience: the meal I had at Sawada was a full-scale transformation, a piece-by-piece poem to starch and sea, not perfect exactly, but a clear indication that a pathway to perfection existed, a stairway to heaven, and that Sawada was climbing it, one step at a time.

This wasn't my first sushi epiphany. On my maiden voyage to Tokyo, I went alone to eat lunch at Mizutani, a Michelin three-star Ginza institution run by Jiro's most famous disciple. There, in a basement restaurant, armed with only three words of Japanese and the one wrinkled button-up I could dig out of my backpack, I learned about the intimacy and artistry of a true sushi experience. (The elegance of the meal came to a crashing halt when I was told Mizutani didn't take credit cards—all too com-

mon in Japan's best restaurants—and the chef personally escorted me to the post office to take out 25,000 yen to cover lunch.)

But Sawada is something else entirely—a former trucker who turned to sushi relatively late in life but with all the manic energy and determination of a man possessed by a single idea: to create the best Edo-style sushi experience in the beating heart of sushi's birthplace.

That means starting each day at 6:00 a.m. at Tsukiji, buying each individual piece of fish from the purveyor who knows the species best. That means investing years in developing a system to serve rice at its ideal temperature and texture the moment the customers settle into their seats. That means constructing an elaborate and expensive refrigeration system cooled not by electricity but by giant blocks of ice. That means serving only six people for lunch and six for dinner. That means ending each night with a terry-cloth towel, scrubbing the hinoki countertop until his arms are sore and his head is slick with sweat and all trace of the fish oils accumulated during service vanish, a cleaning session that marches past midnight, completing an eighteen-hour day that he and his wife repeat six days a week. When I ask Sawada why he doesn't hire someone to clean after dinner service so that he might rest for a bit, he squints his eyes, cocks his head, and points toward the entrance. "You see the name on that door? It says Sawada. I'm Sawada. She's Sawada. Nobody else."

Sawada could probably wake up at 9:00 a.m., get his fish delivered to his door, use a standard refrigerator for cooling his ingredients, have his counters scrubbed by a young apprentice after dinner, and still serve some of Tokyo's most breathtaking sushi. But he doesn't. Because in Japan, it's not about the end; it's about the means.

"It comes down to *kimochi*," says Sawada. "'Feeling.' That's the difference between a good sushi chef and a great one. From start to finish, it's all about feeling. I want you to have the best possible sushi. That's why I go to the market at six a.m. That's why I'm still cleaning at midnight."

Kimochi is a part of all *shokunin*, says Sawada, but especially part of the sushi chef. "Your feelings come out in the sushi. There's no fire. We make it with our hands. You eat it with yours."

With the first bite—and every bite that follows—I realize something I've always been told but never believed: sushi is not about fish; it's about rice. Nigiri—ninety-five times out of a hundred, what Japanese eat when they eat sushi—comprises two components: *shari*, the seasoned rice that forms the base, and *neta*, the slice of fish that rests on top. Anyone can find great *neta* at Tsukiji, the reasoning goes, but only a *shokunin* can master *shari*. "Sushi is eighty percent rice," says Sawada.

Tales of struggle and sacrifice are told of young cooks who toil for years learning the tiny details of proper rice cookery: washing off the excess starch in successive changes of water, calculating the perfect ratio of dry to wet, learning how to properly fan the rice and season it with precise slashes of a wooden spoon. An extraordinary amount of thought goes into Sawada's rice, from the temperature ("It should be as warm as my skin") to the timing ("Rice is at its peak sixty minutes after cooking it"), to the source, which he changes with the rising global temperatures ("The best rice used to come from Niigata, but now it's coming from Hokkaido").

Sawada's *shari* buzzes with a gentle current of acidity, a divisive move among the sushi cognoscenti of Tokyo, many of whom believe rice should be less assertive (so few and focused are the variables in this discipline that a couple extra drops of vinegar added to a mountain of rice constitutes a controversy). But Sawada's *neta* is rich and flush with umami, and the rice's subtle vinegar edge keeps your palate primed for the long road ahead.

From the salty bite of gizzard shad to the supple sweetness of horse mackerel to the crunch and brine of ark shell clam, Sawada guides you through the full spectrum of ocean taste and texture. A giant prawn split into two pieces delivers dessert levels of sweetness. Saltwater eel is equal parts crunchy skin and tender flesh. Smoked bonito, in all its concentrated, fire-kissed intensity, will keep you awake at night.

Behind Sawada, his wife works heating stones, steaming shrimp, wordlessly anticipating everything he will need to continue his thesis. "We move together. She makes me better."

Contrary to popular belief, sushi isn't about freshness; it's about timing. Not just having your rice the proper temperature, but also having your fish the perfect age. Serve fish too soon out of the water and the muscles will be tight and the flavor underdeveloped. Wait too long and the protein turns to mush.

Before refrigeration, fish was either served immediately or marinated in vinegar, but over the years sushi chefs have come to understand that carefully aging fish can bring out its best qualities. The concept, Sawada explains, is the same principle behind aged meat: by removing the water and converting the protein into amino acids, you intensify the flavor of the fish—in particular, the natural umami, the most prized taste in Japan. Tuna tastes most like tuna not when it's still dripping with the essence of the ocean but when it's been allowed to mature for days or even weeks. Every fish has its optimal age: Sawada ages most white fish for two days, scallops and ark shell clams for one week, fattier fish for even longer.

To demonstrate, he offers a flight of tuna: *maguro*, a lean ruby cut a few days out of the water, followed by a lightly marbled, week-old slice of *chutoro*, preceded by an extravagantly fatty *otoro* that floods the brain with a warm rush of endorphins. "Twelve days' aging," he says as he watches me struggle to control my emotions. "Tons of umami." The tuna tutorial concludes with a chunk of *otoro* cooked directly over a hot stone, leaving the outside black and smoky and the inside just warm enough to let loose a tide of fat—a bite I would cross the Pacific for again and again.

Sushi at this level is the finest form of culinary alchemy: cooked rice, raw fish, unmitigated bliss. Along the way, progressions of little mysteries are unveiled: the way an angled knife stroke can relax a thousand tight muscle fibers, how cupping the fish with a warm palm can release just the right amount of natural oils, how the quantity and density of the rice base must be matched to each piece of fish. All these revelations can be tasted on the spot, six feet from where they were born. It is performance art of the highest caliber, one of the few great meals in the world I might not want to share with anyone else, lest they distract me from the theater at hand.

So why does he keep it so small? Why does this man limit himself to just twelve customers a day? When I ask him if he has plans to expand, he tries his best not to look offended. "If anything, we would like to get smaller so we could give more of our attention to our guests. We started as an eight-seat counter, but that was too much, so we downsized to six." Now his greatest ambition is to remove another two chairs.

Lunch ends with a single gooseberry: bright orange, leaves pulled back like a ponytail, no bigger than a marble. I think it's some kind of Japanese thing I don't quite grasp, and maybe it is, but then I crunch down on the berry and the skin pops and releases a flood of sour-sweet juice and I realize that somewhere out there in a field far removed from Tokyo, a farmer with a soul like Sawada is putting everything he's got into these berries.

米 麺 魚

Not far from Sawada, past an eight-story Gucci building, a billion-dollar department store, a 7-Eleven, and a handful of vending machines, there is a small, quiet café where you can drink a cup of coffee from 1954.

Japan may claim one of the world's great tea cultures, but it's no stranger to the coffee bean. Coffee arrived in the country in the eighteenth century, piled high in the bellies of Dutch trading ships. It went relatively unnoticed by most Japanese until, in the early twentieth century, the Brazilian government began sending free coffee beans to Tokyo shop owners. By the 1930s you could find three thousand *kissaten* (called *kissa* for short), traditional Japanese coffee shops, offering Tokyoites a current of caffeine and a respite from city life.

The war put coffee's ascendance on pause. Beans were in short supply for the Japanese, so *kissa* owners roasted soybeans instead, doing little to win over new clientele. At the same time, the Nazis developed a taste for coffee from the Far East and bought up everything they could from Indonesia and Sumatra. When shipments to Western Europe were cut off during the later years of the war, the coffee was rerouted through Japan, where it was to be sent by railroad from China to Germany. When fighting between the Nazis and Russians compromised the train routes, the beans sat all but forgotten in warehouses in Tokyo.

Ichiro Sekiguchi, a sound engineer from Tokyo, was serving in the war at the time and learned that the German-purchased beans were being stored on the outskirts of the city. When the war ended, he decided to go into the coffee business, using what he could of the beans left to languish as the Axis powers met defeat. By the time he opened Café de l'Ambre in Ginza in 1948, he was brewing five-year-old beans from Sumatra. What was born out of necessity turned into a groundbreaking technique. "The coffee had a rich, full taste, like good wine."

Today l'Ambre offers a wide selection of global vintages: '93 Brazil, '76 Mexico, and, the oldest, a Colombian bean from 1954. "Coffee beans are breathing," says

Ichiro. "They evolve and develop different flavors over time." Ichiro's disciples have spread across Tokyo over the decades, infusing the city with a heady dose of cotton-filtered aged coffee, but at 101 years old, Ichiro still shows up to work every day to toast his ancient beans on a roaster he helped design himself decades back. The classic *kissa*, the old beans, and the man himself stand as a stubborn rebuke to the wave of chain coffee outlets, convenience stores, and vending machines that sprang up during Japan's boom years and today make up the vast majority of the coffee market.

I settle onto a stool at the long countertop and choose a cup of Cuban coffee from 1974. A middle-aged barista in a striped turtleneck spends ten minutes dribbling hot water in concentric circles through a vintage Japanese sock filter. The coffee is like nothing I've tasted before, with a round, vegetal quality and only the faintest hint of acidity.

It is not Tokyo's finest cup of coffee.

Until recently, that honor belonged to Daibo-san. But after thirty-eight years of slow filtration, Daibo retired at the end of 2013.

Tokyo's current coffee king is no doubt one of the new-wave wizards at work in Ebisu or Setagaya or Yoyogi, the hip corners of the city, where modern equipment, fresh beans, and time-aged technique combine to make powerful, balanced brews. But Ichiro trades in something more than technical precision—he offers a taste of the past, a reminder that there's always another way to do things.

On my way out, I see Ichiro sitting in his office, hands on his knees, a picture of him as a younger man hanging on the wall over his shoulder. He looks worried. "My supplies are down," he tells me. "I used to have five tons of coffee aging in my storage, but now I'm down to less than a ton." The soul of a *shokunin*: a 101-year-old man worried about inventory.

"What's your secret, Ichiro-san?" I ask. "Coffee, of course. I drink at least five cups a day."

米 麺 魚

Yoshiteru Ikegawa knew that he wanted to cook chicken before he left first grade.

"At home we ate yakitori, but like most people in Japan we did it over gas in a small kitchen. But I'll never forget the smell of charcoal when my parents first took me to a real yakitori."

Despite the early revelation, Ikegawa didn't do what most budding *shokunin* do: he didn't begin to slaughter chickens as a prepubescent boy; he didn't study their musculature and temperament in obscure texts found in dark library corners; he didn't even apprentice under a well-known yakitori chef—at least not at first. Instead, he did what a billion Japanese men had done before him: he became a salaryman. He put on a suit, took the train to work, drank with his colleagues, and remained loyal to his boss. But this wasn't a dream deferred;

on the contrary, it was part of his master plan.

"Most *shokunin* spend their entire lives in kitchens, never learning how to work directly with people," says Ikegawa. "I knew early on that dealing with the customer is one of the most important parts of being a master, so I started with that."

When he felt the business world had taught him the subtleties of customer service—above all, he says, how to give people what they want without their having to ask for it—he left the suit behind and took up an apprenticeship at Toriyoshi, an elegant yakitori bar in Naka-Meguro, where he trained for seven years, studying the bible of the flame-grilled bird. In 2007 he opened Torishiki next to Meguro Station, a lovely low-lit restaurant with a U-shaped bar centered around a small iron grill. His wife glides around the room in a kimono, dispensing drinks and good vibes to happy guests. The master himself stands at attention behind the fire,

the spitting image of a *shokunin*: chiseled facial features, warrior stance, a rolled white bandanna tied tight around his clean-shaven head.

Yakitori, like all great food in Japan, is both perfectly simple and infinitely complex. In its most literal state, yakitori is chicken on a stick grilled over an open flame—conceptually only a step removed from caveman cuisine. It's drinking food, a companion to beer and sake found on the menus of izakaya and clusters of back-alley street stalls that cater to hungry salarymen on their way to the last train.

But yakitori cleans up nicely, too, and room for refinement in the hands of discerning Japanese chefs is infinite. The lack of variables puts all that much more pressure and scrutiny on the few factors each individual can control: the source and intensity of the flame; the provenance of the chicken; the butchering, seasoning, and, above all, careful cooking of its flesh. This isn't a matter of running a skewer through a chicken

Yoshiteru Ikegawa, yakitori master, ready for service

breast and cooking until firm; there are a thousand defining details that must be managed if you take yakitori as seriously as Ikegawa does.

One of the predominant trends in the world of high-end yakitori in Tokyo today is the full anatomy experience. At places like Toritama in Shirokane, owner Shiro Izawa butchers his chickens into thirty-six distinct pieces, a forceful biology lesson for anyone who has dismissed chicken as one-dimensional. For the diner, the question isn't whether you want a skewer of small intestine, but what part of the small intestine you would like: the duodenum or the ileum?

Ikegawa doesn't subscribe to the full-anatomy theory. He doesn't divide the thigh into inner, outer, and middle pieces to challenge your understanding of a single muscle. On a given night, he offers a tasting menu that spans about a dozen cuts of chicken, the same ones you'll find at most respectable yakitori joints in Tokyo: breast, thigh, wing, organs. Seasonal vegetables find their way to the flame, as does the occasional piece of duck or pork, but chicken is the star of Ikegawa's dissertation, a spellbinding treatise on the world of tastes and textures found within a single animal.

In the procession of pieces, which Ikegawa changes based on his read of each guest, you find crunch and chew, fat and cartilage, soft, timid tenderness and bursts of outrageous savory intensity. He starts me with the breast, barely touched by the flame, pink in the center, green on top from a smear of wasabi; a single bite buries a lifetime of salmonella hysteria. A quick-cooked skewer of liver balances the soft, melting fattiness of foie with a gentle mineral bite. The *tsukune*, a string of one-bite orbs made from finely chopped thigh meat, arrives blistered on the outside, studded with pieces of cartilage that give the meatballs a magnificent chew. *Chochin*, the grilled uterus, comes with a proto-egg attached to the skewer like a rising sun. The combination of snappy meat and molten yolk is the stuff taste memories are made of.

What separates Ikegawa from other serious yakitori, what has earned him a Michelin star and keeps his reservation book filled six months in advance, is the amount of care he puts into every last piece of flesh that meets his fire. He tinkers with each skewer as if it's the last piece of meat he'll ever cook, twisting, brushing, dipping, timing, tweaking—employing tight bits of motion to tease out the purest expression of each piece.

Ikegawa embodies the qualities that all *shokunin* share: unwavering focus, economy of motion, disarming humility, and a studied silence that never betrays the inner orchestra his life's work inspires. At any given time, he handles up to a dozen skewers sizzling over *binchotan*, an expensive hardwood charcoal that burns hot for hours, taming the fire with a wooden fan he keeps tucked into the back of his belt. When each piece is ready, he dips it into a large glass jar filled with a sweet lacquer of soy, mirin, and sugar, the indispensable *tare* that sits patiently next to all yakitori grills in Japan. His was a gift from his master, a twenty-five-year-old taste of Toriyoshi that Ikegawa feeds each day like a baker feeds an ancient starter.

After the procession of parts comes Torishiki's *onigiri*, a hulking triangle of rice basted with lavish amounts of rendered chicken fat and grilled until it looks like a lump of gold. I decide to take it back to the hotel to paw it in private, where it will be one of the great rice experiences of my life.

Before the bill, a cup of broth, a simmering distillation of everything that came before it. Chicken tea for the soul, a last respite before night falls over Tokyo.

米 麺 魚

The nighttime starts with a drinkable geography lesson: lemon from Ehime, golden ginger from Kochi Prefecture, and rice shochu from Kumamoto. For

Gen Yamamoto pours the next round.

garnish, a light dusting of *sansho* peppercorn—then served atop a bar made from a giant cross section of five-hundred-year-old Hokkaido oak. The acidity hits first, then the warm sting of shochu, followed by a one-two punch of spice—the scratchy, throat-tickling heat of ginger, the aromatic, tongue-numbing tingle of *sansho*. The young bartender in a crisp white tuxedo looks on and nods, as if to say this is just the beginning.

Gen Yamamoto was born in a small town in Mie Prefecture and came to Tokyo to learn about beverages. He trained in Aoyama Dining Bar in Tokyo before moving to New York for eight years, working as the cocktail man behind a few of Manhattan's best Japanese restaurants. He learned a lot in those years—from serving huge crowds to constructing seasonal menus to speaking fluent English—but all along, he was distilling an idea for a cocktail bar the likes of which the world had never seen. In 2013 Gen returned to Japan and began to build out his dream. "I wanted to try something that you can only do in a city like Tokyo."

Japan has a rich cocktail culture, one studiously built around classic drinks executed with precise technique. Mixologists invest a lifetime in learning how to perfect the hard shake, the gentle stir, the crystalline sphere carved from a giant block of ice. You will find textbook Gibsons and definitive Manhattans in drinking dens from Sapporo to Kagoshima, but you won't find many bartenders in this country pushing the limits of freewheeling cocktail creation.

Gen holds the same respect for refined technique as his colleagues, but he sees an untapped resource in Japan's cocktail culture: the country's bounty of vegetables, citrus, roots, and herbs. "We have amazing local citrus with soft flavors, but they don't mix well with gimlets so you don't see them in other bars. I don't make gimlets." Instead, he draws on the full reach of Japanese climate and topography to build a menu that changes almost daily. Today he's working with papaya and passion fruit from Okinawa, tomato and wasabi from Shizuoka, corn from Miyazaki—almost all of which he sources directly from the farmers themselves. At other moments of the year, you might find Hokkaido squash, Kanagawa carrots, Nagano quince, and a host of rare roots and esoteric herbs with seasons as fleeting as a full moon.

You can order à la carte, but it's the six-course tasting menu that best showcases Gen's vision. As with a great kaiseki feast, there is an arc to the stories he tells with his drinks, drawing heavily on the rituals of the Japanese tea ceremony, where technique, aesthetics, and an unwavering focus on microseasonality combine to create a vivid narrative.

To bring these liquid tales to life, Gen eschews the highfalutin tinctures and technologies favored by many Western bartenders—no volatile distillations, no blowtorched garnishes, no advanced equipment to speak of. He works with three primary tools: a strainer, a stir-rer, and a long wooden muddler. It's the latter that allows him to transform seasonal produce into magic potions, using the blunt face to work fruits and vegetables down into smooth purees that form the base of most drinks. He uses no measurements, choosing instead to build the cocktails slowly, doing little half-stirs with his metal stirring spoon and tasting constantly as he creates.

No music, no wall decorations, nothing to take your attention away from the drinks and their methodical creation. I watch as Gen reduces lipstick-red tomatoes to a fleshy mass with the muddler, then strains the pulp and mixes it with rye vodka from Lithuania, using a tiny spoon and quick, short strokes to emulsify the tomato and vodka. He tastes, adjusts with a splash of vodka, stirs, tastes again, adjusts, adds a pinch of salt, stirs, tastes. He pours the drink into a clear glass cone, then cracks open a passion fruit and spoons the seeds onto the layer of tomato foam that has risen to the rim of the glass, dark orbs hovering delicately on the surface. He sprays a piece of black slate with water, arranges a few loose flowers at one edge and the cocktail at the other.

"Thank you for waiting."

The flavors bloom like a sunrise in my mouth, evolving with each sip: rich and mellow at the top, sweet and acidic in the middle, thinner and stronger with a heavy kick of rye as the drink disappears. It's not simply a tale of taste, but of texture and temperature.

As I journey through the glass, he sets about making the next drink—muddled kiwi from Wakayama, high-proof sake, and a splash of milk. In the foam of kiwi and dairy that settles on the top of the drink he suspends a spoonful of minced fennel, which punctuates each sip with crunchy licorice bursts.

Despite the fireworks in the glass, there is nothing loud or flashy about this man: no waxed mustache or sudden movements. With his shaved head and soft features and quiet voice, he could

be a monk—if you swapped the white tux for saffron robes.

For the final course, he layers twelve-year-old Yamazaki whisky with muddled sweet potato and shavings of dark chocolate: a cocktail whose sweet, smoky, bitter brilliance I'll try and fail to convey a thousand times to anyone who will listen.

米 麺 魚

Not everything is so beautiful in Tokyo. Not every meal ends with a warm ball of rice in your pocket or a sweet potato cocktail in your belly. There are 35 million strong in these streets, after all, and only so many can fit into the sacred shrines scattered throughout the cityscape.

The moments I'm not pursuing the city's *shokunin* I spend mostly on foot, losing myself in the minimalism of Omotesando, the maximalism of Shibuya, the J-pop gyre of Harajuku. Late one night I take a train to Shinjuku, the busiest station on earth, with nearly

4 million bodies traversing its tracks each day. More than home to a frenzied train station, Shinjuku is the heart of Tokyo's entertainment district.

Seventy years ago the neighborhood was all rubble, a smoldering heap of war regrets. Prostitution flourished, and, naturally enough, so did drinking and revelry as ramshackle bars popped up east of the station in the late 1940s. In the years after reconstruction, many of Japan's largest businesses set up shop here, and soon the bulk of the city's skyscrapers sprouted from Shinjuku, creating a dual identity—modern economic might by day, throwback pleasure center by night—that persists today.

I walk under the railroad tracks and into a labyrinth of narrow corridors called Memory Lane, better known as Piss Alley, named for the unsavory smell that once filled these confined quarters before bathrooms joined the party. Today the smell is mainly of yakitori, the lion's share of the shoebox spaces dedicated to chicken parts and cold beer. This is the foil to Torishiki: loud, cramped, drunk—with little subtlety but just enough soul.

In Kabukicho, Tokyo's red-light district, three-story pachinko parlors hum with the sound of retirement checks. Steamy restaurants dispense cheap, instant sustenance—ramen, burgers, dumplings. Yakuza toughs in cheap suits roam the blocks, the not so invisible hand behind most of the night economy.

I pass hostess bars where men with briefcases pay young girls to laugh at their jokes, host bars where middle-aged women pay boy-band look-alikes to tell them they're pretty. It all feels like a twisted simulation, a paper-thin world where people pay top dollar for the promise of a payout, the scent of a woman, the scratching of an itch.

They call this mix of nocturnal carousing *mizu shobai*, the "water trade," a business built on the back of corporate expense accounts during Japan's rapid ascendancy to economic dominance.

Shinjuku's Kabukicho, Japan's largest "red-light" district

Companies may not have footed the bill for the worst secrets that lurk behind these doors, but they paid for the booze and bonhomie that loosened the ties, cemented the deals, and fed the darker sides of those who helped build New Tokyo overnight.

Those darker sides feed strange industries and sad secrets in this part of town. The saddest secret is no secret at all: the Japanese have less sex than people of any other country on the planet. The women call men *soshuku danshi*, herbivores who graze on leaves and pass on flesh, more interested in a virtual relationship than the real thing. The death of romance, some say, is the bane of birthrates, an economic and social crisis bubbling below the surface.

On the edge of Kabukicho, a line of people stretches around the block, all waiting to gain entrance into the Robot Restaurant, home to Tokyo's mad $100 million spectacle. Inside, bikini-clad-women straddle neon tanks, and robots dance and sing in a psychedelic futurama that will take years of the spectators' lives to fully process.

Beyond the lights and the noise, a refuge of Shinjuku's past: Golden Gai, a dense concentration of two hundred–odd bars organized down a series of dimly lit alleys. The spaces are tiny, the prices are high, the bars' motifs as narrow as the alleys they live in: medical gear, horse racing, exploitation films. I try to walk into one, but the owner sees my face and crosses his two pointer fingers into an X.

I find a more welcoming crowd at Bar Plastic Model—a toy-box love letter to 1980s plastic regalia. I order a glass of Nikka whisky while the guy next to me fumbles with a Rubik's Cube. He surrenders after a few minutes and strikes up a conversation in broken English. "You like Japanese food?" he asks. I drop $15, half for the cover charge, and merge back into the drunken alleyway traffic.

The whisky weighs on my eyelids, but the bright surgical lights of the Lawson pull me in like a tractor beam.

From the outside, it looks like the convenience stores back home, but inside exists a very different world—one with a sake section and platters of raw fish and skewers of exotic vegetables simmered in dashi. The young woman behind the counter greets me with more cheer than can be expected at this or any hour. She works with a palpable sense of purpose, disarming surly customers with her smile, meticulously tending to a fryer full of chicken, all the while watching my cautious movements around her store. When I pause in front of the sake, searching for a nightcap, she comes from behind the counter, grabs a small bottle with a silver label, and hands it to me. "*Oishii!*" she says, then goes back to bronzing the skin of her fried chicken.

A convenience-store *shokunin*? A liquor-fueled fever dream? Another lovely paradox? There is beauty to be found in the snack aisle, far from the tiny restaurants with buckling waitlists. It's not always as romantic as it sounds—*karoshi*, death from overwork, is a real thing here—but in the long, strange trip ahead, when the train conductor crisply bows to an empty passenger car or the hotel cleaning lady origamis my towel into a perfect swan or the Lawson clerk fries chicken like a Southerner and picks sake like a sommelier for no other reason than because it's the job she has chosen, Tokyo will seem so much bigger than the world's largest city.

KNOW BEFORE YOU GO

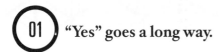 **"Yes" goes a long way.**

Hai, "yes" or "okay" in Japanese, is the most valuable word in the dictionary, a single high-pitched syllable you can finesse into something resembling a conversation. As with *vale* in Spain, tone and inflection can bend the word into a dozen different meanings—from "Yes, I'm a huge fan of this strange and beautiful country" to "Of course I'd like you to soak me in unfiltered sake." Besides, you wouldn't want to say no to the Japanese, would you? Didn't think so.

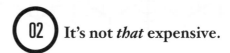 **It's not *that* expensive.**

Legions of potential visitors pass on a trip to Japan because of the misguided belief that the country is unbearably pricey. Compared to Thailand or Central America, it's not cheap; put next to the UK, Switzerland, or any northern European country, Japan looks like a bargain. What is expensive: cab rides, *ryokan* and high-end hotel chains, drinking in nice bars, formal sushi meals, and Japanese beef. What isn't expensive: public transportation, business hotels, drinking in izakaya, conveyor sushi, and beautiful bowls of noodles. You can't survive on $22 a day, but you can sleep and eat pretty well in the big cities for $100.

(03) English is scarce.

Not solar-eclipse scarce but pretty close. Few people in the world speak less English than the Japanese, which means you'll need to sharpen your body language skills, learn a few key phrases, and bring a willingness to laugh at yourself in the long stream of slightly embarrassing situations that will inevitably follow you around the country. Also a smart move: memorize ten or fifteen food words you can use when you get to a restaurant and can't read a single symbol in one of Japan's three alphabets. (See the "Gaijin Glossary" on page 142 for further guidance.)

(04) Japan is a cash society.

It may be surprising to learn that the country that invented the bullet train and robot strippers still relies on hard currency, but places from five-star *ryokan* to top-tier sushi restaurants refuse to take credit cards, which means you'll need to carry a thick wad of yen around at all times. Very few Japanese ATMs work with foreign cards; instead use the machines in post offices and 7-Elevens, the two most reliable ways to get cash.

KNOW BEFORE YOU GO

05 Subtlety is king.

Japan is a society of deep-seated traditions and formalities that can puzzle the outsider, but getting it right can really make a difference for you and your hosts. Some basics to remember: Personal contact is mostly avoided in Japan, so mind your body and be prepared to bow rather than shake hands (a gentle bow for friends and family, a deeper dip from the waist for business relations or people of importance). Be punctual; tardiness isn't tolerated. And in general, avoid anything to cause undue attention to yourself or those around you; though you'll never blend in, Japanese value subtlety over aggressive individuality.

06 Buy your ticket to freedom.

Purchased outside the country (through a travel agency or at international airports), a Japan Rail Pass allows for unlimited travel for up to three weeks on all but a few special trains in Japan. Not only will it save you money and time (a pass costs around $300 for unlimited travel in a week and doesn't require reservations on most trains) but it also turns the country into a traveler's buffet, allowing you to improvise your daily destinations based on your various appetites for culture, climate, and regional cuisine. Go anywhere and everywhere, just never board a train without a bento box and a beverage (more on that subject on page 318).

(07) Smaller is better.

It doesn't matter what you're eating: eel, sushi, noodles, sweets, cocktails. Small establishments are where *shokunin* do their work. It may be intimidating to walk into a six-seat bar, but this is where you will find the good stuff—a place where the chef and the staff (most likely husband and wife) are unwaveringly dedicated to their craft. The most exclusive places require an invitation or a Japanese guest to accompany you, but the country is bursting with warm, intimate establishments dying for a chance to blow your mind.

(08) Don't ask; just do.

Hoping to wander a secret section of the fish market? Want to change seats on a train? Ask and you will invariably be defeated by a series of extended deliberations and bureaucratic consultations—a reflection of the highly structured reality of daily life in Japan. As long as it's not offensive and not illegal, you're better off doing first and feigning innocence later. It might not be the most elegant alibi, but nobody expects gaijin to know what they're doing in Japan.

FOOD GROUPS

MENRUI
noodles

—

SOBA
Japan's most elegant noodle, made from ground buckwheat.

UDON
Thick white noodles, served hot or cold.

SOMEN
Thin wheat noodles, normally served cold for dipping.

RAMEN
Made with wheat flour and alkaline salt to help retain its chew in hot broth (see more on page 174).

AGEMONO
fried

—

TEMPURA
Seafood and vegetables battered in flour, egg, and water (see more on page 224).

KARAAGE
Bite-sized pieces of fried chicken, shrimp, or fish. Classic drinking food.

KATSU
Pork, chicken, or beef cutlets breaded in panko bread crumbs and fried crisp.

KOROKKE
Crispy breaded croquettes made from mashed potato or mincemeat.

NABEMONO
stews

—

SHABU-SHABU
Tableside hot pot of beef, vegetables, and tofu cooked in dashi.

ODEN
Meat, egg, fish cake, and a variety of vegetables slow-simmered in dashi.

SUKIYAKI
Meat and vegetables cooked in soy-spiked dashi and dipped in raw egg yolk.

MOTSUNABE
A popular *nabe* of stewed beef offal and cabbage cooked in dashi.

YAKIMONO
grilled

—

YAKISOBA
Wheat noodles mixed with meat and vegetables and fried on a griddle.

OKONOMIYAKI
Cabbage pancake laced with meat or seafood and topped with a flurry of condiments.

YAKINIKU
Thin slices of meat cooked over a charcoal grill or on a griddle.

YAKITORI
Skewers of chicken and vegetables grilled over a charcoal fire (see more on page 276).

SUSHI
raw

—

SASHIMI
Raw slices of fish, seafood, chicken, or beef.

TATAKI
Torched tuna (and other fish), blackened on the outside, raw in the center.

NIGIRIZUSHI
Single pieces of raw fish pressed over seasoned rice (see more on page 36).

MAKIZUSHI
Rolled sushi of rice and fish or vegetables, wrapped in dried seaweed (nori).

GOHAN
rice

—

ONIGIRI
Pressed rice triangle wrapped in seaweed, often filled with fish or vegetables.

DON
Rice bowls topped with various types of raw or cooked fish and meat.

MOCHI
A soft, sticky rice cake often filled with sweetened beans.

CHAZUKE
Soup made with steamed rice and tea, a classic comfort food.

Sushi

寿司

IN THE
RAW

The most famous and revered of Japan's culinary pillars, sushi comes with a set of rules and rituals that confound most outsiders. In a country where table manners matter, it's easy to look like a jackass when eating raw fish. Here's how to do it right. (Hand and sushi modeling by the great Takashi Saito, one of Tokyo's top sushi *shokunin,* photographed by Sander Jackson Siswojo.)

THE RULES OF SUSHI

—

USE YOUR HANDS

Eat sashimi with chopsticks, but high-end nigiri is delicate, and all but the finest motor skills will test the sushi's integrity. Hands serve as more elegant and perfectly acceptable tools at a sushi bar, as long as they're clean.

RESPECT THE RICE

It's the star of this show, and soaking it in soy sauce would compromise a technique that takes most sushi masters years to perfect. Instead, roll the nigiri over and gently dip the edge of the fish in soy sauce without saturating the rice.

HAVE IT THEIR WAY

True sushi masters serve their pieces how they want them eaten—already seasoned with wasabi and soy. Keep it clean: no ginger (it's there to clean the palate between pieces), no wasabi in your soy sauce, and eat the nigiri in one bite. Always one bite.

KEEP PACE

Great sushi isn't a social outing; it's a communion between you and the chef behind the counter. Part of that means eating nigiri as soon as it's made, at the peak of its deliciousness. Holster your smartphone and save the long conversations for the bar afterward.

赤身
AKAMI (lean tuna)

鯵
AJI (jack mackerel)

中とろ
CHUTORO (medium fatty tuna)

烏賊
IKA (squid)

大とろ
OTORO (fatty tuna)

小鰭
KOHADA (gizzard shad)

車海老
KURUMA EBI (prawn)

穴子
ANAGO (eel)

鰈
KAREI (flatfish)

鰹
KATSUO (skipjack tuna)

蛤
HAMAGURI (surf clam)

卵焼き
TAMAGOYAKI (omelet)

One Night at a
LOVE HOTEL

ORDER YOUR BOOZE

Shochu is a favorite here. Order it by the bottle so you place only one order. Room service staff are hugely afraid of . . . interrupting.

CHECK IN ANONYMOUSLY

Tokyo's Hotel Takamine has some solo guests, but it's still a Love Hotel—a place for discreet liaisons. Check in and pay by computer screen.

8pm   9pm   10pm

BROWSE THE MENU

Takamine is unusual for Love Hotels in that it has a full kitchen. Usually patrons eat before arriving, but for you and your paramour, eating is all part of the warm-up.

FEAST ON THIS

We recommend the braised whole fish head for ¥1950. Succulent.

TAXI IT HOME

No one actually sleeps in a Love Hotel. Salarymen and weary women find white-gloved taxi drivers to return them to the Tokyo they know.

BEHOLD NEGI PORN

Japanese porn is neither subtle nor always consensual. Subway groping and the domination of housewives carrying *negi* (green onion) are common themes.

11pm · 12pm · 1am

RAID THE PLEASURE MINIBAR

It's time to get properly outfitted. The condoms are free, but turn to the minibar for the rest: dildos start at ¥1000.

MAKE YOUR MOVE

The porn bandwidth got crushed with the midnight rush. Nothing to do but get down to business.

Chapter Two
OSAKA

—

This is how it happens: You sit down at a long counter in a restaurant that feels like someone's kitchen. You are alone, a bit nervous, uncertain whether to order a drink or ask the man behind the bar how his day went. He senses your apprehension (after all, he doesn't see your kind around here too often), disappears for a second, then deposits an armful of half-drunk wine bottles before you. Close your eyes and point, he seems to be saying. You abide.

Eventually, the restaurant fills out. A couple in the corner play footsy beneath the gentle heat of the warming griddle. A party of four, the men with spiked hair, the women with skirts and thick-rimmed glasses, slide into the counter seats next to you.

With the first glass of wine, the stilted silence prevails. A plate of warm buffalo mozzarella appears, speckled with pink peppercorns, and something about that combination of tang and spice, cream and crunch, tells you that tonight will be different from the others you've spent in Japan.

With the second glass of wine, your neighbors look over and offer a *kanpai*. Another plate arrives, this one a few pieces of seared octopus, the purple tentacles curled like crawling vines around a warm mound of barely mashed potatoes.

With the third glass of wine you begin to test your Japanese. *Watashi wa Matt-o desu. California kara kimashita.* Even the stone-faced salaryman eating pasta by himself in the corner cracks a smile. Glasses are emptied in your honor.

By the time you move on to sake, you feel the sweat above your eyebrows. At first you figure it's the spirited drinking and the aggressive round of selfies that has taken over the small restaurant, but then you see the old woman behind the counter testing the griddle, showering it with little drops of water that hiss on contact. She lays down a few strips of pork belly, then a ladleful of batter that she lovingly crisps in the sheen of rendered pork fat. She flips it, dresses it with a thick, dark sauce and shaved bonito flakes, which move like flamenco hands as they hit the hot surface, then slides it across the griddle toward you and smiles.

By the time you ask for the bill, the couple has their family album open on the bar and the group of four has nuzzled their stools so close you can smell the pinot gris on their words. You make plans to eat *hakozushi* with one, an off-duty chef; another wants to show you a secret bar that serves only grilled offal. (Back at the hotel, four friend requests await you on Facebook.)

When you leave, the entire restaurant stands to escort you out the door. The man shakes your hand vigorously. The woman hesitates, then wraps her arms around you. You stand there for a second, unsure of how to thank them for such a beautiful evening. Finally, you bow as low and as slowly as possible and step reluctantly away. As you reach the corner, you turn around one last time, just to make sure, and there they are, the entire restaurant, waiting calmly for you to disappear into the night.

米　麺　魚

A well-worn Japanese proverb has it that Tokyoites spend all their money on footwear, Kyotoites on kimonos and formal attire. But Osakans save their funds for food and drink. There's a word for this Osakan propensity, *kuidaore*: to eat until you drop.

Unfortunately, most visitors to Japan will never have the chance to eat themselves stupid in Osaka, because most visitors from the United States and Western Europe don't come to Osaka. They go instead to Tokyo, to bask in the full bulk and breadth of the Japanese urban phenomenon. They travel by train to Kyoto, to tour temples and gardens and capture geisha with their zoom lenses. As well they should. Osaka can't compete with Tokyo's size or stature, and it doesn't have the ancient culture and spellbinding beauty of Kyoto. Travel literature does little to stoke outsider interest. *Lonely Planet* warns readers that "Osaka is not an attractive city"; other guidebooks have similarly grim tidings to share with readers.

But Osaka doesn't seem to mind. After 1,500 years of wildly yo-yoing for-

tunes, the city has developed something of a thick skin. In 645 Emperor Kotoku bestowed upon Osaka, then known as Naniwa, the honor of being Japan's first capital, only to abruptly move the government seat to Asuka just ten years later. In 744 Osaka was once again the capital of Japan, but this stint was even shorter: by 745 Nara had taken up the mantle as Japan's political center.

Come the sixteenth century, Osaka was back on center stage. In 1590 Hideyoshi Toyotomi, considered Japan's second great unifier, completed construction of Osaka Castle, the largest and grandest castle in the country. His son and successor, Hideyori, chose Osaka as his base, but his rival Ieyasu Tokugawa had other ideas. He laid siege to the castle in 1615, driving Hideyori and his mother to suicide, and established as Japan's capital Edo, which lives on today as modern-day Tokyo.

Osaka remained an important commercial center but suffered a series of blows over the next three centuries, including a peasant uprising in 1855 that razed a quarter of the city, and the brunt of the American attack on the Kansai region during World War II. The Americans may have spared nearby Kyoto, but they hit Osaka with the full force of their firebombing campaign, taking aim at the city's railways and extensive industrial complex. Two thousand tons of bombs and ten thousand lives later, the city was reduced to a skeleton of its former self. The rebuild was hasty and in some ways haphazard, robbing Osaka of the pockets of old-world charm that contrast so brilliantly with the modernity in most of Japan's largest cities.

One thing that never changed in millennia of misfortune: Osaka's place as the eating center of Japan. Osaka earned the moniker "the nation's kitchen" as early as the fifteenth century, when its privileged position on the Osaka Bay created a rich, thriving merchant class with the means to eat well (even today *mokarimakka*, "Are you making money?" is a standard greeting in local dialect).

Rice, seaweed, and other staples arrived from all parts of Japan, sent by feudal lords to sell in Osaka's massive system of commodity markets. The city also served as an entry point for Chinese, Korean, and other foreign ships bearing important edible cargo, deepening Osaka's place as a breeding ground for new tastes and big appetites. The table was set for a feast that continues today.

I've barely finished my bento from Tokyo Station when I step off the train in Osaka's Tenma district. Yuko Suzuki, a friend who works with high-end food producers in her adopted city, meets me at the station, and we plunge directly into Tenma's narrow, snaking streets in search of sustenance. Yuko was born to undertake these types of high-calorie missions; not only can she direct you to the city's best place for duck soba but she can also tell you where the restaurant buys its duck and how it grinds its buckwheat.

Our first stop is Tsugie, a smoky pocket square of a bar built around a

Grilling odd cow parts at Tsugie, one of
Osaka's many offal dispensaries

large charcoal grill covered in unfamiliar anatomy. Tsugie serves *horumonyaki*, an Osaka specialty focusing on offal and other off-cuts left behind by most restaurants (and cities with less discerning palates). "In Kyoto, they'd throw this stuff away," Yuko says as we settle into a corner of the bar, "but in Osaka it's the star of the meal."

Yuko tells me about the breed of young Osakan restaurateurs, the kind who have bucked the austere traditions of Japanese restaurant culture to focus on more pressing priorities, namely fun and deliciousness. That means open kitchens, louder music, more banter, less staff, bigger flavors, cheaper prices. Tsugie's owner, Takeshi Yamakawa, could be a poster boy for this ethos: after he takes our order, he bones out a few pounds of short ribs, switches the jazz for metal, fans a bed of charcoal, pours two perfect draft beers, and generally looks like he's having the greatest night of his life.

We start strong with chunks of the cow's third stomach, raw and slippery, slicked in sesame oil and green onion. Later come rosy pieces of flank steak and short rib, soft strips of raw heart with a yuzu chili paste, and gorgeous wedges of grilled tongue dripping with ginger-spiked soy sauce.

There are no seats at Tsugie; all of this is eaten standing up at the bar, washed down with generous amounts of *biru* and sake. *Tachinomi*, literally "drinking while standing," is big in Japan these days, signs of a shifting dining constituency that values good food at low prices over the formalities that dominate *ryotei*, traditional Japanese restaurants. It may not have originated in Osaka, but wander the streets of Tenma after dark and you'll find a well-lubricated mix of salarymen, hipsters, and young couples *tachinomi*-ing like they invented the form.

Later, we deepen our investigation into the drinking-while-standing phenomenon at Mashika, an Italian izakaya in a hip pocket of Nishi-Ku. The

Italian-Japanese coalition is hardly new territory in this pasta-loving country, but Mashika is a different kind of mash-up. To start with, the space isn't really a restaurant at all. During the day, grandma sells cigarettes out of the small space. When the sun goes down, grandson fires up the burners as a crowd of thirtysomething Osakans drink Spritz and fill up on charcuterie, sashimi, and funky hybrids like spaghetti sauced with grated daikon and crowned with a wedge of ocean-sweet saury tataki. The menu follows no particular rules at all. Nobody seems to notice.

Eventually we are joined by Yumiko Nakamoto, editor of *Amakara-techo*, Osaka's largest food magazine. She takes us for a highball break at the spiffy Samboa, where tuxedoed barmen manage to turn a whisky soda into a transfixing ten-minute preparation.

"You see?" Yumiko says, pointing to the tux with the long silver spoon in his hand. "All the details matter. People are just so passionate about food in Osaka.

People want to sit at counters, talk to their neighbors, talk to the chef."

Yumiko, like most people I meet here, is not shy about her Osaka love. She also isn't shy about the rivalry with their Kansai neighbor.

"The French, the Chinese, and the Kyotoites have one thing in common: they all think they're number one. We're not worried about where we rank."

The last stop of the opening Osaka salvo is at Tenpei, another shoebox joint with a six-seat counter and two wooden booths. The menu, all three words of it, hangs from the wall: Gyoza. Pickles. Beer. Gyoza is Japan's take on the Chinese pork dumpling, shrunk down and refined in the same way the Japanese like to shrink and refine most everything. Still, textbook drinking food.

We order the entire menu four times over and take a seat in the booth.

Emiko Urakami, who opened Tenpei in 1952, claims to have invented the one-bite gyoza, now the accepted style across the city. "I made them like that because

WITNESS THE DRAMATIC
TRANSFORMATION OF THE
POSTWORK JAPANESE.

my hands are small," she says, rolling her palms over to show us the proof. "You see this line here; it means I'm going to be rich." Whether or not she invented the form, she certainly mastered it: the mahogany gyoza skin glistens with griddle fat and shatters with the gentlest bite, giving way to a tide of warm pork juice. The table grows silent as we devour the dumplings.

Emiko is plump and ornery and wears the decades of gyoza making like vets wear war on their bodies. "I've been doing this for sixty-two years, feeding lines around the block," she says.

She must really love dumplings, I suggest rather lamely.

"Not at all. I don't really like gyoza."

Exhausted from the march down memory lane, she takes a seat with us at the table and watches intently while four of us try to make 150 dumplings disappear. Every time I put my chopsticks down, she touches my arm and motions for me to keep going. "Eat! Eat!" Nobody at the table wants to let her down,

least of all me, but I don't know how to tell her that this is the fifth stop of the night, that my belly is filled with cow stomach and daikon spaghetti and the warm, mysterious pleasures of a city I'm falling hard for, so instead I just keep eating.

米　麺　魚

On my first morning in Osaka, I see the strangest thing: a man jaywalking. In fact, not just one man, but men and women and young students, crossing side streets and central avenues under the red glow of a stoplight. This might be typical urban behavior in most corners of the world, but jaywalking in Japan is snow-leopard rare. Even in Tokyo, in the small, fuzzy hours of the morning, call girls and yakuza toughs will patiently wait at the city's tiniest, least-traveled intersection for the green light to tell them when to go.

出る杭は打たれる—"The nail that sticks up will be hammered down"— goes one popular Japanese proverb.

Japan is a paragon of order and civil obedience. There are parts of Japanese society so polished, they make Switzerland and Scandinavia look sloppy by comparison. In most regards, this is a glorious virtue: trains are scheduled down to the nanosecond, streets are so clean you can see your reflection in the pavement, and crime—especially violent crime—is all but nonexistent. But for those of us who like our punctual trains with a dash of disorder, Japan can feel stifling.

Osaka understands this. Its guiding proverb has a decidedly more defiant tone: 十人十色: "Ten persons, ten colors." Here the ubiquitous and homogenous spiffiness (some might say stiffness) that defines so much of Japan gives way to a more diverse and familiar tapestry of rich and poor, clean and dirty, highbrow and low. Even by Japanese standards, this is a massive city, with more than 19 million inhabitants in greater Osaka. The guidebooks aren't wrong; Osaka is not a textbook beautiful city. Not a seamless stretch of civilization, but a patchwork of skyscrapers and smokestacks, Gucci and ghettos, that better approximates life as most of us know it.

With all of this in mind, it's not surprising that Osaka is a center of casual food culture. Its two most famous foods, *okonomiyaki* (a thick, savory pancake stuffed with all manners of flora and fauna) and *takoyaki* (a golf-ball-sized fritter with a single chewy nugget of octopus deposited at its molten core), are the kind of carby, fatty, belly-padding drinking food that can sustain a city with Osaka's voracious appetite for mischief. You'll find plenty of both all over the city, but especially at the street food stalls that dot the electric streets of Dotonbori, Osaka's central entertainment district, a high-voltage maze of karaoke bars, gentlemen's clubs, and cheap calories, all punctuated by packs of giant metal animals—dragons, crabs, blowfish—that keep watch over the frothing masses. I've ended more than a few Suntory-soaked Osaka nights there at the elbow of a *takoyaki* cook, that selfless citizen who works tirelessly browning octopus-stuffed batter so that individuals like me might sleep a bit better at night.

But nothing in Osaka is as precious as stomach real estate, and one would be wise to save plenty of space for the city's less-obvious delights. To find the best of Osaka's street eats, you must venture farther afield. Shinsekai is an area known for its rough edges, a once-glorious neighborhood modeled after New York and Paris that became a bastion of seediness and criminal activity in the lean postwar years. But beyond the hucksters and the hustlers, the pachinko parlors and the prostitutes, you will find what you need: *kushikatsu*, tiny skewers of deep-fried meat and vegetables that were invented on these streets. Osaka is lousy with restaurants that have taken the *kushi* concept, cleaned it up, and marked up the price 500 percent, but that's not what you're after. You want your stick fix here in Shinsekai, where

kushi shops line the streets, and with them groups of old couples and construction workers looking for grease. People will proclaim one establishment's superiority over another, but when it comes to fried meat, it's best not to overthink it.

We find a space at the bar of one of three dozen nearly identical establishments and rattle off an order that surprises even the double-fisting plumbers to our left. A meat marathon ensues. Two old guys behind the counter run through the paces, the first doing the three-step shuffle (flour, egg wash, panko bread crumbs), the second working the fryer like a North Carolina line cook. On the counter, a sign lays out the only true rule of the *kushikatsu*: no double dipping. Drop your stick into the thick Worcestershire-like sauce once and be done with it.

The sticks come flying out of the grease, golden and glistening. They taste exactly as they should, of salt and crunch and a general meaty savoriness.

A wedge of raw cabbage is offered as a breath mint of sorts, but in this bar at least, vegetables are a lonely bunch.

The longer we linger, the more the sharp edges of Shinsekai soften. After another round of *kushikatsu*, the oily residue that hangs over this part of town feels like aromatherapy; the electric patter of pachinko begins to sound like Kenny G. By the time we wander back toward downtown Osaka, I'm convinced the most dangerous move you can make in this neighborhood is the double dip.

But you won't find Osaka's most quintessential eating experience under the menacing glare of a local thug in Shinsekai or next to a giant mechanized crab in Dotonbori. You'll find it on an unsuspecting street a few hundred meters from Kyobashi Station, at what looks more like a garage sale or a homeless enclave than a dining establishment. Nothing about Toyo makes sense: the kitchen is housed in the back of a pickup truck, the tables are made from stacks of yellow Asahi crates, and the hours are as

erratic as the decor. But come most days after 4:00 p.m. and you will find a line of young Osakans clutching briefcases and fingering iPhones, eager to take in the Toyo *tachinomi* experience.

Look alive! You will never find a better perch from which to take in the dramatic transformation of the post-work Japanese. It takes place every evening between approximately five and six in cities across Japan, as salarymen and women emerge from gleaming steel structures that hold them captive during daylight hours and beeline it to the closest izakaya to eat and drink away the sting of the workday. The same people who stood so quietly, so tensely in line behind you, soon grow animated. Ties are loosened, hair let down, and *kanpai*s ring out in spirited choruses as rank and order dissolve with each passing sip. From soba to miso to raw-tuna red, the most aggressive transformers wear the stages of devolution on their faces. You want to be near this; this is the Japan that runs antithetical to the one you have constructed in your head. This is the beauty of Japan: it builds a set of beliefs and perceptions during the day, only to destroy them once the sun goes down. Rigid? Reserved? Formal? Find a table, fill it with food and beer and new friends, and watch as all those stiff postures slacken.

Fueling this metamorphosis is Toyo-san, chef and owner of this beautiful mess, a short, muscular man in his late sixties with a shiny bald head and wild-fire in his eyes. He holds forth at the stovetop with a towel wrapped around his neck like a prizefighter, a lit cigarette dangling from his lips and a full-blast blowtorch in his hand. Toyo trades in extremes. Half the food that he sends out is raw: ruby cubes of tuna dressed with a heaping mound of fresh wasabi; sea grapes the size of ball bearings that pop like caviar against the roof of your mouth; glistening beads of salmon roe meant to be stuffed into crispy sheets of nori.

The other half gets the blowtorch treatment. Tuna is transformed into a sort of tataki stir-fry, toasted, glazed with ponzu, and tossed with a thicket of spring onions. Fish heads are blitzed under the flame until the cheeks singe and the skin screams and the eyes melt into a glorious stew meant to be extracted with chopsticks. Even sea urchin, those soft orange tongues of ocean umami, with a sweetness so subtle that cooking it is considered heretical in most culinary circles, gets blasted like a crème brûlée by Toyo and his ring of fire.

From spanking raw to burning inferno and back again, he cooks like a man possessed by some gnawing gastronomic schizophrenia. Every so often he looks up and gives wide-eyed onlookers an enthusiastic thumbs-up, but mostly he keeps to his food and his flame, laughing softly to himself at something we'll never understand. In some corners of Japan's culinary world, where restaurants have roofs and ingredients come with responsibilities, he might be crucified for his blatant disregard for convention

Toyo-san and his flaming tuna, icons
of Osaka

and basic decorum, but in Osaka, where eating is a sport and rules are made to be blowtorched, Toyo-san is a hero.

米　麺　魚

That's not to say Osaka doesn't dress up. After all, this is a city with more boutiques than Paris and more Michelin stars than New York. But even the high-end stuff in Osaka exudes the warm, inviting,　you're-here-to-have-fun-not-whisper-to-your-waiter vibe that you find at more everyday establishments.

At the heart of this ethos is *kappo*, counter-style dining wherein the line between chef and guest is all but dissolved entirely. Chefs talk about the menu, take orders, cook inches from your face, and reach across the counter to serve you dinner. If this sounds familiar, it's because many of the best restaurants in the world right now—Momofuku Ko in New York, L'Atelier de Joel Robuchon in Paris—model themselves after Osaka *kappo*.

You'll find the counter philosophy expressed in a variety of styles across Osaka. Kigawa is the city's *kappo* nerve center, the birthplace of modern *kappo* and still the breeding ground for many of the city's best young chefs. The menu offers a hundred different dishes, all heavily tied to the seasons, all built with the best of Osakan raw materials. At Ka-hala, a favorite of brand-name Western chefs, Yoshifumi Mori serves an eight-course showcase of expensive, obscure local ingredients that concludes with a five-layer mille-feuille of rare beef and fresh wasabi. And at Yamagata, the chef turns his counter intelligence into a treatise on Kansai beef, a *horumon*-inspired showcase of the entire sacred cow: heart sashimi with charred edamame, grilled tongue coated in mushroom miso, and a four-ounce square of tenderloin sauced with barrel-aged soy and fresh *sansho* peppercorns.

But my favorite *kappo*, one of the purest expressions of Osaka-style counter eating, is found down a narrow alley-way just a few blocks removed from the madness of Dotonbori. When you walk into Wayoyuzen Nakamura, the first thing you'll see is Nakamura-san himself standing firmly behind the counter, smiling broadly and bowing as you take your seat. He'll talk to you, ask you about your day, probe the dimensions of your hunger, discuss at length your hopes and fears.

"I can tell right away by looking at you what you want to eat," he says. "I can tell you how many brothers and sisters you have."

After divining my favorite color (blue) and my astrological sign (Aquarius), Nakamura pulls out an ivory stalk of *takenoko*, fresh young bamboo ubiquitous in Japan during the spring. "This came in this morning from Kagumi. It's so sweet that you can eat it raw." He peels off the outer layer, cuts a thin slice, and passes it across the counter.

Then he goes to work. First, he scores an inch-thick bamboo steak with a ferocious *santoku* blade. Then he sears it in a dry sauté pan until the flesh softens and the natural sugars form a dark crust on the surface. While the bamboo cooks, he places two sacks of *shirako*, cod milt, under the broiler. ("Milt," by the way, is a euphemism for sperm. Cod sperm is everywhere in Japan in the winter and early spring, and despite the challenges its name might create for some, it's one of the most delicious things you can eat.)

Nakamura brings it all together on a Meiji-era ceramic plate: caramelized bamboo brushed with soy, broiled cod milt topped with miso made from foraged mountain vegetables, and, for good measure, two lightly boiled fava beans. An edible postcard of spring. I take a bite, drop my chopsticks, and look up to find Nakamura staring right at me.

"See, I told you I know what you want to eat."

The rest of the dinner unfolds in a similar fashion: a little counter banter, a little product display, then back to the burners to transform my tastes and his ingredients into a cohesive unit. The hits keep coming: a staggering plate of sashimi filled with charbroiled tuna, surgically scored squid, thick circles of scallop, and tiny white shrimp blanketed in sea urchin: a lesson in the power of perfect product. A sparkling crab dashi topped with yuzu flowers: a meditation on the power of restraint. Warm mochi infused with cherry blossoms and topped with a crispy plank of broiled eel: a seasonal invention so delicious it defies explanation.

Nakamura watches me eat. He watches everyone eat. Not in a creepy surveillance way, but in a sweetly innocent, I-really-hope-he-likes-this way. Soon you get the feeling that this guy has a body double or two floating around the restaurant, because despite the lavish attention he showers on all of his customers, and despite the fact that he's personally responsible for cooking at least half the plates that cross the counter, he does nothing all night but smile and look unreasonably relaxed behind the bar.

"We don't hide behind kitchen doors," says Nakamura. "This is what makes Osaka food so special, the relationship between the chef and the guest."

In a *kappo* setup, there are no secrets: you know the shrimp soup is laced with both the brains and the roe of the crustacean, plus a jigger of cognac; you see the nail that goes through the brain of the wriggling eel just before it's filleted; you learn that 40 degrees is the perfect angle to transform a pristine fillet of fish into a pile of perfect sashimi. (An enterprising home cook brings home a doggie bag of pro moves after dinner at Nakamura.) If you're going to spend $100 on a meal, this is how you want to spend it, on a dinner that educates and entertains as much as it satisfies.

As I'm paying the bill, an older gentleman with an electric-blue tie sparks up a conversation with the chef. "What's good right now? You have anything you're really excited about?" Nakamura reaches down into one of his coolers and pulls out a massive wedge of beef so intensely frosted with fat that only the sparest trace of protein is visible.

"A-five Omi beef." A hush falls over the restaurant; Omi beef, ludicrously fatty and fabulously expensive, may be Japan's finest Wagyu.

The man bites, and Nakamura gets to work on his dish. He sears the beef, simmers wedges of golden carrots, whisks a fragrant sauce made with butter and vanilla. It's the first time the beef has made an appearance all night, but by the time Nakamura flips the steak, three more orders come in. Suddenly, the entire restaurant is happily working its way through these heartbreaking steaks, and I'm left staring at my bill.

"Are you sure you want to leave?" Nakamura asks, and before I can say anything, he cuts another steak.

米 麺 魚

Of course, there are things to do in Osaka that don't involve fried meat and torched tuna and foie gras masquerading as beef. That is to say, there are nonedible activities here. You can, for example, take in Aleutian otters, Panamanian porcupine fish, and a whale shark the size of a small school bus at the Kaiyukan Aquarium, home to one of the largest collections of sea creatures in the world. You can visit one of Osaka's many awesome and offbeat museums: see rural life transposed onto urban at the Museum of Japanese Farmhouses, witness the world's largest collection of sake drinking vessels at the Museum of National Ceramics, or personalize your own Cup Noodles at the Museum of Instant Ramen. Or spend a day soaking your bones at Spa World, the Epcot Center of *onsen*, where revelers can travel through space and time to bathe in Caprian grottos, Greek medicinal baths, and the Trevi Fountain.

You can give your wallet a workout for the ages. Up near Umeda, you'll find one of Japan's greatest concentrations of department store awesomeness, including a thirteen-story Hankyu that could occupy the better part of a lifetime to fully

The blue-lit backstreets of Dotonbori

explore. (CliffsNotes: Head straight to the basement and you will learn more about the beauty of Japanese food in an hour than in a week of restaurant eating.) Stroll the tree-lined lanes of Midosuji, Osaka's largest and leafiest boulevard, and dream dreams of Armani and Dior. (Or do what I do: dream of all the Omi beef and cod milt you can buy with the money you're not spending on clothing, purses, and other inedible extravagances.) If sprawling commercial centers and polished boulevards aren't your thing, try an afternoon at Tachibana-dori, Orange Street, retail fantasy for the hipster set, comprising a thousand meters of antique shops, boutiques, and pour-over dispensaries, all of which looks to be curated expressly for your Instagram feed.

But ultimately, if you've come to Osaka, you've come to eat, drink, and soak up as much of the bonhomie as possible. And the best way to do that is through a good old-fashioned crawl, in search of the soul of *kuidaore*, a slow,

prodding, improvised evening of binge eating, drinking, and socializing that pushes you, your companions, and the city itself to the breaking point.

On my last night in Osaka, Yuko Suzuki rejoins the rabble, determined to lead us to parts unknown across the nation's kitchen.

The crawl starts where most good crawls end: in a dank basement filled with sake. Shimada Shoten is primarily a sake distributor, with a storefront stocked with a selection of Japan's finest *nihonshu* (the owners tell me they have personally visited over 250 breweries to build out their list), but drop down a secret staircase and you land in the tasting room, with transport barrels and half-drunk bottles scattered everywhere. A group of men who look like they haven't seen daylight all week herald our arrival with a chorus of grunts.

Shimada operates on the honor system. Choose your glass from a stable of beautiful ceramic sake vessels, pick your poison from a series of refrigerators, and at the end of the night, tally up all the damage. Let's go.

We warm up with a sparkling sake from Hiroshima, then move on to a *junmai daiginjo* from Ishikawa Prefecture, one of Japan's best sake-producing regions. You can taste its greatness, a cool shower of stone fruit and spring flowers. One refrigerator houses *koshu*, aged sake, and we take our chances with a twelve-year-old bottle from Kyoto. Aged sake makes up only a fraction of a percent of Japan's total sake production, and remains a controversial beverage, given the vast range of quality found in the end product. This particular *koshu* is as dark and musty as the room we're drinking it in.

We need a landing pad for all this rice wine, so we order the only food they serve in this joint: chunky miso from Wakayama, purple piles of pickled plums, and a strangely delicious cream cheese spiked with sake that pairs perfectly with nearly everything we pour.

Nihonshu sneaks up on you. It goes down gently, floral and cold, coating your throat in the most positively medicinal of ways. There is no recoil, no heartburn, no palpable reminder that what you're drinking is an intoxicant—just gentle sweetness and the earthy whisper of fermentation. The beauty and size of most sake glasses—scarcely larger than a shot glass—adds to the apparent innocence of it all. But once you get started on a proper sake session, with you pouring for your partners and your partners pouring for you and nobody allowing a glass to ever approach empty, it takes on a momentum of its own.

Sake is produced in all but one of Japan's forty-seven prefectures (Kagoshima reserves its distilling ambitions for potato shochu), and the early evening unspools into a liquid road trip. Nagano, Akita, Nara, Sendai, Okayama: we race our way around Japan, testing the harvest from every corner of the country, probing the borders with our tiny glasses, savoring the nuances of climate and topography: the snowmelt from the mountains above Niigata; the pristine waters that flow from the Katsura River outside Nara; the long, sunny days of Okinawa. A proper sake tasting will whisk you around Japan faster than the Shinkansen.

Somewhere in this liquid fantasy my notes degenerate into a series of miso stains and sake splotches and islands of isolated adjectives, which grow increasingly abstract and aggressive as the night inches forward:

Roasted asparagus . . . strawberry fields . . . liquid fireballs!

You could lose yourself quickly down the Shimada rabbit hole, which is probably why it closes at 7:00 p.m. sharp. The owner hustles us out with a broomstick, and we scatter like drunk rodents under the white glare of the streetlights.

"If we're going to make it to midnight, we'll need some real food," says Yuko, ever a beacon of wisdom in our hazy Osaka adventures. "I have an idea."

Osaka is home to a rich, closed-door dining scene, not just formal *ichigen-san okotowari* (invitation-only restaurants found everywhere in Japan) but clandestine spots in private homes and apartments scattered across the city. Madame X (she asked me not to use her real name, to protect her establishment) greets us at the door and ushers us into her apartment, a beautiful sunken space bathed in warm lights, with an open semipro kitchen and a bar with stools overlooking the action. Rendered chicken fat pops and crackles. A wok sizzles with blistered vegetables. Outkast bumps in the background.

We crowd into a nook around a chest-high table with a view of the residential street below. Two men in their late thirties, charming, good-looking dudes still suited up from a long Friday, join the group. They both work for United Airlines, and it is clear from the way they make their wine vanish that this was a week they'd like to forget. "Wait, what are you doing in Osaka?" one asks me, a mixture of merlot and disbelief on his breath.

Madame X returns to flood our table with a selection from tonight's menu: fried tofu floating in dashi and covered with dancing bonito flakes, spring vegetables simmered in dashi and sake, and the house specialty: pizza coverd in *shirasu*, tiny whitefish. The conversation, as it inevitably does in the presence of this foreign journalist, turns to Osaka.

Osakan fun facts ascertained during this stage of the evening:

- *Osakans are hilarious. More than 50 percent of Japan's professional comedians come from Osaka. (Kyotoites, despite living just twenty minutes away, are a decidedly unfunny species, I'm assured by everyone at the table.)*

- *Everyone thinks Tokyo has Japan's best sushi, but they're wrong. Osaka does, because Osaka gets the best fish. Serious eaters from Tokyo take the train down just for dinner.*

- *Osaka sake is really great, because Osaka water is really great. (At which point we switch from French wine to Osaka sake . . . Point taken.)*

- *Osakans love foreigners, even if foreigners haven't fully embraced Osaka. "Please tell people to come." I'm on it, dudes.*

- *Osakans once dumped a statue of KFC magnate Colonel Harland Sanders in the Dotonbori River to celebrate a victory by the Hanshin Tigers in the 1985 Japan Championship Series. The Tigers then went on an eighteen-year losing streak, giving birth to the Curse of the Colonel theory and inciting city officials to dredge the river in search of the shipwrecked birdman. He was eventually found in 2009, though his left hand and eyeglasses remain lost to the canal; only when those are found, Osakans speculate, will the curse be fully lifted.*

- *Osaka is really awesome.*

From Madame X's private parlor we slip our way back into the world of legal establishments. Yuji Kawabata is a well-known restaurateur with six popular izakayas clustered around the Namba area. He's also an artist, a ceramics collector, a deep thinker, and a celebrated drinker. Soul mate material.

His restaurant is closed by the time we arrive, but he ushers us upstairs to

The Osaka night begins to buckle at the knees.

a table, opens a massive bottle of sake, and instructs his kitchen to give us everything they've got. Out comes everything: piles of blistered *shishito* peppers, golden fried sandwiches of taro root stuffed with minced pork, bowls of dashi-braised daikon, a tower of yakitori, including my favorite, *tsukune*, a charcoal-kissed chicken meatball rich with fat and cartilage, meant to be dipped in raw egg yolk. My chopsticks cannot move fast enough.

As we work our way through a second bottle of sake, Yuji presents me with two of his favorite pieces from his ceramics collection, a violet sake pourer from a young Osakan artist and a pimply pink bowl from southern Kyushu. I do what I've been told to do with all gifts: refuse once politely, then accept with exaggerated displays of gratitude.

Not a city, a sensation . . . lights grow, night flows. . . . Osaka decides, we can't say no.

At 2:00 a.m. the airline execs call for a nightcap. As we walk up the stairs to Teppan-Yaro, a bar not far from Yuji's restaurant, I realize that I have been here before, six months ago on my maiden Osaka voyage. That night ended in a blur of whisky shots and air guitars. Somewhere in my parting words was a promise to return soon.

We open the door and the room explodes. A team of line cooks working the griddle raises spatulas in a spirited salute to our posse. The owner, skinny with long hair and the faintest whisper of a mustache, comes from behind the counter and pulls me in close to his chest. "You came back!" Music is cranked. Drinks are proffered. The night begins to buckle at its knees.

Clickety-clack . . . Whisky Pete is back . . . #mayocoma! . . . one-eyed purple people eater.

The Stones bleed through the speakers and the shots ring out and the men work the *teppan* with manic fury. It's unclear if anyone has ordered food, but they keep cooking: *clickety-clack, clickety-clack.*

The drink of the house is a purple potion made with vodka and juice and crushed unicorn horns. A decree has gone out across the bar to drown me in this shit.

I'm not used to this kind of treatment. The tourist is a fragile species in Japan, treated with guarded respect and kept at arm's length. Japanese are unfailingly polite, and most will go to absurd lengths to give you directions or greet you warmly as you enter their establishments. But even then, you are destined to sit on the sidelines of this society and watch it unfold from the outside. Outside that tiny yakitori joint exhaling charcoal smoke and good times. Outside the incredible sushi bar that serves only Japanese-speaking customers. Outside the animated conversation taking place on the stools next to you. This is a dense culture, steeped in a history, a code, and a language that most will never comprehend, and so we stare through the window and wonder what it must be like to understand.

But Osaka leaves the door ajar, if only a crack. Walk into a bar with an open mind and a wide smile, and someone might buy you a drink and ask you what you're up to tomorrow. It might not always be true, doors are walls here too, but everywhere you will see those little slivers of light, and when you see the light, the only thing to do is step into it.

At the end of the night, when our stomachs are stretched to the snapping point and all I can see is purple, the owner turns down the music, quiets the crowd, and makes an announcement in Japanese. Naturally, I understand none of it, but cheer along with the crowd as he punctuates his sentences with hand chops and fist pumps. Until suddenly everyone is staring at me with glasses raised. The owner comes from behind the bar and presents me with a white bandanna, the same one that he and his team of cooks are wearing.

This isn't a polite gift for an enthusiastic foreigner. It's a key to a door I thought was locked forever. And, for this one night in Osaka, it is mine.

揚げ物

OPERATION
IZAKAYA

It's your first night in Japan. All is a mess of incomprehensible signs and inscrutable commuters. Then you find an izakaya—Japan's ubiquitous, openhearted bastion of small plates and big drinks. In this, the most accessible and democratic of all Japanese institutions, you can have it all. Follow these steps, and your first night in Japan may be your best.

01

START WITH SAKE

Izakaya means "to stay in a sake
shop," and rice wine should
propel your tavern experience.
The most important rule of sake:
keep your drinking partners
well lubricated, but never serve
yourself (that's what partners are
for). Start with a midrange *junmai*,
a pure rice wine.

02

GO RAW

Next to first-class sushi bars,
you won't find better raw
fish in all of Japan. Izakaya
sashimi plates typically
deliver a mix of three to five
different types of seasonal
seafood, such as scallop,
yellowtail, squid, or tilefish.
A perfect match for sake.

BRING THE FIRE

Yakitori appears on most menus, but even better is whole grilled fish. Excavating the tastiest bits of a fish head with your chopsticks is izakaya eating at its best.

SCALE MOUNT SAKE

Remember, you're here to drink. Now that you've warmed up, move on to a *junmai daiginjo* from Niigata, Japan's greatest sake-producing region. *Daiginjo* means at least 50 percent of the rice has been polished, giving it a more delicate, complex flavor.

Operation
IZAKAYA

05

TACKLE THE *TEPPAN*

Griddle-cooked staples like *yakisoba* and *okonomiyaki* make it onto most izakaya menus, but it's crispy gyoza, Japan's juicy pork dumplings (best when lashed with chili oil), that offer the best match for your blooming buzz.

06

SWITCH YOUR POISON

Now that you've warmed up on sake, time to wade into deeper waters. Shochu is the distilled drink of choice in Kyushu, packing twice the punch of a typical sake. Try a sweet potato–based *imo* shochu. (No shochu? Make it a highball—a salaryman favorite.)

GREASE UP

Fried food makes the perfect booze sponge. *Karaage* (fried chicken) and *agedashi* tofu (fried tofu) are the most ubiquitous, but crispy oysters and *satsumaage*, fried fish cakes from Kyushu (a perfect match for the shochu!) offer a chance to break new culinary ground.

BE BRAVE

Finish with something from the inevitable section of izakaya oddities: fermented squid guts, cod sperm, fried testicles. There's no better time than right now.

This Is the Beef

和牛
WAGYU 101

DON'T CALL IT KOBE

Kobe is what your local gastropub calls its sliders, not what the Japanese call their high-fat beef. Kobe is a city famous for the quality of its Wagyu (the proper name for Japanese beef), but it represents less than 1 percent of all Japanese beef. Lavishly marbled Wagyu comes from nearly all of Japan's forty-seven prefectures. Want to sound smart? Look for Matsusaka, Omi, or Mishima Wagyu, among the

THERE'S NO BEER IN THAT BEEF

Rumors that Japanese cows get fat on beer, sake, and massages turn out to be greatly exaggerated. Historically, some small part of the Wagyu industry advocated beer or sake to stimulate appetite in the warmer months, while others massaged cows for better fat distribution, but the practice is limited to a tiny percentage of the overall Wagyu game. Most cows live on a diet rich in grains and move very

IT EATS LIKE BUTTER

Wagyu is ranked on a well-defined scale of letters and numbers based on the quality of the beef and the intensity of the marbling. A5, the highest ranking for Wagyu, indicates meat so densely marbled that the red protein is tough to spot. The best Japanese beef eats like European butter, which is a neat trick for protein, but those who love the intense minerality of, say, a grass-fed sirloin may be left wondering, Where's the beef?

IT COSTS A FORTUNE

Whether it's worth it depends on how deep your pockets and your love of beef fat are. Dedicated Wagyu restaurants charge up to $200 for a basic steak dinner. Get your fix with a few bites at a high-end izakaya, or try a Wagyu *sando*—lightly fried beef stuffed between soft bread. You'll find better value with F1 beef, a mix of Wagyu and Angus that delivers much of the extravagant richness of the high-class stuff without the price tag.

The
KNIFE MAKERS OF SAKAI

The blade makes its way from hand to hand, from anvil to grinder to whetstone. The four artisans in this famed knife town south of Osaka create some of the finest edges in a country that still reveres a balanced blade. American photographer Michael Magers crossed Japan in search of *shokunin*, Japan's fading class of master craftsmen, and came to Sakai for these intimate portraits of the men of steel.

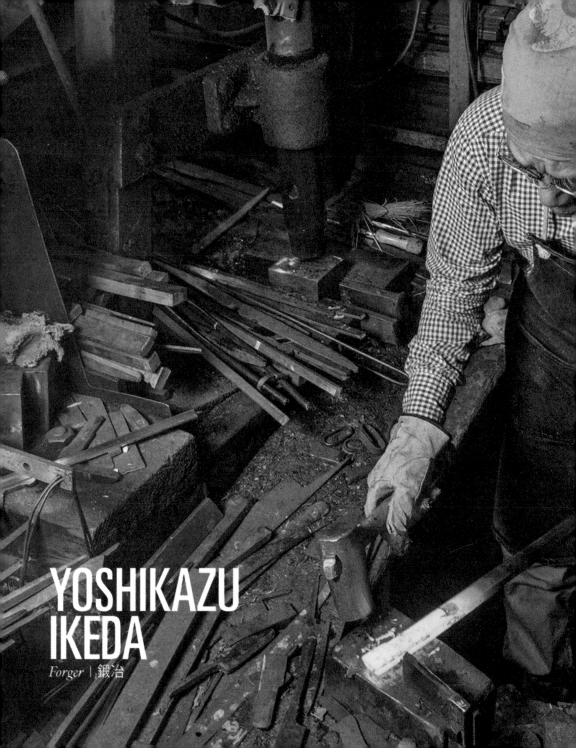

YOSHIKAZU IKEDA

Forger | 鍛冶

SHUNICHI TAHARA

Sharpener | 刃付

KOICHI MORIMOTO
Honer | 刃付

SUSUMU
WAKAI
Setter | 問屋

SANTOKU

三徳包丁

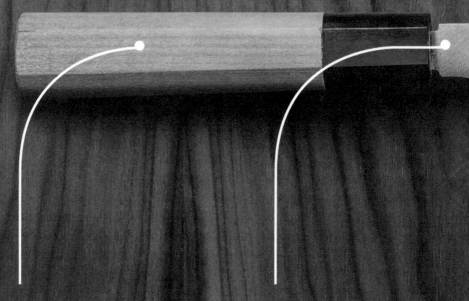

UTILITY BLADE

In a culture with knives for every micro task, *santoku* is the closest thing to an all-purpose chef's knife. *San* = "three" and *toku* = "virtue" or "character." The three virtues are meat, fish, and vegetables.

HIGH-CARBON STEEL

Sakai blades are made by forging together soft ferrite and high-carbon steel at 1,000°C, a delicate process that few blacksmiths have mastered, and can fetch up to $3,000 per knife.

SINGLE-BEVELED EDGE

The edge first takes shape on a
sharpening stone made from whale
bones. The exact angle depends on
what the blade will be used for: there
are configurations for everything from
root vegetables to octopus.

FORGED IN SAKAI

A wealthy port town, Sakai was once
home to Japan's finest sword makers.
Today a small group of dedicated
shokunin continue the tradition by
making the most coveted knives in the
culinary world.

Chapter Three

KYOTO

—

If you blink, you might miss it. You might miss the wet floor at the threshold, symbolically cleansing you before the meal begins. You might overlook the flower arrangement in the corner, a spare expression of the passing season. You might miss the scroll on the wall drawn with a single unbroken line, signaling the infinite continuity of nature. You might not detect the gentle current of young ginger rippling through the dashi, the extra sheet of Hokkaido kelp in the soup, the mochi that is made to look like a cherry blossom at midnight.

You might miss the water.

"I believe water is the most important ingredient in Japanese cuisine," says Toshiro Ogata, chef of the eponymous two-star kaiseki restaurant in the heart of Kyoto. "I always think about different ways to showcase water."

It paints an extraordinary picture, a chef kept awake at night by the most common substance on earth, an ingredient distinguished mainly by its absence of flavor. It would be easy to dismiss as precious lip service, an affectation delivered by a man expected to obsess over the details everyone else overlooks, if not for the fact that every week he drives into the mountains outside Kyoto and comes back with the best water nature provides.

If that's not proof enough of his obsession, there are the first three courses he serves me: a bowl of rice from Niigata Prefecture, steamed seconds before I sit down, shiny with a sheen of warm starch, presented with nothing more than a pod of lightly grilled fava beans; *ichiban* dashi, a stock of seaweed and dried tuna, twenty minutes old, served in an ink-black lacquer bowl; and finally, that same infant dashi, the same inky lacquer, this time with a pearl-white cross section of simmered onion floating in the center, a world of texture in its rings.

As I sip from the bowl cradled in my palms, I watch the line of liquid vanish against the shiny black surface—a moment of peace and mystery. Three courses, three expressions of water, collectively the most audacious and confounding start to any meal I've ever eaten.

Ogata-san is forty-seven years old, but cooks and speaks with a wisdom that suggests he's been on this rock for a few extra orbits. With each new course, he offers up little bites of the ethos that drives his cooking, the tastes and the words playing off each other like a kaiseki echo chamber.

Ark shell, a bulging, bright orange clam peeking out of its dark shell, barely cooked, dusted with seaweed salt.

"To add things is easy; to take them away is the challenge."

Bamboo, cut into wedges, boiled in mountain water and served in a wide, shallow bowl with nothing but the cooking liquid.

"How can we make the ingredient taste more like itself? With heat, with water, with knifework."

Tempura: a single large clam, cloaked in a pale, soft batter with more chew than crunch. The clam snaps under gentle pressure, releasing a warm ocean of umami.

"I want to send a message to the guest: this is the best possible way to cook this ingredient."

A meaty fillet of eel wrapped around a thumb of burdock root, glazed with soy and mirin, grilled until crispy: a three-bite explosion that leaves you desperate for more.

"The meal must go up and down, following strong flavors with subtle flavors, setting the right tone for the diner."

And it does, rising and falling, ebbing and flowing, until the last frothy drop of matcha is gone, signaling the end of the meal. Ten dishes, thirty ingredients, the breadth of kaiseki: boiled, raw, steamed, fried, grilled, all served in their proper order, all part of a poem Ogata pens to this city and to this season. A beautiful piece that I'm not sure I fully understand.

There is no questioning the quality of his ingredients, the scope of his skill, the depth of his dedication, but this is a cuisine so minimalist that it sometimes seems to not exist at all. "Western food is about addition," says Ogata. "Japanese food is about subtraction."

The wet stone, the lonely scroll, the midnight mochi: these are the tiny details that make kaiseki Japan's most elegant and extraordinary and befuddling branch of cuisine. Beautiful and austere, ancient and earnest, never has a cuisine better matched a city. And never has there been a city as mystifying as Kyoto.

米 麺 魚

Over 30 million people a year come to soak up the Kyoto experience, to visit the more than two thousand temples, marvel at the Zen restraint of hundreds of rock gardens, lose themselves in the shadows of towering bamboo forests. UNESCO must appropriate a budget solely for lavishing Kyoto with awards and designations, because over the years the UN has blessed seventeen buildings with its coveted heritage award. Add in the creaky teahouses, the tiny, mystery-filled streets of the Gion, the kimono-clad women, the sword-making men, and you see why Kyoto is considered the cultural heart of Japan, what Pico Iyer, the British essayist who came to the city in 1992 and never left, calls "a citywide shrine to Japaneseness."

Ogata's boiled bamboo in bamboo broth

No shrine to Japaneseness would be complete without its own dedicated cuisine, and *kyo-ryori*, the food of Kyoto, proves to be every bit as decorated as the rest of the city's disciplines. Kyoto claims seven restaurants with three Michelin stars and another twenty-two with two stars making it the most Michelin-dense city on the planet. If the Michelin man doesn't impress you, consider this: in November 2013 Kyoto led a successful campaign to have Japanese cuisine enshrined with a UNESCO Cultural Heritage award, one of only a handful of cuisines in the world to be honored with the distinction.

When I first came to Kyoto, it wasn't for gardens or geisha or UNESCO-blessed shrines; it was for kaiseki. For years I had marveled at it from afar, studied the format and history, read about the quiet practitioners turning dining into an all-encompassing feast for the senses. I had seen its fingerprints all over fine dining in the rest of the world—from the mixture of minimal-ism and naturalism that defines modern haute cuisine to the entire concept of an interconnected tasting menu designed to tell a story larger than the sum of its tastes.

It was the fall, a beautiful time for eating in Japan, when wild mushrooms cover the forest floors and tiny sweet fish swim upstream. In four days I ate five kaiseki meals, a procession of lunches and dinners made with the best imaginable ingredients handled with tremendous precision and served in exquisite settings. There were moments of striking beauty and astounding taste, but those were ultimately overshadowed by the confusion, consternation, and, worst of all, boredom I often felt in these restaurants. Every meal contained the same plate of sashimi, the same vegetable tempura, the same stilted, slightly tense service. I began to feel that kaiseki was a movie whose plot I already knew. In five meals I had five *dobin mushi*, a teakettle filled with conger eel and matsutake mushroom stems, along with a fragrant strip of *sudachi* lime zest, meant to be drunk first, then eaten. The first time, it was an eyes-in-the-back-of-the-head revelation; the fifth time, it felt soulless.

By the time I boarded the Shinkansen back to Tokyo—wallet empty, belly full of mushroom tea—I felt as if I might never need to eat another kaiseki meal in my life.

Was I missing something? Was I bringing my own baggage to the dinner table, hampered by being a foreigner, or did other Japanese find kaiseki so inaccessible? Was a chef who built a menu around water totally fucking insane, or was I the crazy one? The more I thought about it, the more I came to feel for kaiseki the same way I felt for Kyoto: breathtakingly beautiful but encased in amber, more a fossil than a living, breathing creature.

I took my concerns to the people who knew best, the serious eaters of Japan, speaking with friends in Kyoto, Tokyo, and other parts of the country to get their read on kaiseki. I quickly learned that kaiseki is like a Rorschach test for foodies: some see the epitome of elegance and refinement; others see a boring, overpriced cuisine in need of a shake-up. A small group of dedicated chowhounds I consulted spoke reverentially of the importance of kaiseki, its history and impact on Japan, not unlike the way certain Americans discuss the importance of, say, the Constitution. The other, much larger group all offered variations on the same theme: kaiseki is for old, rich people.

I found myself stranded on an island in between, respectful of its beauty and refinement but wary of its rigidity. I continued to feel this way about Kyoto and its famous cuisine until, one day in the fall of 2013, I met Ken Yokoyama, and everything I thought I knew was turned upside down.

米 麺 魚

Whatever you need, Ken Yokoyama has you covered. Need tickets to that

Kabuki show that sold out weeks ago? He knows a guy. Want to eat in that tiny Michelin-starred restaurant all your food-obsessed friends talk about? He'll make a call. Hoping to catch a glimpse of that austere rock garden without all the camera-clutching tourists? He'll do his best, which is always more than enough.

In a city where most doors are locked, Ken carries a skeleton key. As the general manager of the Hyatt Regency Kyoto, it's his job to open doors, but he does so with a subtlety and humility that belie his position. I first meet Ken as a guest of the hotel, which I choose based solely on his reputation, which has spread to certain corners of the country. The accolades, if anything, prove to be understated.

Every morning when I see Ken working the breakfast crowd, I think of the scene in *Casino* in which Robert De Niro is meeting with an exec in the hotel restaurant and both are eating blueberry muffins, only his partner's is exploding with fruit, and De Niro's has only one or two sad little blueberries. So he marches back to the kitchen and tells the dumbfounded chef that he wants every last muffin to have the same amount of blueberries. *The same amount of blueberries.* That's Ken, only not just with muffins, with everything: the petals on the flower arrangements that decorate the lobby, the warm sesame tofu served in the *robata-ya* downstairs, the hand-signed welcome note waiting on your pillow.

The Hyatt was once the indisputable hotel king of Kyoto, "the only non-*ryokan* game in town," as a travel agent friend told me when I first visited. But in late 2013 the Ritz-Carlton set up shop across the Kamo River, opening an aggressively gorgeous hotel rumored to cost $300 million to build. They poached a few of Ken's lieutenants and no doubt went after Ken himself (even if Ken won't admit it), but he seems unfazed. If anything, it makes Yokoyama-san push even harder.

I first recognize the full scope of Ken's reach one fall afternoon a day after we meet. Over a cup of coffee we talk kaiseki, and Ken gently probes the depth of my understanding. Between business dinners, government meetings, and VIP guest treatment, Ken eats kaiseki twice a week, as much as any man in this city, and he brings an anthropologist's eye to the discipline.

After offering up a few quick history lessons, he asks me where I intend to eat. I tell him that Sojiki Nakahigashi, an intimate, modern kaiseki considered Kyoto's most difficult reservation, is at the top of my wish list. "Yes, that would be at the top of my list, too, but as you know, it's not easy even for locals to get in." A few hours after our talk, my phone rings; it's Ken. "Nakahigashi-san will met you tomorrow at five p.m. for a chat. Then at six p.m. he will cook you dinner."

Hasao Nakahigashi grew up in a Kyoto *ryokan*, helping his parents with the cooking that forms a fundamental part of the traditional inn experience in Japan. Later he trained at Hyotei, the grandfather of all kaiseki in Kyoto, in operation since the early seventeenth century, before opening his own restaurant close to the Ginkaku-ji temple in 1992.

Nakahigashi is in his early fifties, with soft features and a gentle smile that exudes a sort of old-soul tranquillity. He wears not a chef's jacket but the white lab coat and tie favored by Kyoto's kaiseki masters. Every morning, before he puts on his coat and tie, Nakahigashi treks to the outskirts of Kyoto to pick vegetables and wild herbs from the hillsides and riverbanks. "The most important part of my cuisine is a strong sense of the season," he says. "If you had to use one word to describe Japanese cuisine, it's *nature*."

The restaurant has a floor made of small, smooth stones and a long polished cherrywood bar overlooking the open kitchen. The centerpiece of the room is a hulking orange *kamado*, a traditional wood-fired rice cooker, the same that has been used for centuries to prepare Japan's sacred grain. As diners arrive, Nakahigashi loads up the rice and feeds the fire.

The meal begins the way all kaiseki meals begin, with *hassun*, a mixed plate of small bites—fish and vegetables, usually—used to set the tone for the feast to come. In a bowl of pine needles and fallen leaves he hides smoky slices of bonito topped with slow-cooked seaweed, ginkgo nuts grilled until just tender, a summer roll packed with foraged herbs, and juicy wedges of persimmon dressed with ground sesame and *sansho* flowers. Autumn resonates in every bite.

While the rice simmers away, the meal marches forward: sashimi decorated with a thicket of mountain vegetables and wildflowers; a thick slab of Kyoto-style mackerel sushi, fermented for a year, with the big, heady funk of a washed cheese; mountain fruit blanketed in white miso and speckled with black sesame and bee larvae. His skills with vegetables bear the mark of a man willing to hunt them down every day at dawn. "The vegetables tell me what to do," he says. "When I pick up a daikon, it says, 'Please bake me, please simmer me.'"

As the meal progresses deeper and deeper into the Kyoto wilderness, the anticipation for Nakahigashi's famous rice grows palpable among his patrons.

"Rice is sacred to the Japanese people," he says. "We eat it at every meal, yet we never get tired of it." He points out that the word for rice in Japanese, *gohan*, is the same as the word for meal.

When he finally lifts the lid of the first rice cooker, releasing a dramatic gasp of starchy steam, the entire restaurant looks ready to wave their white napkins in exuberant applause.

The rice is served with a single anchovy painstakingly smoked over a charcoal fire. Below the rice, a nest of lightly grilled matsutake mushrooms; on top, an orange slice of compressed fish roe. Together, an intense wave of umami to fortify the tender grains of rice.

Next comes *okoge*, the crispy rice from the bottom of the pan, served with crunchy flakes of sea salt and oil made from the outside kernel of the rice, spiked with spicy *sansho* pepper. For the finale, an island of crisp rice with wild herbs and broth from the cooked rice, a moving rendition of *chazuke*, Japanese rice-and-tea soup. It's a husk-to-heart exposé on rice, striking in both its simplicity and its soul-warming deliciousness—the standard by which all rice I ever eat will be judged.

米 麺 魚

Before you rush off to drop $300 on an eight-course kaiseki dinner, take this simple questionnaire:

▪ *When I eat out, I like to do so in a quiet, contemplative way.*

▪ *I care a lot about the bowl my soup is served in.*

▪ *I prefer subtle flavors to aggressive ones.*

▪ *I am a big fan of negative space.*

▪ *For me, eating is a form of meditation.*

▪ *I am capable of feeling wonder at a single perfect ingredient.*

▪ *I like to wander alone in the woods.*

If you've answered yes to all the statements, congratulations, you have kaiseki in your DNA! Head directly to a very old, very serious restaurant and embrace the subtlety. A handful of affirmatives and you should book a table during your time in Kyoto and give it a shot. All nos? Save your money for sushi.

Regardless of your feelings on the form, the importance of kaiseki on Japanese culture cannot be overstated. Kaiseki draws on a diverse wellspring of influences, all of them intimately associated with the long, storied history of Kyoto itself.

In AD 789 the capital of Japan moved from Nara to Kyoto, where it remained uninterrupted until 1869. For more than a millennium, all life flowed through Kyoto—all political maneuvering, all artistic creation, all of the country's best ingredients for consumption by the elite. This is where Ieyasu and Hideyoshi ruled; this is where Kabuki and geisha were born. Modern Kyotoites' sense of pride ruffles the feathers of many other Japanese, but for the people of Kyoto, the city's long-spanning reign serves as empirical evidence of its superiority: *When Tokyo has been capital of Japan for more than a thousand years, then we'll talk.*

This sense of confidence stretches to all sides of Kyoto culture, but it's felt especially strongly in *kyo-ryori*, traditional Kyoto cuisine. You'll hear that the dashi is more elegant, the tofu more refined, the vegetables more dense with the flavors of Japanese terroir. If you listen closely, you will hear elaborate tales of ancient family traditions and heroic battles and extravagant courtly precedents that gave birth to Kyoto's status

as one of the great eating cities of the world. Kyotoites may allow that Tokyo has a deeper overall food scene, if only for its size, but the belief of anybody born and bred on the food of the ancient capital is that Kyoto is ground zero for Japanese cuisine. And nowhere are its tenets and techniques better displayed than through kaiseki.

By the end of Kyoto's thousand-year run, kaiseki had emerged as the dominant cuisine for the local elite, with four principal branches reflecting the city's multilayered history: court cooking, a regal cuisine soaked in pageantry developed around the imperial presence during the early years of Kyoto's reign as capital; *shojin ryori*, vegan cooking, the humble yet elaborate meals formed around Buddhist-temple dining (*kaiseki* literally means "a stone in the stomach," a reference to fasting Buddhist monks who used warm rocks to ward off hunger during the long, hard winters of meditation); *obanzai*, traditional home cooking that showcases the bounty of Kyoto, in particular its vegetables; and, most important, *chakaiseki*, the cuisine of the tea ceremony, the fountain through which nearly all traditional Japanese culture flows.

Tea came to Japan from China around the same time Kyoto was settling into its role as the country's new capital. Back then, it was consumed primarily as a form of medicine, but in time it developed into an important social ritual, one that grew more elaborate and grandiose as the years went on.

Sen no Rikyu would change all that. Born in 1522 in the nearby port town of Sakai to a wealthy merchant father, he studied tea from an early age and rose quickly in the ranks of Kyoto's tea luminaries, going on to serve as tea master under Japan's two most powerful warlords at the end of the sixteenth century. Nobunaga Oda was one of Japan's fiercest and cruelest rulers, a man best known for his blatant and bloody disregard for history, tradition, and Japanese formalities. And yet he was a lover of the tea ceremony, the most formal and traditional of all Japanese endeavors, which he used as a civilized way to discuss politics. When Nobunaga was betrayed and killed in 1582, Rikyu's talents with tea were employed for a new boss: Hideyoshi Toyotomi, a former servant to Nobunaga who would go on to be one of Japan's three great unifiers.

During his time serving Hideyoshi, Rikyu began to reshape the dynamics of the tea ceremony. Building on the Japanese idea of *wabi-sabi*, appreciation for the imperfect and the inconstant, Rikyu worked to bring the tea ceremony back down to earth, to replace the ostentatious public ceremonies held by the Kyoto elite with private, reflective experiences designed to tease out in participants a deeper appreciation for the finer points of the moment—the shadows in a rock garden, the brushstrokes on a scroll, the gentle bitterness of the tea itself.

Rikyu achieved this by stripping away all nonessentials from the cere-

Most students will spend decades studying and still not become official tea masters.

mony. He traded lavish halls for wooden huts, golden kettles for iron pots, elaborate ceramics for simple wooden cups. Free from fancy distractions, participants could achieve the deeper meditative state the tea ceremony was supposed to evoke.

In 1591 Rikyu's relationship with Hideyoshi turned sour. Some scholars speculate Hideyoshi grew resentful of Rikyu's growing influence in Kyoto; others point to a statue Rikyu erected of himself in Hideyoshi's compound as the source of the ruler's ire. Whatever the rift may have been, Hideyoshi ordered the grand tea master to commit seppuku, death by his own blade, which Rikyu did after serving up one last cup of tea to students and friends.

Four hundred years later, Rikyu is not only viewed as the father of the modern tea ceremony but he is also by extension one of the chief architects of kaiseki.

It has been said by more than a few smart people that to truly understand Japanese culture, you must first understand the Japanese tea ceremony.

Packed into this single event you can experience the purest expression of the cornerstones of Japanese culture: flower and garden arrangements, calligraphy and scrolling, architecture and dress. And, of course, cuisine. Food became a part of the tea ceremony as a way to line the stomach before drinking strong beverages, but what started out as a light snack gradually grew to a meticulous multicourse feast.

Today kaiseki exists as a stand-alone experience, separate from the elaborate four-hour tea ceremonies that still take place in many corners of Japan, but appropriating many of the same aesthetic anchors—scrolls, flowers, rock gardens—to carry on Rikyu's enduring vision: an experience of gentle nourishment, a meditation on imperfection, a communion between man and nature.

米 麺 魚

The morning after the Nakahigashi dinner, I find Ken waiting in the lobby. "Well?"

"A beautiful meal from a beautiful man," I tell him, before running through a few of the highlights. But he senses something in my voice, some distant reservation that even I don't register.

"But?"

"No buts. No, no. How could there be buts when there's a six-month waiting list? The rice was lovely. The guy is obviously a genius."

He arches his eyebrows, cocks his head slightly.

"Okay, maybe there is something. I'm not really sure what it is, but it just feels like I'm missing something, like maybe I don't have all the pieces of the puzzle. Or maybe I'm just ill suited to kaiseki."

We both stand there in the lobby in silence. Finally Ken speaks up.

"What are you doing tonight?"

"Why?"

"Be here at ten p.m. There's something I want to show you."

A few ticks after ten, we're in a taxi heading west across Kyoto. Eventually we come to a river framed by a dark mass of mountains behind it. The taxi pulls up to a freestanding two-story wooden building, what looks like someone's riverside residence.

A family of four greets us at the door, bowing as we approach. Ken carries a gift from the Hyatt, little cakes and sweets from their pastry kitchen in impeccable packaging. "My favorite," says the older man, as he bows to accept the gift and welcome his late-night visitors.

As we step inside the house, I realize that it's actually a restaurant, but it doesn't look like any of the kaiseki places I've eaten in before: small and creaky, with a handful of tables and a long counter—more an izakaya than a sanctuary for quiet reflection. The room smells of grilled fish and sesame oil, but there are no customers to be found. I see two sets of chopsticks, two sake glasses, and two stalks of bamboo set at the bar. We take a seat, and the old man and his son join two other cooks behind the counter. Packed inside the bamboo is a sorbet made from *shiso*, an herb with a flavor somewhere between mint and basil, a bracing shotgun start. Ken gives a nod, and the procession begins.

We start with a next-generation miso soup: Kyoto's famous sweet white miso whisked with dashi made from lobster shells, with large chunks of tender claw meat and wilted spinach bobbing on the soup's surface.

The son takes a cube of topflight Wagyu off the grill, charred on the outside, rare in the center, and swaddles it with green onions and a scoop of melting sea urchin—a surf-and-turf to end all others.

The father lays down a gorgeous ceramic plate with a poem painted on its surface. "From the sixteenth century," he tells us, then goes about constructing the dish with his son, piece by piece: First, a chunk of tilefish wrapped around a grilled matsutake mushroom stem. Then a thick triangle of grilled mushroom cap, plus another grilled stem the size of a D-sized battery, topped with mushroom miso. A pickled ginger shoot,

a few tender soybeans, and the crowning touch, the tilefish skin, separated from its body and fried into a rippled wave of crunch.

The rice course arrives in a small bamboo steamer. The young chef works quickly. He slices curtains of tuna belly from a massive, fat-streaked block, dips it briefly in house-made soy sauce, then lays it on the rice. Over the top he spoons a sauce of seaweed and crushed sesame seeds just as the tuna fat begins to melt into the grains below.

A round of tempura comes next: a harvest moon of creamy pumpkin, a gold nugget of blowfish capped with a translucent daikon sauce, and finally a soft, custardy chunk of salmon liver, intensely fatty with a bitter edge, a flavor that I've never tasted before.

The last savory course comes in a large ice block carved into the shape of a bowl. Inside, a nest of soba noodles tinted green with powdered matcha floating in a dashi charged with citrus and topped with a false quail egg, the white fashioned from grated daikon. The chefs cheer as I lift the block to my lips.

It happens fast, ten courses in just over an hour, and it unspools so quickly that there's no time for talking or processing everything they serve us, but by the time we emerge from the restaurant under a bright bank of Kansai stars, I know that I've just eaten one of the great meals of my life.

米 麵 魚

If anyone could be expected to carry the torch for classic Kyoto cuisine, it's Shunichi Matsuno. He was born in Gion, the ancient geisha district of Kyoto and the spiritual center of kaiseki. His dad ran a private teahouse, one of the most exclusive institutions in a city built on exclusive institutions. Down the street, one aunt owned a famous soba shop and another a grilled eel restaurant, two sturdy pillars of *kyo-ryori*.

And yet, when he graduated from university, Shunichi wanted to be a salary-man—a wage warrior far away from the smoke and steam of the kitchen. But the cooking gene was strong in Shunichi, and when the business suit began to chafe, he decided to continue the family legacy, albeit with his own restaurant safely removed from the rest of the Matsuno clan.

"The Gion was filled with drunk people treating women badly. Lots of prostitution. I knew I needed to get away from the center of Kyoto." So he came to Arashiyama, six miles due west, and bought a house along the Oi River with a sweeping view of the area's guidebook beauty.

"Being next to the river and the mountains, we hear the water from the kitchen, we see the leaves change from our window."

Tempura Matsu was a true tempura restaurant for only three years. The fry business was slow, so Shunichi began to experiment with other dishes to serve alongside the tempura. It was those dishes that customers loved and came back for. Gradually the menu grew in scope and ambition, incorporating the structure of traditional kaiseki but without being bound to its strict tenets.

He ran the restaurant with his wife, Toyomi, and when his daughter, Mariko, and his son, Toshio, were born, as is tradition in Japan, they eventually became a part of the business.

I learn all this one morning in the back of Shunichi's station wagon on the way to Kyoto's central market. Toshio is riding shotgun, arguing with his dad over the quickest backstreets to take through the city. It's been nine months since the midnight meal with Ken at the Matsu counter, and barely a day has passed when I haven't thought about that crunchy tilefish skin, that miso lobster, that icy soba finale. After nearly a dozen kaiseki meals and a world of ambivalence, I felt like I finally had a breakthrough, something unequivocally worthy of the towering fame of Kyoto's cuisine, and I needed to know—and taste—more.

The benchmark for innovation in Western cuisine is high these days. Ever since Ferran and Albert Adrià of Spain's El Bulli blew the doors off the traditional French model of dining that dominated high-end restaurants for decades, unleashing on the world a palette of foams, gels, powders, and spheres to paint with, the modern kitchen has become the seat of a creative arms race. Centrifuges and thermal circulators share counter space with mortars and pestles, young chefs use liquid nitrogen like old chefs use freezers, and restaurants collaborate with physicists, chemists, even perfumists, in the search for the next big discovery. Ambition announces itself with a megaphone at these places, above all on the plate, where a tableau of strange tastes and textures paint precious—and sometimes delicious—pictures.

But in Japan, creativity takes a back seat to tradition. Chefs remain more dedicated to perfecting the old than uncovering the new. Here innovation

Shunichi and Toshio Matsuno,
in the kitchen at Tempura Matsu

means adding a few extra grams of *katsuobushi* to your dashi, buying your tuna on Tuesday and serving it on Thursday, driving to the mountain to get your water. By this measure, what I tasted at Tempura Matsu was radical, if not downright heretical.

Most visitors to Kyoto will wind up in the Nishiki Market, the spellbinding sprawl of pickle purveyors, tofu artisans, and prepared-food specialists that runs horizontally through five blocks of downtown. But Kyoto's legions of chefs do most of their shopping at the less beautiful but more functional wholesale market, a cavernous collection of bulk seafood, meat, and vegetable dealers. As with most of Japan's commercial markets, you need a special ID just to survey the goods.

The menu at Tempura Matsu is a constantly evolving animal, with dishes rotating on and off daily, if not hourly. Every night after service, Toshio and Shunichi draw up the next day's menu, but final decisions aren't made un-til they've done their market run and tasted as many of the menu's protagonists as possible. "Too many chefs in Kyoto cook by the calendar, not by taste," says Shunichi. "We would never write a monthly menu because if the product isn't good, you still have to use it, and that doesn't make sense."

Instead, the two of them bound from one stand to the next, tasting everything in their path, making adjustments as they go. Shunichi is a large man, half bald, with a light frost of white stubble and a round face that looks borrowed from a manga character. His default facial expression is a smile that could melt an ice bowl of soba, punctuated by the occasional furrowed brow reserved for contemplative moments. Dressed in sweatpants, a bubbly jacket vest, and long-sleeved black shirt, he could be an emcee a few rhymes past his prime.

The shopping starts with Shunichi's tuna man. When the fishmonger sees us coming, he pulls out a large katana blade and saws thin slices of meat off the tail, which he dresses with soy and passes our way. "These ones don't have a lot of fat because they're jumping so much right now," says Shunichi. "They swim around the world to get away from their wives, and then they end up in my kitchen. Ha! Ha! Ha!"

He tells the man to bring out the *otoro*, the prized belly meat, which next to the lean tail meat looks like a winter snowstorm. Shunichi, convinced, peels off 10,000-yen notes from a thick wad he carries in his sweatpants.

We stop at a sea urchin vendor a few stands down who lines up a selection of Hokkaido and Kansai *uni* for us to taste. "You see? The Kansai *uni* isn't sweet enough yet," Dad says to his son. "We'll use it mostly later in the season, when it improves, but for now we'll stick with Hokkaido."

As we move through the market, gathering the building blocks for today's menu, Shunichi offers a running commentary on everything we pass. "See these eels? They're caught one by one in

a net. The difference in taste is unbelievable. . . . Hokkaido asparagus is famous, but these are too fat to be delicious. . . . You know what these are? Dried sea cucumber ovaries. The most expensive ingredient in the world."

Purveyors offer us tea, ply us with samples, pull Shunichi aside to show him a special product they've saved just for him. He happily bellows out his opinions on any and all market constituents, including the vendors themselves, but when it comes time to discuss prices, he goes quiet. He'll grab a vendor by the arm, usher him to the side and whisper, often using a little piece of cardboard to cover his mouth so others can't read his lips.

He takes an enormous amount of pride in the product he procures and the prices he pays, a result, he says, of the relationships he's cultivated over four decades at the market and the fact that he always carries cash. "A meal that could cost forty thousand yen anywhere else in Kyoto costs only fifteen thousand at our place. I know how to get value."

But while purveyors all vie for his attention, not everyone loves his bargaining tactics. "They call my dad the little devil in this market," says Toshio. He leans in to add, "Sometimes I think the same thing."

"What did you say?" Shunichi asks, inspecting a large snapping turtle crawling across the market floor.

"Nothing, Dad," he says, shooting me a little wink. "How does the turtle look?"

"Delicious." After a bit of negotiating, he settles on a 3.7-kilogram turtle, not something on the shopping list today, but he likes the rim of yellow fat he spots beneath the shell.

After a breakfast of ramen and fried rice, we make the morning's last purchase just outside the market maze. Shunichi has arranged to meet one of Kyoto's top sushi chefs, who moonlights as a high-end wild boar dealer. The chef emerges from between two delivery trucks with a white plastic bag in his hand and quickly passes it off to Shuni-chi, as if it were a brick of Colombia's finest.

"Three-year-old virgin boars are the most delicious," he says, peeking into the bag. "The fat is perfect."

It's late April in Kyoto, not long after the last of the cherry blossoms have vanished, which means *takenoko* (bamboo) season is in full bloom. Seasonality is a dominant tenet of Japanese cooking across the country, but in Kyoto, it dictates nearly every calorie consumed across the city. At this very moment, a thousand prep chefs are peeling back the fibrous layers of bamboo bulbs.

The Matsunos buy their bamboo from Yoshiaki Yamashita, a farmer whose family has been farming bamboo on the outskirts of Arashiyama for centuries. "He's Japan's number one bamboo farmer. He's the emperor's *takenoko* supplier. Very high-class stuff."

The key to great bamboo, Yamashita tells me, is space. Bamboo trees can reproduce for six years, but their roots need room to spread, and the sun needs room to bake the forest floor. More than a farmer, Yamashita is a constant gardener, pruning branches, keeping the trees to a height of six meters, using rice husk to sow nutrients back into the soil.

The best bamboo is found deep underground, safely away from sunlight, turning the harvest into something resembling a truffle hunt. We walk carefully and quietly through the forest, looking for little cracks in the earth that indicate a baby bamboo trying to make its way to the surface. When we spot cracks, Yamashita comes by with a small pick and gently works the soil until he reaches the bulb.

Most bamboo you see is ruddy brown or purple, but Yamashita's *takenoko* comes out lily white, tender, and sweet enough to eat like an apple.

"You have to cook it right away, otherwise you begin to lose the flavor," says Shunichi. He pulls his cell phone from his sweatpants and calls the restaurant.

"Tell them to start boiling the water. We're coming back."

米 麺 魚

For a place filled with so many outsiders, Kyoto is the ultimate insider's town. Everywhere you turn you find reminders of the line that exists between you and them: not just the restaurant menus dense with Japan's three alphabets, but the hidden pathways, the dancing curtains, the portals to a world that your imagination will work fiercely to construct as you wander through the shadows of Kyoto's oldest streets.

To understand just how deep the divide runs, consider the case of Ken. He is the ultimate insider, as deeply connected to this city, its culture, and its most august citizens as anyone you'll meet, yet he will never be anything but a guest in this city, a Yokohama-born transplant with Kyoto in his heart but not in his blood. Even if he had been born here, it would make no difference; Kyotoites count their history not in years or decades but in centuries.

Robert Yellin, an American expat who runs one of Kyoto's greatest ceramics

The veiled light of a *ryokan* entrance

galleries, tells it like this: "You aren't officially a Kyotoite until you're seventh generation. If you're sixth generation and your family has been here for two hundred years, you're still an outsider."

I count my Kyoto history in hours, a ship anchored in port for the night. I find myself constantly fighting the urge to abandon caution and good manners and breach the curtains into Kyoto's higher dimension. Reason and decorum save me the embarrassment, though; instead, late at night, I'll wander the smallest streets of the Gion in hope that one of those doors will suddenly slide open, an arm will reach out, like a Hollywood hand plunged into the frigid sea to save a sinking body, and pull me into the wondrous universe inside.

I have only a vague notion of what goes down in the house of the geisha. I imagine streams of sake poured from ancient ceramic sculptures by hands specifically designed for its dispensing. Long, electric conversations confronting the mysteries of our existence. Beau-tiful plates of food packed with textures and flavors unknown to the outside world. Busy hands, sweaty brows. Intellect and innuendo. When I close my eyes really tight, I see the last candle of the night casting an orange glow against the gossamer veil of a rice-paper door.

But I have no way of verifying any of these suspicions. Unless your family tree begins with a Tokugawa *bafuku*, or you have befriended the daughter of a Grand Master of Tea, your imagination will do most of the feasting in this town.

It's not all mirages, though. One afternoon, I sit in on a master tea class. Five students—two men, three women, all but one over sixty—spend hours practicing to make a smokeless charcoal fire in a hole in the tatami floor. Later, one by one they whip hot water and matcha powder into a frothy emerald cup of tea with *chasen*, bamboo tea whisks. An older woman in a purple kimono serves me one; I turn the cup three times to honor its creator, as I was taught before, then drink it down in one long gulp.

Thick, vegetal, astringent—nearly a meal on its own. There are three stages one must pass before reaching the status of master; the woman who makes my tea has spent two decades in the class and remains mired in the first stage. "I know I still have much to learn before I can move on to the next level," she says, eyes closed, head bowed.

One early evening, with the sun dipping just below the crest of the mountains that loom over the city, I meet with Yoshihiro Murata, the head chef of Kikunoi, one of Kyoto's most venerable kaiseki institutions. Murata ranks among Japan's best-known chefs, the man behind the successful UNESCO bid to honor Japanese cuisine. We meet in a private room upstairs at his restaurant, just me and him and five people in suits from various government branches. Upon learning that I am from the United States, he offers up a small lesson on global cuisine: "Western cuisines are based on fat," he says, "but Japanese gets its flavor from umami, which

has zero calories. That's why we live longer than everyone else."

Another day, Ken takes me to meet Setsuko Sugimoto, matriarch of one of Kyoto's ancient clans, a family that traces its roots back seventeen generations, to when the city was the center of Japan. Her home is among the oldest in Kyoto, so closely protected by the city that to rearrange a piece of furniture requires approval from multiple government offices. She serves us a traditional *obanzai* dinner, Kyoto-style home cooking: *chazuke*, steamed rice-and-tea soup, and a salad of tofu scraps speckled with dried fish. "We're starting to lose these traditions," she says, ladling the soup from an ancient wood-fired stovetop.

But inevitably, most of the moments that aren't spent at the kaiseki counter are spent wandering—past the shops where *wagashi* artisans shape sweetened beans into works of edible art, through the temples and shrines that dot the winding Philosopher's Path, across the canal and into the evening glow of Shirakawa Dori, a street whose beauty leaves me breathless every time I walk it.

I dream strange dreams when I am in Kyoto. One night, I am called upon by Obama to broker a trade negotiation between Japan and the United States. The next, I iron a suit jacket that stays forever wrinkled. An anxiety lies awake in me that no flower arrangement or seasonal scroll or dimly lit path can uproot. I'm not sure if it comes from the doors I can't open or the people who guard their thresholds. Maybe it's the shoes that never slip off my feet, the density of Japanese words in my mouth, the chopsticks that feel like tree branches. I cycle through metaphors, looking for one that makes sense of what I'm feeling: Kyoto is a Christmas feast, and I'm stuck at the kids' table. Or maybe Kyoto is a poem of immense but impenetrable meaning.

And yet, even after all the doubt and restlessness, all the unsettling stimuli, when I see a young *maiko*, a geisha-in-training, emerge from behind the curtains and fill a quiet street with her clomping wooden shoes, the whole world stops. My knees buckle and my palms sweat and in that second where everything grows wonderfully fuzzy I remember that this is where the story begins. That they are the music makers, and we are the dreamers of dreams.

米　麺　魚

By the time we get back to Tempura Matsu, the morning market haul is in various stages of undress. In Kyoto's more renowned restaurants, ingredient transformation is a delicate act—a bit of knifework, a gentle boil, a brushstroke of soy. But at Tempura Matsu, transformation takes on a more aggressive tone.

The 3.7-kilogram snapping turtle is alive no more; its shell bobs just above the water line of a simmering stock, flavoring a dashi made with leeks, ginger, sake, and mirin. The wild boar braises in a bath of white miso studded with mountain herbs and wedges of daikon. The bamboo goes directly from the trunk of the car into a massive pot of boiling water, the first step in a multipart process that will transform the tender bulbs into five separate dishes for the day's menu.

The restaurant employs five cooks who collectively have spent more than a century working in the Matsu kitchen. Kazuhiro Nakagawa, the youngest of the crew, handles the rice, the most straightforward but in some ways most stressful job on the line—rice must always be perfect in Japan. Hirofumi Oyagi works the tempura station, gently stirring batter with chopsticks, floating little drops into the hot oil to take its temperature. The same way an owner and his dog grow to resemble one another, Hirofumi and his pot have nearly become one over the decades, his eyes and hair cast-iron black, his face moist and craggy from forty-two years in front of the fryer.

If you sat on a stool and watched Takashi Shingu long enough, you would eventually unlock all the secrets of Japanese cooking. He skewers Wagyu and salmon and sacks of cod sperm and begins to grill them slowly over a charcoal fire. He turns pufferfish and squid into perfect dominos for sashimi. He nails a still-slithering eel to the cutting board, skins it with one swift motion, fillets it with one more, and has it cooking in a bamboo steamer splashed with sake before its muscles have stopped moving. He's been at Matsu since he was in high school, nearly four decades on the line, and he moves through the day's cooking like a man who has never wanted to do anything else.

Grilling, steaming, stewing, slicing, frying: the wheels of kaiseki turn with incredible ease and fluency at Tempura Matsu. With all the pieces in place, father and son both disappear upstairs to prepare for service. When Toshio comes back down, he's changed from his market clothes into a crisp white chef's jacket with a tiny Matsu kanji monogrammed on the left breast. Toshio's thirty years old but looks a decade younger, with boy-band good looks and a tommy-gun laugh that makes everything sound like the funniest moment of his life.

Toshio trained under Alain Ducasse, arguably the greatest French chef cooking today. "I taught Ducasse how to cook on hot stones," he says with a sort of sweet seriousness that dispatches any doubts you might have about the claim. "Now he's using it in all of his restaurants, but because he's so famous, people think we're the ones copying him." When Toshio looks over at me, he seems concerned that my pen isn't moving. "Please make sure to write that down."

Toshio also spent time in the kitchen at Kitcho, Kyoto's most renowned kaiseki temple, where dinner starts at $400 and dishes read like an edible history of Japan's ancient capital. You won't find many like him in the kitchens of this city: a young, hypertalented chef with one eye fixed on Kyoto and the other scanning the horizons of global cuisine.

Of course, Toshio's true master has always been his father. It was his father who taught him to how to bone a fish, how to fry a vegetable, how to fit two opposing flavors together. Normally the son of the owner, regardless of résumé, would be relegated to a supporting role in any Japanese kitchen—especially in Kyoto. But the father-son dynamic at Matsu is like none I've seen anywhere else in this country, one built on open collaboration, constant feedback, and a deep respect for each other's talents.

"When customers like a dish, they often ask who created it," says Shunichi. "But we always do it together. The base comes from one of us, but the final is a collaboration."

"Don't listen to him!" says Toshio, lining up plates for sashimi. "I came up with a dish yesterday and my dad said it was no good, but then the customers really liked it and he said he did, too. It happens all the time." He says it with a playful smile, but you can see by the way he works the kitchen, by the way men who were cooking here before he was born follow his orders with exacting

discipline, that Toshio is ready to push Kyoto cuisine forward.

"Kyoto is a place trying to hold on to its past," says Shunichi. "Many of the young chefs training at the important restaurants in the city will go on to open the exact same kind of kaiseki place. Of course we're always chasing perfection, but not at the cost of new ideas. We don't change tradition; we build on top of it."

That's where Toshio comes in, says his father. "He's the future of this place, so I need to empower him with the ability to do what he needs to do to adapt. Times change. We have different backgrounds and we combine them and that's what makes Tempura Matsu what it is."

At 11:30 a.m., the guests begin to arrive. First, a couple from Hong Kong with their six-year-old son settle in at the countertop; then a group of four businessmen in suits are led to a private table. Later, a single woman from Tokyo and two young men from Singapore, back for their third visit, fill out the countertop.

Father and son roam freely through the kitchen, Shunichi tasting sauces and plating sashimi, Toshio buzzing from one station to the next, whisking, slicing, skewering, creating dishes on the fly. Mom and daughter work on the other side of the counter, handling reservations, recommending sake, delivering dishes to customers seated in the restaurant's quiet second floor, removed from the immediate action of the kitchen.

As I learned that first night with Ken, the Matsu service philosophy revolves around guest interaction and kitchen spectacle. "Anyone can make delicious food. It's about pleasure, having fun," says Shunichi. "It's different when you can look a customer in the eyes, when you can see her smile." Throughout lunch, they make jokes and ask questions and do a good bit of the cooking and plating directly on the countertop, to the wild delight of the diners.

But as service wears on, Dad begins to tire. He goes from plating and tasting and teasing to standing in the center of the kitchen, arms folded, watching over his restaurant. Ten years ago he suffered a heart attack, losing the use of his right hand in the kitchen in the process. You'll never hear him complain, but occasionally, in a quiet moment, he speaks obliquely about the mounting health problems. When he says Toshio is the future of the restaurant, it's not a platitude; it's a forecast.

"Maybe I won't continue the way we're going," says Toshio, when I ask him about the future of Tempura Matsu. "I don't see myself copying my father. I don't think that's the right thing to do."

From a strict skills standpoint, Toshio is more than ready to blaze his own trail. I've seen few chefs with his touch, his versatility, his innate ability to create delicious, meaningful food. But this is his father's kitchen, his father's meticulous creation. Shunichi spent a lifetime ignoring the rules of Kyoto to build a bridge to the future, and now his son fears that he might have to cross it alone.

米　麺　魚

One morning I rent a bike and ride west, away from the old city. I ride with a backpack full of salty snacks and green tea, the Golden Pavilion of Kinkaku-ji my nominal destination. I don't pedal for long before discovering that most of this city lives and breathes in the vast space between Karasuma Station and Arashiyama, shopping for flat-screens, drinking canned coffee from vending machines, catching buses and trains like the rest of Japan.

Halfway to the pavilion, I hit a red light on a busy street corner. While I wait, life passes me by: cars honk, schoolgirls in plaid skirts eat French fries from a takeaway bag, a man passes out flyers for a cell phone sale down the street. For three light cycles, I just stand there, eyes glazed, wondering what to make of this strange city before me.

It's not the Kyoto we come for, and if you want your vision of this city to be as unblemished as the Gion's baby-smooth streets, it's best to stay east of the Kamo

River. Most visitors—gaijin and Japanese alike—would rather not spoil the view, but head west on foot or by bike or taxi and you will see the "other" Kyoto, a Kyoto without brooding red bulbs, rake-groomed gardens, powder-white layers of face paint.

This is a Kyoto that feeds itself the same way most of Japan feeds itself: with big steamy bowls of shoyu ramen, grilled skewers of chicken hearts, egg salad sandwiches from Lawson. For this Kyoto, traditional kaiseki is a source of pride, not a source of sustenance.

If places like Kikunoi and Ogata exist to nourish Old Kyoto (and the affluent visitors who come to immerse themselves in its unflinching antiquity), GiroGiro represents the tastes of a more modern city—young, hip, more concerned about value and good times than adherence to historical standards.

GiroGiro is a kaiseki restaurant, but only in the most liberal definition of the term. It's true, the third course they serve is sashimi, the sixth tempura, the last rice and miso soup, all in accordance with kaiseki code, but the similarities between it and the earnest institutions that have turned Kyoto into the Milky Way of Michelin stars stop there. The list of differences runs long.

To start with, there's the noise. Conversations echo off the ceilings, laughter bounces off the walls, the collective commotion a stark contrast to the pin-drop silence observed at most kaiseki restaurants.

The cooks: bright shocks of spiky hair, tattoos, loud and animated and quite possibly drunk—literally the polar opposite of almost every other cook you'll see in Japan.

The crowd looks scarcely different from the cooks: young, nicely toasted, aggressively hip. There seems to be more facial hair in this one room than in the rest of the country combined.

The price: at 3,500 yen, dinner at GiroGiro costs roughly one-tenth what you might pay at top-tier kaiseki in Kyoto, opening up the reservation book to an entirely different set of demographics.

If Nakahigashi is classical and Tempura Matsu jazz, this is punk rock kaiseki, done with attitude, volume, and a disdain for rules and expectations. There will be no scrolls to consider, no flower arrangements to admire, no ancient pottery to appreciate. As for the food, well, it's more manipulated, more dressed up, than anything you'd find in traditional kaiseki.

"In many ways, the more expensive the food, the more simple it's going to be, and that's hard to get as a beginner," says Shota Okuda, who has been cooking at GiroGiro for six years. "We have to develop techniques to work with the ingredients we can afford." Many of the resulting creations display a generous vision and a deft touch, like a bowl of rice spiked with sesame seeds and daikon, pressed fish roe and fresh strawberries, a tightrope balance of sweet and savory. Or the crispy fish cake covered in a sauce of whipped tofu and juicy segments of grapefruit—a dish with the type of contrasting tastes and textures you wish more kaiseki chefs would employ.

Other times, the limitations of a $35 kaiseki dinner are more noticeable. The final course of steamed rice and grilled *anago*, served with mushy, flaccid eel, made me long for the crispy soy-shellacked *anago* at Ogata.

But nobody here seems to mind. Young couples hold hands under the countertop. An apple-cheeked diner plies the staff with shots of whisky. A waitress, victim of the patron's generosity, stumbles delivering desserts to the last customers.

"Kyoto is ultimately a very young town," says Okuda, "and the university students can't go to traditional kaiseki, but they can come here with a date."

GiroGiro isn't the only restaurant pushing the kaiseki envelope. Jimbocho Den takes the traditional format and infuses it with whimsy and wizardry, serving dishes like Wagyu stained with beet blood and Dentucky Fried Chicken in a mock KFC box. At Ryugin, chef Seiji Yamamoto combines a *shokunin*'s ingredient obsession with highfalutin techniques borrowed from modern-ist kitchens in the West. Both are ex-ceptional places to eat, but both are in Tokyo, far from the standards and stric-tures of Kyoto.

Compared to these, GiroGiro, with its wobbling waitresses and Sid Vicious line cooks, is an especially aggressive addition to the kaiseki canon. Perhaps the most audacious part of GiroGiro is its location, along the Shirakawa Ca-nal, a few blocks from the Gion, one of the oldest and loveliest parts of Kyoto. The past literally pushing up against the future, the conundrum of kaiseki, of Kyoto, and in many ways of all of Japan, captured in a single restaurant with a funny name.

Is this the future of kaiseki? Half of Kyoto shudders at the thought. The other half is lining up for a reservation.

米 麺 魚

As the last of the lunch customers make their way out the door, Matsuno-san seats me at the counter and says something in Japanese to his son that could mean only one thing: keep it coming.

First, a sizzling stone, the same one Toshio introduced to Ducasse years back. Today it's filled with rice and gin-ger juice and baby firefly squid, which crackle wildly as he tosses it all like a scalding salad and pushes it over to me. The squid guts coat the rice like an ocean risotto, give it body and funk, while the heat from the stone crisps the grains like a perfect bibimbap.

By now the other cooks have all stopped working; even Shunichi has stepped out of the kitchen to talk with his wife. It's just Toshio, and you can tell by the way he wriggles his shoulders and glides between stations that he lives for this moment.

Next comes *chawan mushi*, a delicate egg custard studded with wild mountain vegetables and surrounded by flowers

Toshio creates a new dish while his father looks on.

from the bamboo forest. A dish as old as Kyoto itself.

Toshio plucks two sacs of cod milt from the grill, slides them off the skewer into a squat clay box filled with bubbling miso. He comes back a second later with a scoop of *konawata*, pickled sea cucumber organs. A dish as new as the spring flowers blooming just outside the window.

One by one, the market stars reappear on the plate.

A black-and-gold-lacquered bowl: Toshio pulls off the top to reveal thin slices of three-year-old virgin wild boar braised into sweet, savory submission with Kyoto white miso and chunks of root vegetables.

Uni—Hokkaido and Kansai—the first atop a wedge of taro root dusted with rice flour and lightly fried, the other resting gently on a fried shiso leaf. Two bites, two urchins, an echo of the lesson in the market this morning.

Shunichi comes back to the kitchen and shuffles up behind his son, watching his moves closely.

He's on to sashimi now, fanning and curling slices of snapper and fugu into white roses on his cutting board. Before Toshio can plate the slices, Shunichi reaches over and calmly replaces the serving plate his son has chosen with an Edo-era ceramic rectangle more to his liking.

Three pieces of tempura—shrimp, eggplant, new onion—emerge hissing and golden from the black iron pot in the corner, and Toshio arranges them on small plates with wedges of Japanese lime. Before the tempura goes out, Shunichi sneaks in a few extra granules of salt while Toshio's not looking.

By now Dad is shadowing his son's every move. As Toshio waves a thin plank of sea cucumber eggs over the charcoal fire, his dad leans gently over his shoulder. "Be careful. You don't want to cook it. You just want to release its aroma."

Toshio places a fried silverfish spine on a craggy ceramic plate, tucks grated yuzu and *sansho* flowers into its ribs, then lays a sliver of the dried eggs over the top. The bones shatter like a potato chip, and the sea cucumber detonates in my mouth.

A golden light bleeds through the window, framing the spirals of steam rising from a copper teakettle. Outside, the river sparkles at the foot of the mountains. At this hour, Tempura Matsu looks magnificent.

It's way past lunchtime. Normally the entire family would be upstairs, eating lunch together, a moment of peace, the day's first, before the dinner rush. But not today.

Toshio uses tongs to pluck a burning log of *binchotan* charcoal from the fire, sets it on an inverted Japanese roof tile filled with sand, and places it all before me. "This is an idea I just came up with," he says with a mischievous little smile.

He pinches two slices of densely marbled Japanese beef between chopsticks and lays them directly over the *binchotan*, a cloud of smoke rising on contact.

Shunichi inches in tight, eyebrows raised in an expression somewhere between surprise and doubt. He doesn't do or say anything, though. He doesn't grab the salt. He doesn't look for a new plate. He just stands there, close enough to breathe on his son's neck, watching him cook a dish that neither of them has ever tasted.

お土産
THE ART OF
GIFT GIVING

OMIYAGE
お土産

The word for gift giving, a touchstone of Japanese culture, is *omiyage*, which literally translates to "product of the earth," a local food from the place you were coming from. But while food (or drink) usually makes the best gift, there's more to *omiyage* than that.

TSUMARANAI
つまらない

Westerners are often tempted to hype their gifts. The Japanese, not so much. When giving a gift, use the customary line: *tsumaranai mono desu ga*: "It's nothing, actually, but please accept it." They in turn may decline it a couple times, but you should persist.

MEIWAKU
迷惑

One job of the gift giver? Avoiding *meiwaku*—annoyance. Don't give a heavy bottle at the beginning of a night out. And don't get something needlessly expensive: custom requires a return gift worth about half the value, so your rich gift costs them.

MEIBUTSU
名物

The best gift of all may be the most classic: *meibutsu*, the most famous foods of any given region of Japan. Hairy crab from Hokkaido, grapes from Yamanashi, and so on. It's not a unique choice, but creativity isn't the goal here. Besides, *meibutsu* are delicious.

TAKKYUBIN
宅急便

Not ready to pack a hairy crab in your suitcase? Grapes don't travel well, either. Fortunately there is the ingenious *takkyubin* transport system, which will express-ship local products anywhere in Japan for reasonable rates.

Japan's
GREATEST FOOD JOURNEYS

In a country shaped by its regional specialties, the travel dilemma isn't where to go, but what to eat. These are the answers you're looking for.

03

GRILLED RICE NABE
in Akita

COW TONGUE
in Sendai

SAKE
in Niigata

02

FUGU
in Yamaguchi

04

01

06

NAVY CURRY
in Kanagawa

TATAKI
in Kochi

CHICKEN SASHIMI
in Miyazaki

05

01 **UDON** *in Takamatsu*

 02 **SOBA** *in Nagano*

 **03** **SEAFOOD** *in Hakodate*

 **04** **STREET FOOD** *in Osaka*

 **05** **PORK AND SHOCHU** *in Kagoshima*

 06 **YATAI** *in Fukuoka*

UDON IN TAKAMATSU

Perhaps no city in Japan is better known for one dish than Takamatsu and its udon. Hundreds of restaurants dedicate themselves to Sanuki-style udon—thick al dente noodles afloat in dashi and topped with everything from raw egg to tempura to braised beef. Not sure where to go? Wave down one of the taxis marked with bowls of udon, and they'll deliver you to the city's finest noodle dispensaries.

SOBA IN NAGANO

Soba culture gets deeper and more delicious the higher you climb, and mountainous Nagano produces some of the country's finest buckwheat noodles. Here you can have your soba cold and naked, hot and swimming in dashi, topped with wild duck and tinged black with charcoal. Both Kusabue and Fujiki-an have been in the soba game for a few centuries—worthy places for your noodle

SEAFOOD
IN HAKODATE

Hakodate at the southern tip of Hokkaido offers one of the finest displays of seafood you'll find anywhere on the planet. The morning markets teem with wild salmon, hairy crabs, giant sea scallops, and golden mountains of sea urchin roe. The best way to enjoy it all? A breakfast *donburi*, bowls of steamed rice topped with any or all of Hokkaido's finest raw materials.

STREET FOOD IN OSAKA

Osaka's reputation as a center for good times and cheap food is well earned: the city abounds with casual eateries, lively bars, and street stands dispensing quick bites with potent flavors. *Kuiadore*, Osakan dialect for eating yourself stupid, is a founding principle in Japan's most freewheeling city, and it should be the primary objective while in Japan's second city. One could survive very happily on *takoyaki*, *okonomiyaki*, cold beer, and the good vibes of the Osakan citizenry for weeks at a

PORK AND SHOCHU IN KAGOSHIMA

There's something deeply lovable about this southern Kyushu city: maybe it's the spewing Sakurajima volcano, the sprawling sea views, the seedy entertainment district. Probably it's the abundance of Japan's best shochu (with over a hundred distilleries in the city) and *kurobuta* cuisine—shabu-shabu, tender braises, and ramen all made with black-footed Berkshire pork. Combine both in as many of

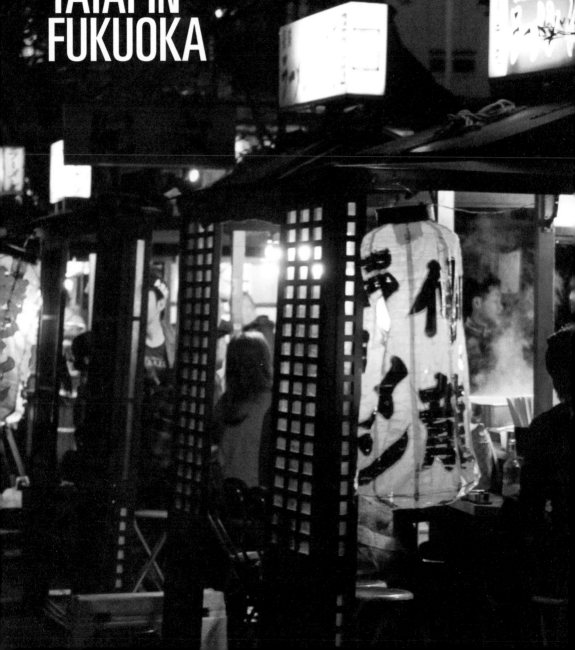

YATAI IN
FUKUOKA

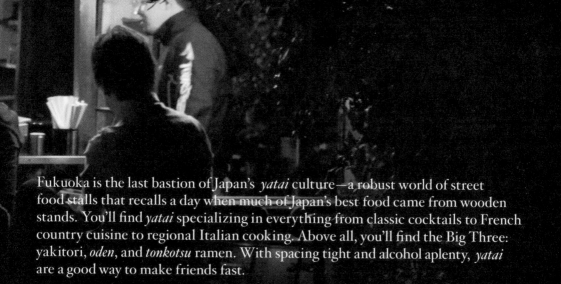

Fukuoka is the last bastion of Japan's *yatai* culture—a robust world of street food stalls that recalls a day when much of Japan's best food came from wooden stands. You'll find *yatai* specializing in everything from classic cocktails to French country cuisine to regional Italian cooking. Above all, you'll find the Big Three: yakitori, *oden*, and *tonkotsu* ramen. With spacing tight and alcohol aplenty, *yatai* are a good way to make friends fast.

GAIJIN GLOSSARY

OISHII 美味しい
Delicious.

If there is one word that will bring visitor and host together, this is it. Said with a slight twinkle in the eye, it can melt all the barriers of language and culture into a warm broth of love for one's fellow man.

SUMIMASEN すみません
Excuse me.

Personal space in Japan is highly valued and yet nearly impossible to defend. *Sumimasen* and its expat-impatient variety, *excuse-me-masen*, are the Purell of jostling: a word you can just lather on any situation to defuse and disinfect.

DOZO どうぞ
Please, go ahead.

Like *vale* in Spain or *doch* in Germany, *dozo* in Japan is a multitool of a word. It adds politeness—not an undervalued commodity in Japan—to any situation, whether you're letting someone pass in front of you or handing over a present.

DOKO どこ
Where?

It's not just that most people don't speak English; most street signs and place names are not in the Romaji alphabet, and guidebook and Internet addresses routinely fail. *Doko* is your friend.

TABEMASU 食べます
To eat.

You did come to Japan to eat, yes? Say this word (remember, the *u* is silent in Japanese) with a question mark at the end, and you will immediately be led to Japanese food.

OMAKASE お任せ
I leave it up to you.

It's the equivalent of putting yourself in the chef's hands—most common at high-end sushi bars but also used in many top restaurants. Say it when you want to be taken on a boundless gastronomic adventure, or when you have no idea how to order à la carte.

ITADAKIMASU 美味しい
I receive this food.

Use this and *gochiso sama deshita* to bookend mealtime, and you will win hearts everywhere you go. This is essentially a small blessing to be intoned just before you begin eating, aimed at those who prepared the food for you.

GOCHISO SAMA DESHITA ご馳走様でした
It was quite a feast.

After you finish eating, say this incantation to thank and praise the cook. When you return for lunch the next day, they'll give you a hero's welcome.

Chapter Four

FUKUOKA

——

Toshiyuki Kamimura eats four hundred bowls of ramen a year. That's a bowl every day for lunch or dinner, plus one for breakfast about once a week. For that weekly breakfast bowl he usually goes to Ganso Nagahama out toward the ocean, a legendary spot located in what looks like an auto-parts warehouse that stays open twenty hours a day. "Sometimes I can't wait until lunch," says Kamimura, who consumes his ramen with a sense of urgency, conveying thick ropes of noodles into his mouth and sliding them down his throat like a duck, barely pausing to chew, "so I eat with the taxi drivers getting off the late shift."

His first memories of eating ramen come from his childhood in Kagoshima, the city at the southern tip of Kyushu famous for its fat-strewn pigs and potato-based liquor. Back then, Kamimura's parents would have ramen delivered from a local restaurant as a treat for the family. Even with the distance of time and the warm mist of nostalgia, Kamimura can't help but put a critical spin on those infant ramen moments. "By the time it got home, the broth was cold and the noodles were compromised. It wasn't impressive ramen."

He moved to Fukuoka, the capital of Kyushu, when he was seventeen in order to study photography at Fukuoka University. It was in that first year living on his own that Kamimura had his ramen epiphany. The transformative bowl came from Ichiran, now a popular national chain of middling quality but back then a gateway to a new life: "It was a whole different experience. I had no idea ramen could be so good."

In the twenty years since, he has gone from being a passionate consumer to one of Japan's most important ramen bloggers. When it comes to food writing, the Japanese are avid consumers of data, and the nascent ramen blogging industry specializes in chronicling every aspect of Japan's chief noodle obsession. On his website, Junction 9 (named for a local intersection with a concentration of killer ramen), Kamimura reviews hundreds of shops across Kyushu, offering detailed analysis on broth strength, noodle type, and topping cohesion. He's also a frequent contributor to *Ramen Walker*, the most prominent of Japan's dozen or so ramen magazines, among other publications, and appears regularly on television, offering his take on the pressing ramen issues of the day.

Ramen bloggers aren't just passive observers of the noodle soup phenomenon: they create trends, drive or deflate business, and generally analyze ramen creation, consumption, and culture down to a microbial level. In some cases they eventually find themselves on the other side of the counter, stirring the soup and kneading the noodles. They, as much as the bandanna-wearing chefs and the legions of slurping salarymen, are the heart of modern ramen culture.

To be a ramen writer of Kamimura's stature, you need to live in a ramen town, and there is unquestionably no town in Japan more dedicated to ramen than Fukuoka. This city of 1.5 million along the northern coast of Kyushu, the southernmost of Japan's four main islands, is home to two thousand ramen shops, representing Japan's densest concentration of noodle-soup emporiums. While bowls of ramen are like snowflakes in Japan, Fukuoka is known as the cradle of *tonkotsu*, a pork-bone broth made milky white by the deposits of fat and collagen extracted during days of aggressive boiling. It is not simply a specialty of the city; it is the city, a distillation of all its qualities and calluses.

Indeed, tell any Japanese that you've been to Fukuoka and invariably the first question will be: "How was the *tonkotsu*?"

Ramen, despite its reputation as a cheap fast food, is a complex pillar of modern Japanese society, one loaded with political, cultural, and culinary importance that stretches far beyond the circumference of the bowl. And all those big ideas start here in Fukuoka, ground zero for the ramen craze, a dizzying galaxy of bone-broth dispensaries that can be overwhelming for the noodle novice.

I'm not a novice, not exactly. Like most Westerners, my ramen history begins with a brick of dried noodles and a silver spice packet, a three-for-a-dollar subsistence plan that propelled

me through the lean college years. Later came the real thing, first in the early ramen boom of New York, later in noodle crawls around Tokyo that opened my mind to how sophisticated and staggeringly delicious the best bowls could be.

But this kind of ramen world, one where every block houses a bowl that could make your knees buckle, is brand-new territory, and objective is nothing if not ambitious, naive, and slightly hazardous to my health. I'm stalking the million-footed beast: not just a bowl that will make my stomach dance, but an experience that will help me better understand how a bowl of noodle soup from China came to define Japanese food culture in the twenty-first century. Any local can take you to a handful of her favorite shops, but it takes the discerning eye of a ramen blogger to understand the details. That is why I've enlisted Kamimura-san to be my ramen guru, my noodle-soup interpreter, a spirit guide in a journey to better understand the bowl behind the city, and the city behind the bowl.

米 麺 魚

In the broadest sense, a bowl of ramen comprises four principal constituents: *tare* (a seasoning base), broth, noodles, and toppings. (Of course, ramen wonks like Kamimura could nitpick these parts into dozens of subcategories.)

Let's start from the top of the bowl and work our way down. In theory, toppings can include almost anything, but 95 percent of the ramen you consume in Japan will be topped with *chashu*, Chinese-style roasted pork. In a perfect world, that means luscious slices of marinated belly or shoulder, carefully basted over a low temperature until the fat has rendered and the meat collapses with a hard stare. Beyond the pork, the only other sure bet in a bowl of ramen is *negi*, thinly sliced green onion, little islands of allium sting in a sea of richness. Pickled bamboo shoots (*menma*), sheets of nori, bean sprouts, fish cake,

raw garlic, and soy-soaked eggs are common constituents, but of course there is a whole world of outlier ingredients that make it into more esoteric bowls, which we'll get into later.

While shape and size will vary depending on region and style, ramen noodles all share one thing in common: alkaline salts. Called *kansui* in Japanese, alkaline salts are what give the noodles a yellow tint and allow them to stand up to the blistering heat of the soup without degrading into a gummy mass. In fact, in the sprawling ecosystem of noodle soups, it may be the alkaline noodle alone that unites the ramen universe. "If it doesn't have *kansui*, it's not ramen," Kamimura says.

Noodles and toppings are paramount in the ramen formula, but the broth is undoubtedly the soul of the bowl, there to unite the disparate tastes and textures at work in the dish. This is where a ramen chef makes his name. Broth can be made from an encyclopedia of flora and fauna: chicken, pork, fish, mushrooms,

of the few foods in Japan that

rule book.

root vegetables, herbs, spices. Ramen broth isn't about nuance; it's about impact, which is why making most soup involves high heat, long cooking times, and giant heaps of chicken bones, pork bones, or both.

Tare is the flavor base that anchors each bowl, that special potion—usually just an ounce or two of concentrated liquid—that bends ramen into one camp or another. In Sapporo, *tare* is made with miso. In Tokyo, soy sauce takes the lead. At enterprising ramen joints, you'll find *tare* made with up to two dozen ingredients, an apothecary's stash of dried fish and fungus and esoteric add-ons. The objective of *tare* is essentially the core objective of Japanese food itself: to pack as much umami as possible into every bite.

With all these variables in play, the potential combinations are limitless, but in Fukuoka, the single-minded dedication to *tonkotsu* is so relentless that all other ramen is beside the point. Kyushu has long been the center of Ja-

pan's pork industry, and no dish better expresses the potential of the pig better than *tonkotsu*. To make sure I fully understand the Fukuoka-*tonkotsu* connection, Kamimura starts me off at one of his favorite shops, Ramen-Ya Mototsugi.

Watching Kamimura review a ramen shop is like watching a detective work a crime scene. He starts with the *noren*, the cloth awning that invariably hangs from a shop's entrance. "If it's greasy ramen," he says, reaching up and rubbing the yellowing drapes with a nod of approval, "it will look like a dirty shirt."

Next, he inhales deeply. *Tonkotsu* is legendary for its fragrance, which, when emanating from the most intense shops, can assault your olfactory system from a three-block radius. It's a barnyard smell, pure sweaty-foot funk, and it's everywhere in Fukuoka, a misty aroma that hangs over the city the way fog clings to the hills of San Francisco.

"When I walk into a place and smell the broth, I can imagine how it was made," says the ramen whisperer as we slip into the shop. I draw in a deep breath, and my head swims with the memory of pigs passed.

After he orders, Kamimura turns his attention to the noodles. Are they cooked in individual baskets for easy timing, or are they dropped coil by coil into an open pot of boiling water? Most cooks go the basket route these days, but Kamimura prefers the purity of a free boil. "I respect the talent it takes to cook it all together—it takes real touch and intuition."

All the while, he's watching for little precursors of quality: the way the ramen cook shakes the water from the noodles after they're done cooking so as not to dilute the precious broth; the careful hand-slicing of a roll of *chashu* so that it melts on contact with the hot soup; the judicious layering of *negi* and nori and other garnishes to elongate the textural juxtaposition.

"I work hard to gather all the information necessary to make my judg-ments. If you don't poke your head into the kitchen, you never know," Ka-mimura says.

Our first bowl of ramen arrives. It's a muscular rendition, the spitting defini-tion of Hakata-style *tonkotsu*: pale, thin, straight noodles, thick ivory broth, two slices of *chashu*, and little else in the way of toppings. Sesame seeds, ground white pepper, and electric pink pickled ginger are the holy trinity of table con-diments in Fukuoka, but Kamimura isn't much for accessories. He wastes no time in cracking his wooden chopsticks and breaching the surface, but I wade in more cautiously.

Most Japanese food is a collective ex-perience: the sushi chef feeds you piece by piece, the yakitori arrives in a great heap for divvying up, and the shabu-shabu bubbles away between you and your dining partners. But not ramen. With ramen it is just you and the bowl—the most intense and intimate of all food experiences in Japan. You may belly up to the bar with friends or colleagues in tow, but once your bowl arrives, all talking ceases as you turn your attention entirely to the task of conveying noodles and soup from bowl to mouth. No conversing, no pausing, no "How is the soup working out for you?" from the waitstaff. You bow your head, let the steam wash over you, and don't look up again until you can see the bottom of the bowl.

Inexperienced eaters will require some practice before they learn to handle the volcanic temperatures of a proper bowl of ramen. Waiting for it to cool, though, will prove an unnerving experience for both you and the chef. The only way forward is to abandon Western decorum and embrace the slurp, the calculated introduction of air that cools the noodles upon entry. A ramen shop in full feast mode sounds like a car vacuum suctioned against your front seat. It will take a few scaldings and a few stained shirts, but until you learn to properly slurp, expect to be lapped by grandpas whose bowls are dry before you've had

the chance to slip the first noodles past your lips.

When we finish our bowls—Kamimura in three minutes, me in twelve—beads of sweat have gathered above my brow. I look up, almost surprised and slightly embarrassed to find I'm not alone in the shop.

"Next stop," he says, and we step outside, swallowed by the bright lights of a Fukuoka night, in search of another bowl.

米　麺　魚

Kyushu, as the southernmost of Japan's four main islands, has always been a gateway to the outside world. In fact, for much of Japan's modern history, it was the only way in and out.

When the shogun Tokugawa Iemitsu closed Japan's borders in 1635, ushering in two centuries of virtual isolation, Nagasaki on Kyushu's west coast remained the only open port in the country. It became a tiny door through which cultural artifacts from the outside world could enter. Portuguese missionaries brought tempura and Christianity. The Koreans introduced a rich ceramics culture. And the Chinese arrived with their noodle soups, including *champon*, a Nagasaki specialty of pork, seafood, and egg noodles that some believe to be a precursor to Japanese ramen.

At the same time, Kyushu maintained a wild, rebellious edge. For much of the seventeenth and eighteenth centuries, it became a clubhouse for buccaneers and misfits, a refuge where pirates could take advantage of Japan's lack of centralized power and public order to loot and pillage. By the nineteenth century, much of this rogue energy had coalesced into one of Japan's mightiest military factions. It was in here, in Satsuma in 1877, shortly after the inception of the Meiji era, that the last samurai took a final stand against imperial Japan.

Kyushu later became a home of industry—steel and iron, mostly—and as such took on an outsize role in World War II. The southern island became a favorite target for American attacks, starting with the 1944 bombing of Yahata. In fact, Yawata Steel Works in Fukuoka Prefecture was the original target for the second atomic bomb, but because of cloud cover, Nagasaki was razed instead.

Like the rest of Japan, Kyushu recovered quickly, rebuilding and expanding industry in the postwar years. Since then the region has been working hard to position itself as a top destination for domestic and foreign tourists. The arrival of the Shinkansen in 2004 has made the southern island more accessible than ever: board a bullet train in Kyoto, and you'll barely have time to crack a bento box and down a Kirin before you pull into Hakata Station.

Despite the ease of access, just 3 percent of American tourists in Japan ever make it to Kyushu, something that will feel like a gross oversight to anyone who has spent time in the region. This is a land for coastal cruising and mountain bounding, for hot mud baths and cold

Fukuoka dusk reflected in the Naka River;
nightlife here is among the best in Japan.

potato liquor. Above all, it's a place to eat. In Kagoshima in the south, the list of local specialties (black-footed pigs, fried fish cakes, tiny, sweet sardines) is exceeded only by the world-class shochu on offer at every bar and restaurant. In Miyazaki, on the southwestern coast where Japan's surfing community chases the country's best break, chicken is king, from blackened, charcoal-coated thighs to the scourge of Western hygienic sensibilities, chicken sashimi.

But Fukuoka is the center of island life—gastronomically and otherwise. The island's capital was originally divided into two urban centers: Fukuoka for the well-to-do to the west of the Nakagawa River, and Hakata for the common folk settled in the east. The two were officially merged in 1889, but the two names are still used by locals and urban planners (who named the airport after the former and the train station after the latter).

It's a city with a broad yet gentle appeal—not a love-at-first-sight des-tination, but a slow-burn kinda place. *Monocle* named it the tenth most livable city in the world in its 2014 survey, a fact you're likely to hear repeated more than a few times while in town. Indeed, on paper, it stacks up favorably to any city you know: great weather, lovely coast-line, plenty of parks and open spaces, fantastic food, electric nightlife. Unlike other parts of Japan, which can strike visitors as wondrous, fantastical places, spend a few days in Fukuoka and you might find yourself saying, "I could see myself living here . . ."

Here with the high-skirts and hus-tlers working the corners of Naksu. Here with the hipsters and the book-worms buying jean jackets and sipping matcha lattes on the narrow streets of Daimyo. Here with the tuna-cheeked businessmen bellying up to the *yatai*, the local street food vendors, for one last round and a bowl of something warm before heading home. Fukuoka has an edge, a certain samurai resistance about it, and nowhere is the spirit of nonconformity more apparent than in its street-food scene.

Fukuoka is the last bastion of *yatai* culture in Japan, a reminder of a past when all of Japan's most famous foods—sushi, soba, skewers—could be found at these pushcart street stands. While *yatai* have effectively been banned across Japan, you will still find them all around Fukuoka, gathered in clusters along the river and in pockets of city nightlife centers like Tenjin and Naga-hama. They take shape every evening at dusk and disappear every morning at dawn, and in the hours between they serve everything from *oden* and yakitori to craft cocktails and escargot.

Kamimura takes me to his favorite *yatai*, a collection of covered stands next to a famous shrine where the owner works the crowd in a full kimono and headband. Most *yatai* seat eight people hip to hip, but this is Fukuoka's largest, a tented stand that could house your high school algebra class. It's early by *yatai* standards, but the group of young

suits next to us is already soaked in sho-chu and offers up spirited *kanpai*s when our own drinks arrive. After skewers of grilled chicken parts and a few more rounds of shochu, they pay their bill and move on, but it's clear that a few more *yatai* stops await before the night is through. Kamimura looks almost wist-ful as he watches them go.

"*Yatai* life is slowly dying in Fukuoka. There used to be three hundred *yatai*. Now there are a hundred and fifty." *Yatai* have been fighting for survival for the past two decades as business owners have decried their low-rent competitive advantage and local residents have railed against the bad behavior—the noise, the smell, the public urinating—of *yatai* cus-tomers, many of them tourists, most of them drunk.

After a few rounds of shochu and some skewers of cheese grilled directly over charcoal, the ramen arrives—a small bowl dotted with bamboo and nori and a single thin slice of roast pork. Kamimura seems to sense my disappointment.

"There are very few *yatai* that serve good ramen. They have limited space, so they use soup and noodles made by someone else. Others have very limited hours so it's impossible to have the same quality as a restaurant. And because it's for after drinking, the style tends to be light. But you have to respect *yatai* for their history and for still being one of the most popular places to eat ramen here."

Kamimura is an enthusiast, a man who in private will tell you that a noodle should have been a millimeter wider but publicly, on his website and in magazines, will always try to find the positive side behind every bowl. Rather than calling a bowl small or overpriced, he says, "It's perfect for a snack." Instead of calling a broth overly fatty and without nuance, he'll say "It's best for hardcore *tonkotsu* lovers."

That's not to say Kamimura's ramen writing isn't deeply informative; the man will lay out details about ingredients and techniques with encyclopedic exactitude. But the overall tone is always one of respect and enthusiasm for the craft. "No matter what happens in my life, ramen has always been there for me."

This is our fifth bowl of ramen over the past eight hours, and I've reached my limit, but Kamimura shows no sign of slowing down. He looks over at me and eyes the small puddle of pork broth and tiny tangle of noodles before me. "You going to finish that?" It's not a clever technique to inspire me to soldier on; it's a legitimate desire to leave no soup unslurped. For every bowl I eat, Kamimura eats two—not for research (he's been to all of these places dozens of times), not to avoid waste (all nonramen food that makes its way to the table is essentially ignored by him), and certainly not because he's hungry (by my back-of-the-napkin math, he is ingesting north of 5,000 calories' worth of ramen a day during our time together). No, Kamimura does it for the same reason he reviews packaged ramen at home and feeds his baby boy pork broth and makes his wife pull over every time they drive past an unknown shop: because his dedication to ramen is boundless. He doesn't love ramen like you love pizza or like I love *The Sopranos*; he loves ramen like Antony loved Cleopatra.

In Japanese, you would call Kamimura an *otaku*, one with a deep, abiding dedication to a single topic. A nerd. *Otaku* commonly describes manga fanatics and video game savants. But just like the chefs he admires, Kamimura is a craftsman, and his commitment to ramen writing approaches *shokunin* status, a dedication so all-consuming that everything else in his life is a footnote.

Sometimes, he says, that love may go too deep. Eating more than a bowl of *tonkotsu* a day will wear on a man's body, and Kamimura is no exception. "I've gained ten kilos in the last three years. I'm afraid my blood is more fat than blood now. My doctor is concerned."

But the torment goes beyond the physical; the knowledge that somewhere, in some corner of Fukuoka or Kyushu beyond, lurks a bowl of unknown provenance and deliciousness is enough to keep a man like Kamimura up until the small hours of the night. When we part each day after our ramen adventures, there's a hint of sadness in his demeanor, as if he thought our hunt would go on forever. When he waves good night, it's not with an open palm but with two fingers pressed together like chopsticks, which he shovels toward his mouth.

米 麺 魚

The earliest footprints of ramen in Japan can be found around the turn of the century, as Chinese migrants in areas like Yokohama, Hakodate, and Nagasaki, the first ports opened to the outside world after hundreds of years of isolationism, began selling the soup to construction workers. Back then it was called *shina soba*, "Chinese noodles," and was sold mostly from street

Kamimura Toshiyuki working on one of his
four hundred annual bowls of ramen.

carts and, oddly enough, Western-style restaurants. The dish was a humble convergence of noodles and a light salt-based broth, but also a sign of Japan's shifting eating habits, one that signaled an increasing appetite for wheat and meat.

Whatever it might have been before the war, the events that took place between 1937 and 1945 would put ramen culture on an entirely different trajectory. Strict food rationing meant *shina soba* all but disappeared during World War II. When the atomic dust finally settled, the Americans moved in and began to reshape Japanese eating habits in profound ways.

Japan had long struggled to feed its own citizens, given its small land mass and high population density. But with the country pockmarked by fire bombings and much of the young male population lost to the war, the Japanese became deeply reliant on American supplies as they fought to ward off starvation. Chief among the imports: American wheat and lard, the basis for a bowl of ramen.

In his excellent book *The Untold History of Ramen*, George Solt points out that these two ingredients, along with garlic, became the basis for what the Japanese called "stamina food," belly-filling staples like gyoza, *okonomiyaki*, and ramen that became lifelines in the scavenger years following the war. Rice harvests were largely compromised by the war, so American flour became the building block for postwar recovery, and eventually the reindustrialization of Japan.

Some scholars, including Solt, argue that the shift from rice to wheat consumption during these years was a carefully crafted political objective undertaken by the Americans and supported by the Japanese government. It also became a powerful weapon for the United States' quest to contain the spread of communism across the Far East. Internal memos between the chief architects of the postwar world—

Truman, Eisenhower and MacArthur—discussed American wheat shipments down to the last ton.

Propaganda abounded. "Eating Rice Makes You Stupid," read one flyer put out by a consortium of wheat producers. Another popular leaflet, circulated by the Civil Information and Education Section, showed a muscle-bound American foisting a tray of buttered bread loaves:

Protein is a body builder. Wheat flour contains 50% more protein than rice. America is spending $250 million for your food. Learn to use it properly to get the full benefit.

A sketchy nutrition lesson and an even sketchier claim of American altruism (Japan was forced to pay the Americans back for the food aid they provided), but because this was a vulnerable and humbled Japan, the message caught on. Between 1956 and 1974, U.S. wheat exports to Japan nearly tripled.

On August 25, 1958, Momofuku Ando, a Taiwanese-born owner of a small salt company, released the first package of instant ramen noodles, a triumph of industrial food science that would redefine ramen for generations of busy moms, hungry bachelors, and desperate stoners. It would also represent the first taste of ramen most of the world beyond Japan would ever experience, a gateway to an ever-expanding world of noodle soups. (Today 100 billion servings of instant noodles are consumed annually worldwide.)

By the 1960s Japan had passed from postwar fallout into a period of rapid reindustrialization, and the workforce turned to ramen for fuel. As cities like Tokyo and Osaka began to rebuild and expand, small ramen shops sprouted across the cityscapes to feed the growing body of construction workers at the heart of Japan's unprecedented growth. In a matter of three decades Japan went from a broken nation to one of the world's greatest economic powers, a turnaround of staggering speed and remarkable scope. Behind every step forward was a bowl of ramen feeding the fires of industry.

The 1980s marked ramen's arrival into a whole new social stratosphere. Ramen was no longer a simple staple; it became a craft food, an object of obsession, a means of expression for legions of new cooks. Whereas most Japanese food is bound by tradition and a set of unspoken rules, ramen fans embraced innovation and experimentation. Microtrends—crinkled noodles, burned garlic oil, double broths—took shape overnight. The culture of queuing, now an honored pastime in Japan, was bred into acceptance in the boiling years of ramen ascendance.

Everyone wanted a piece of the action. Salarymen, disenchanted by the soulless demands of New Japan and its economic might, traded their briefcases for stockpots and began to boil their way back into a more rewarding life. (So common is this phenomenon that it has its own name: *datsu-sara*, "salaryman escapee.") Young cooks took up the profession in droves, brandishing bandannas, self-branded tees, and a swag-ger that spoke of a new era of Japanese identity.

By the time Hideto Kawahara was twenty, ramen's transformation from a humble Chinese noodle soup to a Japanese cultural juggernaut was complete. But it still had yet to hit its apex. Hideto's father was a ramen man; in 1963 in Fukuoka he opened Daruma, a small shop serving a thick, dark bowl of *tonkotsu* to a loyal local clientele. Ramen was one of the few corners of the culinary world where young cooks and entrepreneurs could make an immediate impact, but by the time he was old enough to cook, Hideto—a competitive breakdancer, a hat-to-the-side b-boy popping and locking his way across Japan—was more interested in break beats than pork bones.

But Hideto couldn't dance forever, so at twenty-eight years he gave up the floor spins and the helicopters and waded into the simmering waters of the ramen world. But he didn't do what sons had been doing for a thousand years in

Japan: he didn't learn from his father. "My father told me he didn't want me to imitate his ramen. He wanted me to develop my own."

Instead, Hideto spent five years training down the street from his dad's shop, and then branched off to start his own, which quickly grew into a popular local chain in Fukuoka. By the time he opened in Tokyo's Asakusa neighborhood in 2001, he had a camera crew following his every move for a documentary TV show. "That was a rough time in my life. I was going through a divorce and I had this huge opening. So much pressure." When the store finally opened, there were three-hour waits for Hideto's ramen.

Today Hideto is forty-eight years old. He still wears his hat to the side, still rocks the gold chain, still looks like he could drop into a 720-degree headspin at any moment, but he's now ramen royalty, owner of seventeen shops across the globe, including ramen counters in New York, Hong Kong, Singapore, and

Cambodia. He's just one part of a faction of Fukuoka-based chains that have together reshaped ramen on a global scale in the new millennium.

For the better part of thirty years, sushi was Japan's primary culinary export. But come the mid-aughts, when sushi bars had infiltrated cities across the globe and spicy tuna rolls could be found in every supermarket from Milwaukee to Melbourne, a new taste of Japan found its way to Los Angeles and New York. David Chang and his Momofuku Noodle Bar in New York's East Village was an early and influential player in the ramen game, but it wasn't until Fukuoka's most famous export, Ippudo, opened a few blocks west, on Fourth Avenue, in the winter of 2006 that ramen hit full fever pitch. Now you can find ramen shops in Midwestern malls and roving food trucks, and even your weird aunt Agnes can't stop talking about those strange and delicious Japanese noodles she had last spring.

The Japan represented by sushi is

a very different country from the one represented by ramen. The former was a hushed, refined, serious country of fine taste and even finer economic means, but ramen represents a less intimidating, less exotic Japan, one dominated by bright lights, bold flavors, and the electric pulse of youth-driven pop culture.

Fukuoka, more than any other city in Japan, is responsible for ramen's rocket-ship trajectory, and the ensuing shift in Japan's cultural identity abroad. Between Hide-Chan, Ichiran, and Ippudo—three of the biggest ramen chains in the world—they've brought the soup to corners of the globe that still thought ramen meant a bag of dried noodles and a dehydrated spice packet. But while Ichiran and Ippudo are purveyors of classic *tonkotsu*, undoubtedly the defining ramen of the modern era, Hideto has a decidedly different belief about ramen and its mutability.

"There are no boundaries for ramen, no rules," he says. "It's all freestyle."

As we talk at his original Hide-Chan location in the Kego area of Fukuoka, a new bowl arrives on the table, a prototype for his borderless ramen philosophy. A coffee filter is filled with *katsuobushi*, smoked skipjack tuna flakes, and balanced over a bowl with a pair of chopsticks. Hideto pours chicken stock through the filter, which soaks up the *katsuobushi* and emerges into the bowl as clear as a consommé. He adds rice noodles and sawtooth coriander then slides it over to me.

Compared with other Hide-Chan creations, though, this one shows remarkable restraint. While I sip the soup, Hideto pulls out his cell phone and plays a video of him layering hot pork cheeks and cold noodles into a hollowed-out porcelain skull, then dumping a cocktail shaker filled with chili oil, shrimp oil, truffle oil, and dashi over the top. Other creations include spicy arrabiata ramen with pancetta and roasted tomatoes, foie gras ramen with orange jam and blueberry miso, and black ramen made with bamboo ash dipped into a mix of miso and onions caramelized for forty-five days.

"It's important to make the right ra-men for the right place. If I do what I do here in New York, it doesn't work," he says. "They want less salt and less fat in New York. Gluten-free noodles. New Yorkers are tough."

Suddenly Hideto jumps up from the table and announces that he needs to go. He leaves me with a bowl of industrial-strength *tonkotsu*—pig heads viciously boiled in sixty-liter iron vats for forty-eight hours—and a rundown of his itin-erary for the next week: first to Sin-gapore, then to Phnom Penh for the opening of his first Cambodian shop, then to New York to roll out a new line of dry ramen dishes, back to Hong Kong to scout new locations, then home to Fukuoka for thirty-six hours before re-peating the loop. The world, he says, is hungry for ramen.

米 麵 魚

Hideki Irie doesn't look like a typi-cal *tonkotsu* ramen cook. He walks into his restaurant in a shiny black bubble jacket, sunglasses perched on his head, a sparkly watch on each wrist. Even in his uniform, with the black collar popped like a Michigan frat boy, he manages to exude a sense of attitude that feels completely foreign in this country. But ramen may be the one corner of Japa-nese food culture where swagger is an acceptable ingredient, and Irie projects it with gusto.

We've met at his shop Mengekijo Genei, which eschews the typical ra-men curtains in favor of a thick wooden door and trades a traditional counter-top setup for stadium seating, each stool positioned for optimal intake of the kitchen action below. Cooks in the center toast garlic and shrimp oil in siz-zling woks while a young kid behind a glass wall on the left feeds yellow balls of dough into a pasta machine to make the night's noodles.

Before turning to ramen, Irie was a private investigator, a job that he dis-misses today with a single shake of the head. "I wasn't happy doing it. I would

Hideki Irie, the Ramen Chemist,
with his finely tuned bowl of *tonkotsu*

walk around with this horrible look on my face." One day during his sleuthing years, he visited a ramen shop in his hometown of Kumamoto owned by a friend. Something clicked when he saw the simplicity of it all: hot soup, happy people. "My friend told me, 'It's the most rewarding job in the world.'"

He left the investigating behind and took up a job behind the counter at Tenyo Ramen, where he spent five years learning the ins and outs of the craft. He discovered early on what he didn't like about ramen: he didn't like short-cuts; he didn't like cheap ingredients; he didn't like monosodium glutamate. The last point remains one of heated debate in the ramen community. In some kitchens, tubs of MSG sit openly on the counter like salt and pepper, ready to be spooned generously into each bowl before being passed across the counter. But many of the young modern ramen chefs have made it a mission to find maximum flavor without MSG.

Proponents say MSG is a natural flavor enhancer, a crystalline source of umami that has been openly harnessed for its savory powers for generations. Detractors claim it's unsafe, a catalyst for rogue headaches and strange neural reactions—or, at the very least, a dubious substitute for finesse in the kitchen. No matter what your reasons may be for keeping it out of your restaurant, one thing is certain: not using MSG puts you at a distinct disadvantage in a crowded, powder-happy market like Fukuoka. For a place to survive and thrive, it must find other ways to harness flavor.

This became Irie's obsession. He started out by learning to brew his own soy sauce. "Almost all chefs buy soy in the store, but the product is lousy. If I could develop my own soy, nobody could copy my recipe." The resulting potion took a year of research to master and costs $200 a liter to make—which, Irie says, is worth every yen. "Joel Robuchon wanted to buy it from me, and I told him no," he says, speaking of the French chef dubbed by the Michelin guides as "the greatest chef of the century." "I don't want Robuchon copying my ramen."

With the super soy calibrated, he set about tinkering with different combinations of umami-rich products until he found the perfect mix for his *tare*: kelp, shiitakes, bonito, oysters, sardines, mackerel, dried scallops, and dried abalone.

"I'm a ramen chemist," he says, talking about the time he spent three days straight in the library studying the science of taste. "I can engineer any flavor. I could make you a bowl of *tonkotsu* without using pork."

Irie is part of a generation of enterprising ramen chefs intent on pushing the soul of this traditional comfort food to its most sophisticated and refined expression. After listening to him talk about his top-secret *tare*, his $200-a-liter homemade soy sauce, his years spent studying MSG, you get the sense that the 800 yen he charges for a bowl may represent one of the greatest bargains in the entire food world. And maybe it does.

But I'm not so sure Kamimura is convinced. It's clear that he respects Irie's talent and his desire to innovate, but Kamimura is a *tonkotsu* purist, a man who would rather pay 400 yen for a bowl of pork bones and store-bought soy sauce than twice that much for a bowl refined down to its last milliliter. Ramen should be made by blue-collar cooks, not white-collar chefs. Most of the men in Fukuoka might agree, judging by the crowds I see gathered around places like Ganso and Shin Shin, classic joints serving throwback bowls for throwback prices.

But that's clearly not the audience Irie is aiming for. *Tonkotsu* has always been an almost all-male sport, but look around Genei and you see a different clientele entirely: couples, single women, families—signs of a shifting culture.

"There are two methods to develop a ramen shop in Fukuoka," says Kamimura. "The first is to provide a single taste and dedicate yourself just to that taste. The second way is to offer a variety of flavors and changing menus. At least Hide-Chan and Genei keep their classic ramen while they experiment with new flavors. It has to be that way, because that brings in a wider variety of clientele."

Irie serves me three ramens, including a bowl made with a rich dashi and head-on shrimp and another studded with spicy ground pork and wilted spinach and lashed with chili oil. Both are exceptionally delicious, sophisticated creations, but it's his interpretation of *tonkotsu* that leaves me muttering softly to myself. The noodles are firm and chewy, the roast pork is striped with soft deposits of warm fat, and the toppings—white curls of shredded spring onion, chewy strips of bamboo, a perfect square of toasted seaweed—are skillfully applied. Here it is the combination of *tare*, the culmination of years of careful tinkering, and broth, made from whole pig heads and knots of ginger, that defies the laws of *tonkotsu*: a soup with the savory, meaty intensity of

a broth made from a thousand pigs that's light enough to leave you wanting more. And more. And more.

"I have no doubt that I make the best bowl of ramen in Japan," Irie says. Fighting words, to be sure, but the man may have a point.

米　麺　魚

Tonkotsu, like many of the world's great dishes, was born out of a happy accident. The idea of replacing traditional chicken bones with pork bones was already in practice in Kurume in the early 1930s, adapted from the Chinese in nearby Nagasaki. As the story has it, one night an old cook at a *yatai* left the soup on the stove too long, turning the broth thick and cloudy with melted marrow and porky intensity. It caught on quickly, spreading from *yatai* to *yatai*, and soon double-boiled pork-bone soup became the official ramen of Kyushu.

At the Kurume train station, twenty-five miles south of Fukuoka, a miniature bronze replica of the original *yatai* stands as a reminder to all of where one of Japan's most famous dishes comes from. Kamimura takes me by the statue to pay our respects to ramen history, but he talks grimly about Kurume's ramen scene. He speaks of a ramen town where nobody gets along, where factional beefs and claims to history cloud the already cloudy soup, a town where the shop that invented *tonkotsu* can't even make a decent bowl anymore. (Which is why we're genuflecting to the statue instead of the still-operational original *yatai*.)

But the trip isn't merely a historical pilgrimage; Kurume still claims a few of Kamimura's favorite shops. We start at Rai Fuku Ken, a tiny shop next to the train station that has been serving *tonkotsu* since shortly after it was invented down the street. The owner, Akira Yoshino, is a second-generation shop owner and the current president of the Kurume *Tonkotsu* Ramen Association. Round-faced and rosy-cheeked, with a black bandanna tied tightly across

his forehead, Yoshino views himself as a guardian of the true *tonkotsu*.

"I'm proud to know that ramen has spread to places like New York and Europe," he says, "but Kurume people like Kurume ramen, and the style that people around the world know as *tonkotsu* is not the original *tonkotsu*. We care only about keeping the soul of Kurume ramen alive."

His is a Goldilocks bowl: medium body, golden in color, made from all parts of the pig cooked over twenty-four hours with nothing but water from the Chikobe River nearby. It asserts itself, coats your throat on the way down, but it doesn't stick to your ribs the way the most intense bowls do.

It's the next stop, though, that I've been waiting for. Kamimura has been whispering all week of a sacred twenty-four-hour ramen spot located on a two-lane highway in Kurume where truckers go for the taste of true ramen. The shop is massive by ramen standards, big enough to fit a few trucks along with

The same stock has been simmering
at Maruboshi since 1955.

those drivers, and in the midafternoon a loose assortment of castaways and road warriors sit slurping their noodles. Near the entrance a thick, sweaty cauldron boils so aggressively that a haze of pork fat hangs over the kitchen like waterfall mist.

While few are audacious enough to claim ramen is healthy, *tonkotsu* enthusiasts love to point out that the collagen in pork bones is great for the skin. "Look at their faces!" says Kamimura. "They're almost seventy years old and not a wrinkle! That's the collagen. Where there is *tonkotsu*, there is rarely a wrinkle."

He's right: the woman wears a faded purple bandanna and sad, sunken eyes, but even then she doesn't look a day over fifty. She's stirring a massive metal cauldron of broth, and I ask her how long it's been simmering for.

"Sixty years," she says flatly.

This isn't hyperbole, not exactly. Kurume treats *tonkotsu* like a French country baker treats a sourdough starter—feeding it, regenerating, keep-

ing some small fraction of the original soup alive in perpetuity. Old bones out, new bones in, but the base never changes. The mother of all ramen.

Maruboshi Ramen opened in 1958, and you can taste every one of those years in the simple bowl they serve. There is no fancy *tare*, no double broth, no secret spice or unexpected toppings: just pork bones, noodles, and three generations of constant simmering.

The flavor is pig in its purest form, a milky white broth with no aromatics or condiments to mitigate the purity of its porcine essence. Up until now, Kamimura has worked his way through bowls of ramen with the methodical persistence of a librarian cataloging books, but something in him changes with the first slurp of Maruboshi's bowl. His eyes light up, he wiggles his shoulders, and a childish smile breaks out across his face. "What do you think? What do you think?"

For Kamimura, it's not just a strength thing—it's a soul thing. He respects craftsmen like Hideto and Irie, but their calculated compositions don't move him the same way that a straight bowl of bone broth does. It takes time to draw out the soul of ramen—some say hours; others, like Kamimura, say lifetimes.

When the owners spot Kamimura, they hurry over to our booth, offering paper cups of coffee to go with our mystic soup. Kamimura mentions that he's been reviewing more instant ramen than ever lately, and the woman disappears and comes back with a cardboard box stacked with sixteen individual packets of Maruboshi's take-home product. But his attention isn't with the owners or the packaged noodles or the steaming cups of coffee. No, it's aimed squarely at me. He catches my eyes, then looks down at my unfinished bowl, then back up at me. I know what he wants, and after twenty-eight bowls over the course of five days, I'm more than happy to give it to him, but first, he needs to ask.

"You going to finish that?"

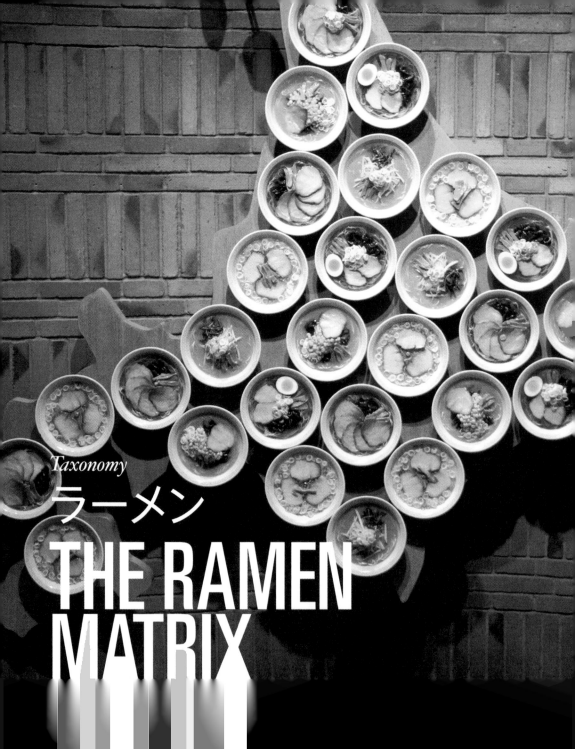

ラーメン

THE RAMEN
MATRIX

Japan is a land of a million bowls of ramen. With over 200,000 shops
and a world of microtrends and funky innovations, ramen is Japan's most
personalized and boundless staple. Behind the specialty bowls, though, there
are at least twenty-two accepted regional styles of ramen that bring order to
the complex noodle ecosystem. Here, in part, are the most famous of Japan's
regional ramen species.

 01

HAKODATE SHIO

As one of Japan's first ports open to the outside world, Hakodate has a long ramen history. Light and clear like consommé, *shio* (salt) ramen is the closest reflection of the original Chinese ramen.

Where to eat: Ebisuken (Hakodate), Afuri (Tokyo)

 02

SAPPORO MISO

The thickest and richest of Japan's regional ramens, designed to get people through Hokkaido's Siberian winters. Red miso and wok-fried *chashu* and vegetables make up the soul of the bowl. Butter and corn, two Hokkaido staples, are optional.

Where to eat: Menya Saimi (Sapporo), Hanamichi (Tokyo)

03

HAKATA TONKOTSU

The king of regional ramen, made
exclusively with pork bones boiled
for up to forty-eight hours, creating
a milky white broth thick with
melted marrow and collagen.
Served with straight, thin noodles.
Where to eat: Mengekijo Genei
(Fukuoka and Tokyo)

04

KAGOSHIMA HYBRID

Kagoshima ramen cooks cut
a *tonkotsu* base with chicken
and vegetables for a lighter
version of Hakata *tonkotsu*.
Noodles are flat, broad, and
cooked soft, and the *chashu*,
made from local *kurobuta* pig,
is Japan's best.
Where to eat: Ramen Kokinta,
Tontoro

TOKYO SHOYU

Chicken-based broth spiked with a generous amount of shoyu (soy sauce) and often a current of *niboshi* (dried sardine). Expect curly yellow noodles, *menma* (pickled bamboo), seaweed, and a soy-soaked egg. Along with *tonkotsu*, the most common style of ramen in Japan.

TOKYO TSUKEMEN

Thick room-temperature noodles slicked with warm pork fat and served with *chashu* and a concentrated broth for dipping. One of the most popular ramen trends of the past decade, perfect for steamy summer afternoons.
Where to eat: Rokurinsha

ASAHIKAWA SURF-AND-TURF

Blending the best from the two extremes of Japan: pork *tonkotsu* from Kyushu mixed with the best seafood from Asahikawa's northern Hokkaido backyard to create a complex broth of land and sea.
Where to eat: Santouka (throughout Japan)

DREAM MACHINES

Our favorite picks from Japan's ubiquitous
army of vending machines

BOSS COFFEE
Vending-machine
coffee can be
sickly sweet, but
Black Boss delivers
the caffeine high
without the sugar
crash. Red buttons
on the machine
mean hot coffee;
blue means cold.

POCARI SWEAT
Even more
appetizing than
its name is the
salty-sweet rush
of electrolytes it
delivers. Pocari is
for the morning
after a long night of
chuhai and Yebisu.

CHU-HI

A version of the highball made with shochu instead of whisky, *Chu-hi* contains twice as much alcohol as most beer. Best consumed as a pre-karaoke aperitif.

YEBISU

Lesser known but the best of Japan's major beers, malty and smooth. When you spot this rare beast in the vending wilderness, rustle up some change.

FEAR NOT!

Conquering Japan's greatest cultural challenges

NATTO

Soft, slimy, with a fermented tang, *natto* is everything Westerners don't want in food. But the dish—made from soaked, steamed, and funkified soybeans—is served at breakfast through much of Japan. (It is also a common way to test a gaijin's appetite for real Japanese food.) How to handle? First, spike it with hot mustard and soy-based *tare*, then just close your eyes and think of England.

WAGASHI

There are two genres of desserts in Japan. *Yogashi* are European-style cakes and pastries (universally excellent throughout Japan); *wagashi* are traditional Japanese sweets. The charms of *wagashi* can be elusive if you're not used to sweet rice, adzuki beans, and sticky textures for dessert. The trick is to embrace the subtlety:

...egret having chosen a *ryokan*, a traditional Japanese inn, right ...time the innkeeper wakes everyone up for breakfast at 7:00 a.m. on ...t don't rue: spending a day or two in a *ryokan* is the quickest route to ...ling the futon-sleeping, robe-wearing, big-breakfasting, hot-tub-loving ...oul.

ONSEN

Sitting naked in a communal bath might not sound like a relaxing time, but when you slip into the therapeutic waters of a hot spring, all worries will evaporate. Prepare yourself: First, strip down. No bathing suits, no underwear. Cover tattoos (often banned because of their connection to yakuza). Scrub yourself head to toe

Chapter Five

HIROSHIMA

———

It starts with a *thwack*, the sharp crack of hard plastic against a hot metal surface. When the ladle rolls over, it deposits a pale-yellow puddle of batter onto the griddle. A gentle sizzle, as the back of the ladle spackles a mixture of eggs, flour, water, and milk across the silver surface. A crepe takes shape.

Next comes cabbage, chopped thin—but not too thin—and stacked six inches high, lightly packed so hot air can flow freely and wilt the mountain down to a molehill. Crowning the cabbage comes a flurry of tastes and textures: ivory bean sprouts, golden pebbles of fried tempura batter, a few shakes of salt,

and, for an extra umami punch, a drift of dried bonito powder. Finally, three strips of streaky pork belly, just enough to umbrella the cabbage in fat, plus a bit more batter to hold the whole thing together. With two metal spatulas and a gentle rocking of the wrists, the mass is inverted. The pork fat melts on contact, and the cabbage shrinks in the steam trapped under the crepe.

Then things get serious. Thin wheat soba noodles, still dripping with hot water, hit the *teppan*, dancing like garden hoses across its hot surface, absorbing the heat of the griddle until they crisp into a bird's nest to house the cabbage and crepe. An egg with two orange yolks sizzles beside the soba, waiting for its place on top of this magnificent heap.

Everything comes together: cabbage and crepe at the base, bean sprouts and pork belly in the center, soba and fried egg parked on top, a geologic construction of carbs and crunch, protein and chew, all framed with the black and white of thickened Worcestershire and a zigzag of mayonnaise.

This is *okonomiyaki*, the second most famous thing that ever happened to Hiroshima.

米 麵 魚

Fernando Lopez makes an unlikely candidate for one of Hiroshima's greatest *okonomiyaki* chefs. He was born in Guatemala City in 1963. His father worked for Guatemala's health services, spraying DDT to combat the plague of malaria that gripped Central America in the 1960s. He spent a lot of his time on the road, often in the beds of other women. "He wasn't a good man," says Lopez.

His father had Mayan blood, with dark skin to match his dark hair. His mother was fair, with wavy hair and a sweet smile. When little Fernando was born with light skin, blue eyes, and curly hair, his father refused to believe the boy was his, and so Lopez was raised mainly by his grandmother, separate from his four brothers and two sisters.

Even when his father did finally accept Fernando as his own, it wasn't an easy relationship. At fifteen, Lopez decided to stand between the man he barely knew and a beating aimed for his mother, and years of abuse and philandering came to a head. His father left, never to come back, and the boy who'd grown up alone was left to absorb the blame for chasing away the man of the house.

Lopez survived, working hard to overcome the early challenges life had posed for him. He studied accounting for a year in college, and eventually took a job managing the books for a popular Italian restaurant in Guatemala City.

Fernando Lopez in the early
moments of *okonomiyaki* prep

He soon discovered that the managers were skimming off the top, along with other criminal activity, and he fretted over what to do with this sensitive information. When one of his coworkers turned up dead in a ditch, he knew it was time to leave Guatemala, possibly for good.

He landed in New Orleans on a visa sponsored by an uncle who had lived in the States for years. He planned to stay for three months to study English, but instead took a job busing tables at an Italian restaurant. The chef had a temper issue, and one day the entire kitchen staff walked out on him. He recruited Lopez to help out in the kitchen, but the young Guatemalan knew nothing about cooking. "He fired me every fifteen minutes. It was a mess."

Soon after, while working as a dishwasher at the Fairmont, he met Andre LeDoux, a well-traveled hotel chef who would become his kitchen mentor—the first of a series of teacher-student relationships that would shape Lopez as a cook and a man. LeDoux made him a deal: Lopez would teach him Spanish, and he would teach Lopez how to cook. When LeDoux became chef of the French Quarter institute Arnaud's, he took Lopez with him, and Lopez's real education began in earnest. "At first you're a slave, you're everyone's bitch, and they can do whatever they want with you. But that's how you learn." He moved from station to station, mastering the classics of the French Creole canon: shucking and roasting oysters, making roux for gumbo, sautéing frog legs in garlic butter. "There were twelve of us feeding six hundred people a night. People walked out on him. They couldn't take the stress. But I loved it."

When LeDoux left Arnaud's to run the kitchen at the Sheraton Surfrider in Honolulu, Lopez followed him across the Pacific. The Sheraton's kitchen staff was on strike, so Lopez entered as a scab, stuffed in a van and slipped into the kitchen under the cover of darkness. He cooked nonstop for forty-three days and nights, until the strike broke and Lopez was left without a place in the kitchen. He took a job as a valet at a hotel where, one night, a young Japanese woman in a beat-up Toyota Corolla with a bad paint job pulled into the parking lot and changed his life. "Nobody else wanted to park the car because it was so beat up, they thought they wouldn't get a tip." He didn't get a tip, but he got a date out of it.

Makiko Yonezawa was from Hiroshima. Her family owned a *ryokan* back home, and she had come to Hawaii six years earlier to study the hotel industry. They connected right away, but Lopez's timing wasn't great: Makiko returned to Japan a few months after they started dating to help with the family business. Lopez soon followed with a surprise visit, a grand gesture of young love that didn't sit well with Makiko's parents. They didn't like the idea of their daughter dating a foreigner, but her father pulled Lopez aside before he returned to Hawaii and told him that if they re-

mained together for a year, then they could talk seriously.

Fernando and Makiko married in 1992, in a small civil ceremony in Hawaii. For their honeymoon, they took Amtrak around the United States, looking for a place to build a life together. They loved Chicago, Denver, and Seattle, but the cold and the rain scared them off. In Phoenix they fell hard for the spice-charged food of the Southwest, and they hatched a plan to open a Tex-Mex restaurant together in Hawaii. But things didn't go exactly as planned. Real estate was outrageously expensive in Honolulu, and neither of them qualified for the kind of loan they would need to build a business. So in 1995, with dwindling prospects in the States, they made the move to the Far East, to southern Japan, transporting their dream of opening a Southwestern restaurant to the heart of Hiroshima.

米 麺 魚

People around town tell me to look for the giant wooden egg. "The Giant

Wooden Egg!" they say, raising their voices and stretching their wingspans out to mimic its shape—a brown oblong structure eight stories high, inside which I would find the secrets of Hiroshima's most sacred food.

The egg in question is home to Otafuku, Hiroshima's famous sauce maker, which doubles as the de facto museum to Hiroshima-style *okonomiyaki*. Maybe it's the exposed ribs, the empty spaces, the nearly naked aspect of the looming wooden structure, but the building looks less like an egg and more like the skeletal remains of the Atomic Bomb Dome, which stands as a memorial to the nuclear attack on Hiroshima. It seems like a grim architectural echo for the global headquarters of a company best known for its sticky-sweet *okonomiyaki* topping.

That echo, however, turns out to be intentional. Otafuku ties its sauce intimately to the city it comes from, and also to the defining horror that destroyed old Hiroshima and remade everything that followed. It was in the wake of that horror that *okonomiyaki* took shape.

Issenyoshoku, "one-coin Western food," gained popularity in the early 1900s as a cheap after-school snack for kids, a crepe rolled with onions and bean sprouts and often sold in candy shops. In the years immediately following the war, as the survivors of the bomb tried to stave off starvation, the snack became a vital part of Hiroshima's revival.

In a matter of seconds, the bomb leveled every eatery in the city center, in essence wiping Hiroshima's restaurant culture clean. With nothing else to work with, loose pieces of sheet metal, the bones of buildings lost to the bomb, became street *teppan*s, makeshift griddles heated from below with coal from the shipyard and used to cook whatever scraps of food could be thrown together: a few shreds of cabbage, loose vegetable bits, an egg or a touch of protein for the most fortunate. As American forces arrived in Japan with surplus wheat supplies, cooks in Hiroshima used flour and water to stretch and bind the dish.

The Otafuku tour begins the *okonomiyaki* story a few years later, after the dust had settled, after the desperation had ebbed. On the main floor of the museum, the first stop is a reconstructed *okonomiyaki* ya-san from the 1950s. Like many of the early wave of *okonomiyaki* shops, it was connected to a home, perhaps with a small convenience store for daytime commerce, selling gum and cigarettes. More than anything, the ad hoc diners were a way for war widows to earn some money. The reconstructed space has the plastic feel of demonstration food, punctuated by a few original accents: metal *hera* (spatulas) from the period, a small black-and-white television with old newsreels, a menu board offering *okonomiyaki* with egg for 15 yen and without for 10.

As Japan recovered from the post-war depression, *okonomiyaki* became the cornerstone of Hiroshima's nascent restaurant culture. And with new variables—noodles, protein, fishy powders—

added to the equation, it became an increasingly fungible concept. Half a century later it still defies easy description. *Okonomi* means "whatever you like," *yaki* means "grill," but smashed together they do little to paint a clear picture. Invariably, writers, cooks, and *oko* officials revert to analogies: some call it a cabbage crepe; others a savory pancake or an omelet. Guidebooks, unhelpfully, refer to it as Japanese pizza, though *okonomiyaki* looks and tastes nothing like pizza. Otafuku, for its part, does little to clarify the situation, comparing *okonomiyaki* in turn to Turkish pide, Indian chapati, and Mexican tacos.

There are two overarching categories of *okonomiyaki*: Hiroshima style, with a layer of noodles and a heavy cabbage presence, and Osaka or Kansai style, made with a base of eggs, flour, dashi, and grated *nagaimo*, sticky mountain yam. More than the ingredients themselves, the difference lies in the structure: whereas *okonomiyaki* in Hiroshima is carefully layered, a savory circle with

A wall of sticky-sweet *okonomiyaki* sauce on display at Otafuku's headquarters.

five or six distinct layers, the ingredients in Osaka-style *okonomiyaki* are mixed together before cooking. The latter is so simple to cook that many restaurants let you do it yourself on tableside *teppan*s. Hiroshima-style *okonomiyaki*, on the otherhand, is complicated enough that even the cooks who dedicate their lives to its construction still don't get it right most of the time. (Some people consider *monjayaki*, a runny mass of meat and vegetables popularized in Tokyo's Tsukishima district, to be part of the *okonomiyaki* family, but if so, it's no more than a distant cousin.)

Otafuku entered the picture in 1938 as a rice vinegar manufacturer. Their original factory near Yokogawa Station burned down in the nuclear attack, but in 1946 they started making vinegar again. In 1950 Otafuku began production of Worcestershire sauce, but local cooks complained that it was too spicy and too thin, that it didn't cling to *okonomiyaki*, which was becoming the nutritional staple of Hiroshima life. So Otafuku used fruit—originally orange and peach, later Middle Eastern dates—to thicken and sweeten the sauce, and added the now-iconic Otafuku label with the six virtues that the chubby-cheeked lady of Otafuku, a traditional character from Japanese folklore, is supposed to represent, including a little nose for modesty, big ears for good listening, and a large forehead for wisdom.

Today Otafuku is the primary engine behind Hiroshima's massive *okonomiyaki* industry, and as such, they invest no small amount of time and energy in making sure the city is checkered with successful vendors dispensing dark rivers of its saccharine sauce. That means connecting business owners with cabbage and pork purveyors to keep the *teppan*s humming. That means schooling potential entrepreneurs in the economics of restaurant management. That means helping train the next wave of *okonomiyaki* masters: disgruntled salarymen, ambitious home cooks, even the occasional Guatemalan immigrant.

米 麺 魚

Lopez and his wife were determined to bring the flavors of Phoenix and Santa Fe and El Paso to the people of Hiroshima. The only problem was that no one in Japan had ever heard of Southwestern food.

After Lopez presented his plan to a local builder, the contractor told Lopez bluntly, "I don't build restaurants that fail."

Lopez and his wife shuffled through ideas—pizzeria, bistro, sandwich shop—but nothing felt right. Eventually the conversation turned where conversations in Hiroshima normally turn when the subject of food comes up: *okonomiyaki*. "Why don't you open an *okonomiyaki* restaurant?" friends and family started to ask.

Why not open an *okonomiyaki* shop? Let's consider the reasons: Because Lopez was born seven thousand miles away, in one of the roughest cities on the planet. Because he didn't look Japanese, speak Japanese, or cook Japa-

nese. Because *okonomiyaki* isn't just a pile of cabbage and noodles and pork belly, but a hallowed food in Hiroshima, stacked with layers and layers of history and culture that he couldn't pretend to be a part of. Because even though they might accept an Italian cooking pasta and a Frenchman baking baguettes, they would never accept a Guatemalan making *okonomiyaki*.

But friends and family insisted it was a good idea—"Everybody knows and loves *okonomiyaki*," they would say, still confounded by the idea of fajitas—and Lopez, with few decent alternatives, agreed to attend a business workshop put on by Otafuku. By the time he emerged three days later, head full of inventory lists and *teppan* technology, he was convinced enough to give it a run.

Otafuku provided the framework for running a business, but he still needed to learn how to cook *okonomiyaki*, so he sought out an apprenticeship. Lopez knew a guy who knew a guy working at Hassho, one of Hiroshima's greatest *okonomiyaki* restaurants, where every night a line filled with hungry locals and guidebook-clutching tourists snakes around the block of Hiroshima's neon Yagenbori entertainment district. He was in.

The master-apprentice relationship, in many ways, is still the beating heart of Japanese food culture, an age-old tradition that supersedes stages and cooking school as the primary engine of culinary education. Unsurprisingly, apprenticeships tend to be formal endeavors, and each style of cooking comes with its own set of rules and expectations. Serious tempura students can expect to spend five years filtering oil, stirring batter, and looking over their master's shoulder before they're deemed ready to fry. In the sushi world, the apprentice might begin with a year of washing dishes, another few years cleaning and cooking rice, and eventually dedicate a decade to quietly observing the master slice and serve fish before being released into the wild to test his skills. I once met a

fifty-five-year-old man in a Matsumoto *karaage* restaurant who had been apprenticing under his father for twenty-seven years. After three decades, the dad didn't let the son fry the chicken.

By these standards, the *okonomiyaki* apprenticeship is relatively relaxed. Lopez spent just three months working at Hassho, learning quickly the dozens of steps that go into constructing Hiroshima's most sacred staple. "I had an advantage that most of these guys don't have: I was a professional cook. I picked it up pretty fast."

In ninety days, Hassho's owner, Ogawa Hiroki, passed along to Lopez an arsenal of tiny tricks and vital techniques it had taken him a lifetime to accumulate. Lopez learned that bean sprouts in May behave differently from bean sprouts in October. He learned that fresh noodles, cooked to order, make an *okonomiyaki* superior to one made with the prepackaged, precooked soba everyone else uses. He learned that touch and finesse are the most vital items in an *okonomiyaki* cook's toolkit, because every *okonomiyaki* behaves differently.

When Lopez had metabolized the meaty lessons of *okonomiyaki*, Hiroki didn't just pat him on the back and wish him good luck. He took an early and spirited role in assuring that Lopez would succeed on his own. He helped design the layout of the restaurant; he made sure the *teppan* was three centimeters thick and had overlapping burners to better hold in the heat, just as he had designed it himself so many years ago; he connected Lopez with all the right purveyors, including the guy with the gorgeous eggs with double yolks that his regulars so adored.

When a new *okonomiyaki* restaurant opens in Hiroshima, an elaborate flower arrangement adorns the front of the shop, a gift from the master to the apprentice as the latter tries to win over a new clientele. It's both a sign of respect and an easy way to establish the bona fides of the new business owner. (It's also a subtle but looming reminder to the apprentice that he better keep his shit together and not bring dishonor to the master.) When Okonomiyaki Lopez opened in the spring of 2000, Hiroki sent an elaborate $200 arrangement, a sign with his shop's logo, and a metal stand to hold it all out in front for the public to see.

But business was slow. To start with, *okonomiyaki* joints are everywhere in this city, two thousand in total across greater Hiroshima, and it's not easy to set yourself apart from the competition. It doesn't help that Okonomiyaki Lopez is located on a quiet street in Yokogawacho, the working-class neighborhood where Makiko's family once owned its *ryokan*. This is the kind of area where small neighborhood restaurants rule, and Lopez didn't fit the profile of your Tuesday-night cook. "People would sit there and watch me with huge eyes, trying to figure out who this guy was making their *okonomiyaki*."

Less than 2 percent of Japan's 126 million citizens are immigrants, making it one of the most homogenous countries on the planet (a 2012 study in the *Journal of Economic Literature* placed it third to last in terms of ethnic diversity, with only North and South Korea ranking lower). Chinese and Koreans, many of whom have lived here for generations, account for more than half of whatever diversity there is, meaning very few Westerners call Japan home. Part of this stems from Japan's historic aversion to non-Japanese—from the sealed borders of the Tokugawa shogunate to the forced assimilation of the Ainu in Hokkaido. Modern immigration laws, among the most draconian in the world, and a deep dedication to a belief in Japanese superiority on the part of today's most conservative leaders, have done little to make Japan a more inclusive society.

The Japanese are heroically hospitable when it comes to foreign visitors, but for immigrants the welcome mat can be harder to find. Even if you do make it here, adapt to the culture, commit a thousand kanji characters to memory,

denounce your birth country, and feel deep down in your soul that you are as Japanese as pickled fish and electronic toilets, you will always be an outsider.

Being from Guatemala, which at last count had just 145 citizens calling Japan home, means you're more outside than most. "A lot of people think Guatemala is a coffee brand. 'Oh, you're from the coffee brand!'" says Lopez. "Japanese people forget about Central America. They think Mexico is attached to South America."

Knowing they were up against a formidable headwind, Lopez and Makiko worked hard to make inroads in the neighborhood. So did Hiroki, who created special cards announcing Okonomiyaki Lopez that he distributed around Yokogawacho. He instructed Lopez—who was studying Japanese in night school and by now beginning to grasp some of the many social formalities that dominate basic interactions in Japan—to follow up with free samples of his *okonomiyaki* and to solicit feedback from potential customers.

"Many said I could do better," says Lopez. "I mean, if you ask them their opinion, they're going to tell you."

In those early days, Lopez and Makiko cooked side by side. She was pregnant with their first child, but she had trained in kitchens before and proved a talented *okonomiyaki* cook. Plus, since she was born and raised in the neighborhood, her mere presence behind the counter gave Lopez a sparkle of authenticity.

The combination of the *oko* offensive and the husband-and-wife dynamics worked to slowly win over the neighborhood. The biggest breakthrough, though, came from the most unlikely source of all: Guatemala. A customer from the neighborhood came in one afternoon while Lopez was making salsa for a staff meal. He saw a pile of chopped jalapeños and asked Lopez to throw a few in with his *okonomiyaki*. Lopez tried to dissuade the man, told him that jalapeños are spicy and wouldn't match well with the *okonomiyaki*, but the customer insisted. He loved it, and came back every day for weeks, ordering the same thing, until finally another customer saw the off-menu alteration and came along for the ride. Soon the spicy supplement became a Lopez staple, and he was forced to add it to the regular menu.

Today the jalapeño *okonomiyaki* remains the most popular item at Okonomiyaki Lopez, much to the owner's chagrin.

"Jalapeños don't belong in *okonomiyaki*."

米 麺 魚

I eat a lot of *okonomiyaki* when I stay in Hiroshima, which is to say, I survive on *okonomiyaki* alone for many days at a time. I eat it in tiny shops down tiny alleys without names on the door. I eat it in the famous places with long lines and dense clouds of savory steam fogging up the windows. I eat it in Okonomi-mura, a four-story building dedicated entirely to *okonomiyaki*, with twenty-six vendors wilting their way through vast sierras of cabbage. (I'm reminded constantly

There are more than two thousand *okonomiyaki* shops
in the greater Hiroshima area.

during my time in Hiroshima that Okonomi-mura is the most popular food theme park in all of Japan.) I eat it with the salarymen at noon and the hustlers at midnight; I eat it with pork and beef, shrimp and scallops, oysters and squid.

My main takeaway, from a strict culinary perspective, is this: if handled improperly, made in a hurry, or constructed from subpar ingredients, Hiroshima-style *okonomiyaki* is little more than prosaic drinking food—*yakisoba* made vertically instead of horizontally.

Made with care, constructed with a deft hand, put together with finesse and talent and a few shakes of soul, it is a glorious amalgamation, so vastly superior to Osaka's version as to not even warrant a comparison. But nothing about *okonomiyaki* feels particularly Japanese—not the flavors, not the format, and certainly not the bulk. Which, ultimately, might explain its popularity: after a breakfast of *natto* and a lunch of grilled mackerel and steamed rice, there's nothing like tuck-ing into a 1,500-calorie disk of destiny to remind you of the primal joys of eating. (Unsurprisingly, it's a dish that wins the hearts and stomachs of Western visitors almost instantly.)

Friday lunch at Okonomiyaki Lopez is one of the busiest shifts of the week, a time for a final splurge for the professional set before the weekend begins. I've been watching Lopez make *okonomiyaki* all week now, and occasionally I've grabbed a spatula and made a mess of his *teppan*, but the pace of today's business allows little time for gaijin high jinks; I take up a chair at the end of the bar and watch the great feast unfold.

Two female pharmacists in lab coats are the first to arrive, followed by a pair of older salarymen with impeccable suits and polished briefcases. Then a mother and her young son. By 11:20 every seat is taken, and the *teppan* crackles with the sound of sizzling pork belly and wilting cabbage.

The restaurant is small, even by *okonomiyaki* standards, with a narrow prep kitchen, a sixteen-seat counter, and a U-shaped *teppan* that stretches nearly the entire width of the shop. From appearances alone, it's tough to tell where the fantasy of Lopez Southwest ends and the reality of Okonomiyaki Lopez begins. The chairs are covered in poncho patterns, the shop logo shines bright with yellow, red, and green, and the menu contains a few tastes of a dream deferred, including a Guatemalan tongue stew and chicken fajitas, which sit warming in green and red enamel pots at the edge of the *teppan*.

It's clear a lot has changed since the years of goosing the neighborhood with free samples. Lopez looks comfortable behind his stainless steel perch, with a white flower-studded bandanna wrapped tight around his head and a denim Otafuku apron covering his chest that reads: "Eat *Okonomiyaki* All Together a Happy Happy Home!!"

Lopez makes his *okonomiyaki* with a mixture of repetitive precision and intense personal interest. As soon as a cus-tomer walks in the door, before she can even sit down, he drops a ladle of batter onto the griddle and begins to build. The precise layering of ingredients, the way he cups the cabbage between two spatulas, the little beads of water he splashes on the *teppan* to take and adjust its temperature: all point to a man who knows that the difference between commodity and craft is razor thin.

Unlike many of the *okonomiyaki* cooks I see around town, who look as if they changed their suits and ties for aprons and bandannas in a phone booth, Lopez works the griddle like a guy who has filleted a few fish, reduced a few sauces, ruined a few soufflés in his life. For someone with his rolling-stone résumé, you might think a single savory concoction would be a death sentence, but he exudes a deep sense of calm behind the sizzle and the steam.

"People ask if I ever get bored of making the same thing. Are you kidding me? They have no idea what goes on in my head just to make this one *okonomiyaki*."

To illustrate his point, Lopez gives me a primer on cabbage. Cabbage evolves throughout the course of the year, coming from different prefectures across Japan—from the wintry mountains of Nagano to the dry flats of Fukuoka—and as the seasons change, so too does the cabbage's behavior on the *teppan*. In spring, it wilts fast and burns quickly, in the fall it retains liquid and requires a longer, slower cook. "It took me a full year just to figure out how to manage my cabbage."

Multiply that by noodles, eggs, crepes, proteins, and the capricious nature of the griddle, and you begin to understand why he doesn't seem eager to add items to his menu or build more restaurants or do anything else besides make *okonomiyaki* exactly where he's been making it for fifteen years. That might be the most Japanese thing about Lopez: his ability to accept tiny details like a vegetable's water content and griddle heat distribution as challenges worthy of a life's dedication.

Behind Lopez, tracking his every move, are two apprentices. Futoshi Mitsumura, thirty-one, left behind a moderately successful stint as a punk rock drummer in Tokyo to return to Hiroshima and learn to cook the soul food of his hometown. He's been here for one year, and still does most of his work behind the scenes, boiling noodles, chopping cabbage, refilling bottles of Otafuku sauce.

Hidenori Takemoto, thirty, could be the poster child for the salaryman convert, an uninspired mechanic at Toyota who found his true muse in the leafy layers of this Hiroshima specialty. "At Toyota, I did what I was told and there was no praise for a job well done. With *okonomiyaki*, I get immediate response." He's been working behind Lopez for over a year now, and he shadows his master with quiet confidence, cracking eggs, flipping crepes, splashing noodles with helpful doses of hot water. He already has a space picked out for his restaurant, where he will bring Lopez-style *okonomi-*

yaki, jalapeños and all, to the people of Shikoku.

The line of people waiting for a seat at the counter continues to grow, until a small group—a pair of parking attendants, a young guy with huge headphones and a bubble jacket—forms outside. Makiko suddenly appears, apron-clad and spatula-ready, and takes her place beside Lopez at the *teppan*. She still works the griddle but mostly during the restaurant's busiest moments (the Lopez family—husband and wife, two boys, in-laws—all live in a house attached to the restaurant). She shakes spices and fries eggs and efficiently begins to finish the *okonomiyaki* her husband starts, then slides them across the griddle to waiting customers. *Okonomiyaki*, in the best places, at least, is eaten with a *hera*, a thin metal spatula, directly off the *teppan*—a dish, as Lopez likes to say, that continues to evolve down to the last bite.

These days Okonomiyaki Lopez shows up on the top-ten lists of many local experts, including a perennial slot as one of Hiroshima's best *okonomiyaki* shops on Tablelog, Japan's massive restaurant review website. But a certain contingent of Japan's food cognoscenti still have a hard time believing that *okonomiyaki* could come from a Guatemalan. Lopez remembers a few years back when a local journalist wrote a book dedicated to Hiroshima-style *okonomiyaki* and its many purveyors. He ate at Okonomiyaki Lopez a few times, and politely returned months later to give Lopez a finished copy of the book. Only, Lopez wasn't listed with the other *okonomiyaki* shops; he was written up in the "Other" section. (Two of his students, however, had made the real shop list.)

"Some people say I've Westernized *okonomiyaki* just because I'm Western," Lopez says, with the affectless delivery of someone who appears constitutionally incapable of getting worked up over anything, a walking Venn diagram of Latin American humility and Japanese restraint. He can talk openly about the most extraordinary things—an abusive father, a transcontinental romance, the challenges of being an immigrant in Japan—with the same shoulder shrugs and steady monotone he saves for discussions about vegetables. It's tough to say if this temperament came with his Japanese citizenship or if he's been carrying it around with him since he left Guatemala, but it plays well at the *teppan*. With the right set of eyes, you might even mistake Lopez for a local.

Today's customers look comfortable at Okonomiyaki Lopez. They drink beer and take pictures and talk up the man behind the griddle—a sharp contrast to the studied silence of many Japanese restaurants. He chats with old women and young couples as they place their orders, asking regulars about family members, telling stories about mutual friends.

"Out there in the streets of Hiroshima, you don't talk with people. You live in your own world," he says. "But here, you pull up a stool, watch the cooking, and you get to know your neighbor."

米 麺 魚

One afternoon, as I sit scraping my way through a Lopez jalapeño *okonomiyaki* at the restaurant counter, an old woman takes a seat next to me and places a large to-go order. She looks surprised to see a foreigner in the restaurant and tells me as much in near-perfect English. We get to talking about the types of things strangers talk about until she, unprompted, tells me that she is a *hibakusha*, a bomb survivor.

"I was two years old when it happened. We lived a kilometer and a half from the center. Some people survived the initial blast in this neighborhood, but the heat was so intense that it burned for three days and many eventually died. My three older brothers died in the rubble when our building collapsed. My mother and I were the only ones from my family to survive."

We both sit quietly, staring at the little waves of heat rising off the surface of the *teppan*. After a few minutes, she breaks the silence.

"I've spent my whole life thinking about how amazing it is that in the same apartment four people died and two people lived. Life is full of mysteries."

Is it possible to write about Hiroshima without writing about the splitting of atoms? Is it possible to walk its streets and visit its markets and eat in its restaurants without thinking about oblivion? I think about it constantly, wonder why I can't get past it, wonder if I lived here if I would ever get past it. Even as I type these words, I feel a current of guilt coursing through my digits, as if I owe it to the people of Hiroshima to leave it alone, to let them get on with living.

The earth this city is built on was ready to move on before its surface had cooled. They say that after the bomb dropped and nearly blasted Hiroshima out of existence, the grass and flowers grew back almost immediately. Not months or years after the bodies had been burned and the radiation dissipated; by August 12, 1945, just a week

after the *Enola Gay* gave birth to the nuclear age, the city was blanketed in green. "Weeds already hid the ashes, and wild flowers were in bloom among the city's bones," John Hersey wrote in *Hiroshima*, his wrenching minute-by-minute account of the aftermath of the first atomic bomb. "The bomb had not only left the underground organs of plants intact; it had stimulated them."

A modern city was transposed onto the ruined one with remarkable speed: skyscrapers were erected, a new system of streets and avenues laid out, and a sprawling memorial dedicated to peace took shape along the water. When Emperor Hirohito came in 1947 to visit the orphans of Hiroshima, he didn't find a city mourning; he found a city rising.

"This was no beaten people who welcomed the Emperor to their city," Allen Raymond, a correspondent for the *Herald Tribune*, wrote at the time. "I have seen most of the war-damaged sections of the world, and one could not find a healthier, stronger, more cheerful

207

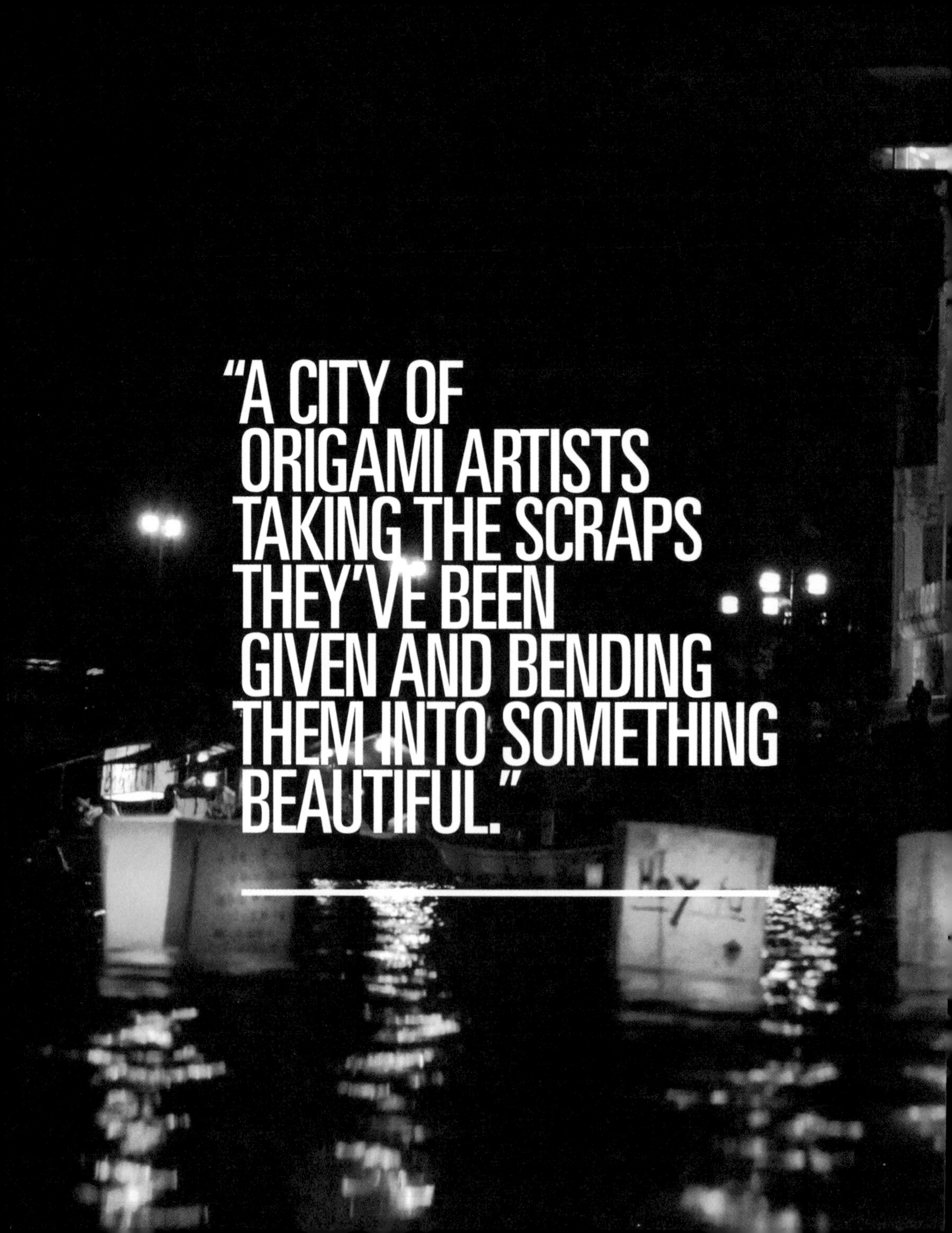

"A CITY OF
ORIGAMI ARTISTS
TAKING THE SCRAPS
THEY'VE BEEN
GIVEN AND BENDING
THEM INTO SOMETHING
BEAUTIFUL."

population anywhere than that of Hiroshima. The city is simply crawling with new life and energy." American correspondents were known for dispensing self-serving boosterism in the wake of the war, but so many I meet in Hiroshima tell me various versions of the same story: *We were looking forward, not backward.*

Every morning I walk from the city center to Okonomiyaki Lopez, crossing the wide boulevards designed by the Americans, cutting through generous parks, where local women hunt wild vegetables in the bushes, getting swallowed by the shadows of buildings electric with the energy of an animated workforce. Men slurp noodles; women sell shoes; kids ride bikes: Hiroshima is nothing but a city being a city.

But every night I walk home along the Motoyasu River, seven murky fingers that splinter the city into a small archipelago, and all I can see is the past. The looming mountains, where people fled that first morning to higher

ground, away from the smoldering remains. The T-shaped Aioi Bridge, the original target for Little Boy, until the bomb drifted west and detonated above a hospital instead. The river, where survivors trapped in the center submerged themselves to escape the incendiary temperatures of the burning city. The river, where the skeleton of the Atomic Bomb Dome casts a pale light on the water, a spectral reminder of Hiroshima's haunted past.

Once known as the Industrial Promotional Hall, the building was located just 160 meters from where the bomb detonated. Everyone inside was killed instantly, but besides a few scars across its facade, the structure survived intact. Many people, frightened by the eerie bones of the building in the city center, wanted to see it flattened and forgotten, but the government elected to keep it, and now it shimmers across the water like an optical illusion—a reminder of either the senselessness or the resilience of man, depending on how you squint your eyes.

Every night I think: How can the walls possibly be so smooth? How can those windows be so square? How can that dome up top still be so round? I think: After all it's been through, how does it still have the strength to stand? It begins to follow me into my dreams, just one of the many ghosts that chase me around the city.

Those ghosts show up in the form of impromptu tales told at the Lopez counter. Most are stories of impossible survival. One old man, between bites of a squid *okonomiyaki*, recounts to the entire restaurant how he walked behind a building just as the bomb blew, unknowingly saving himself from its incinerating temperatures. Another day, with a full counter of diners around us, Makiko tells me the story of her mother, ten years old and working in a factory, building plane parts for the war, who survived when two pieces of machinery collapsed onto each other, creating a protective A-frame above her tiny body. "My mom always says, 'No

wonder we lost the war, we had little girls building the weapons.'"

I try to take all of this in, to think of something appropriate to say, but nothing comes out. Being American, with a grandfather who stormed the shores of Okinawa and whose cohort likely celebrated the news of the bombing, makes it only more complicated. The emotions swirl and take shape inside you, one after the next, a tarmac procession of loaded cargo waiting to take off: guilt, regret, rationalization, anger, acceptance, ambivalence. My internal chaos contrasts sharply with the extraordinary sense of calm transmitted by everyone I meet, especially the gentle *hibakusha* at my side, sharing her story, patiently waiting for her dinner.

I can't help but try to connect the dots—the smiling old woman with the vanished family, the stone monuments to peace, the people who gather around this improbable postwar food—and when I do, this is all I can see: a city of origami artists taking the scraps they've been given and bending them into something beautiful.

A few minutes later Lopez hands her a bag stuffed full of food—three pork *okonomiyaki* to go—and her face lights up like Christmas Eve.

"His *okonomiyaki* is very good," she says, then shuffles off into the night with her bag of goodies.

I fight off a few tears and look up at Lopez. He shakes his head. "She always orders *okonomiyaki* with udon. I can't get her to try it with soba."

米　麺　魚

Ever since its owner developed tendinitis in his shoulder back in 2008, Okonomiyaki Lopez has been closed on Saturdays, a reality that doesn't sit well with the parents-in-law. "In Japan, when you're young you're supposed to work hard all the time. My mother-in-law's friends in the neighborhood ask her why we take Saturdays off." He says this with the subtle grin of a man who long ago stopped worrying about the opinions of his in-laws.

Behind the smile, Lopez is nervous, pacing slowly in front of the shuttered shop. He has been meaning to drop in on one of his apprentices for months now, ever since he opened his shop behind Hiroshima Station. He sent flowers, of course, along with a bright Okonomiyaki Lopez shop sign, but today would be the first time tasting the student's work. To add to the pressure, Lopez has invited along Hiroki, his master, to help assess the quality of the Lopez school of *okonomiyaki*.

Hiroki picks us up in front of the shop in his van, and master and student embrace like old friends. "You look good," says Lopez. "I've been worried about you." The reunion is spoiled in part by a bit of troubling news Hiroki has just received: a former student of his suddenly died last week, and now Hiroki, as cosigner on the restaurant lease, is expected to inherit the shop. The bank delivered the news earlier this week.

Hiroki is seventy-one years old, and clearly in no shape to be running an-

When the crowds descend, Lopez's wife, Makiko, joins him at the *teppan*.

other man's *okonomiyaki* shop. He has spent the past few years in a two-front battle against liver and colon cancer, and after three operations and rounds of chemo, his body is starting to give out on him. But his dedication to his students, he says, takes precedence. "The bank told me I either have to pay or go back to work. So I'm going back to work."

Hiroki was born in Nagasaki a year after the bomb and moved to Hiroshima in 1968. He was working as a bartender in the early 1970s when an *okonomiyaki* place opened upstairs and the owner offered to train him. Ten years later he opened his own branch and began, little by little, to make the changes to the ingredients and techniques and cooking implements that have come to define one of Hiroshima's most famous and influential strains of *okonomiyaki*.

Since then, he's trained over fifty students in the art of Hassho-style *okonomiyaki*, an open-door, open-book philosophy that runs counter to the guardedness you find in many corners of

the culinary world. "I have no secrets. I want people to do well."

Okonomiyaki Masaru shares more than a few things in common with Okonomiyaki Lopez: the long U-shaped *teppan*, the bright colors and Latin music, the crowds that descend upon the place as soon as the sun goes down. We arrive unannounced, and Hiraoka Masaru looks dumbstruck when he sees Lopez and Hiroki walk through the door. He greets us nervously, then retreats to the *teppan* to tend to his cabbage.

Hiroki watches him work, quietly, carefully, throwing off tiny nods of approval as he analyzes the methodical construction of Masaru's *okonomiyaki*: the oval shape of the crepe, the freshly boiled noodles, still dripping with water, the double-yolk eggs, the rising heat off the surface of the *teppan*.

Hiroki grows silent for quite some time, looks lost in the midst of the *teppan*, as if he's staring into a lava lamp of his life. Is he thinking of the fifty young men who have chosen him as their guide? The foulmouthed kid from Hokkaido, the one who got rich fast in Tokyo, the Guatemalan who surprised everyone? Or is he thinking about the one who just slipped away, and the painful path ahead of him?

Masaru is not his student, which makes the familiarity of his moves all the more meaningful. Why the thick *teppan*? Why fresh noodles? That's the way master did it. Why two yolks? Why? Why? Because that's how master taught me—the simple answer to the most important food questions of Japan.

Three generations, three branches of an *okonomiyaki* discipline responsible for feeding Hiroshima the food it craves. To Masaru's right, chopping cabbage, is a fourth branch, his own disciple, who will spread the gospel in some unknown direction. He'll call it not Hassho style or Lopez style but Masaru style to his customers and to his own students one day, yet the fountain of his inspiration is seated right next to me, cancer-riddled, hard of hearing, watching the

little waves of his legacy ripple across Hiroshima.

"I haven't changed anything. This is exactly as Lopez-san taught me," says Masaru, wiping off a trail of sweat inching down his forehead. "My goal is to reach his level, to make it just like his. I'm not there yet, but my customers will tell me when I am." With this last part Lopez blushes just a bit. With this last part, Hiroki snaps out of his silence, mumbles his approval, and blushes a bit too.

Another order comes in, and Masaru rushes back to the other side of the *teppan* and gets to work. He spackles the crepe with the back of the ladle, packs the cabbage lightly, lets the noodles dance across the hot surface, paints it with a generous stroke of Otafuku sauce. And when everything is ready, stacked high and bubbling, double yolk dripping down the side, he grabs a handful of jalapeños and scatters them over the *okonomiyaki*.

"It's our bestseller."

Food History
THE EVOLUTION

600

Rice arrives from China, beginning a long regional trade relationship in which the Chinese and Koreans export vital cultural cornerstones (tea, Buddhism, ceramics, various culinary staples) and the Japanese reward them with a mixture of respect and resentment.

1543

Portuguese sailors shipwreck off the coast of Kyushu, bringing with them the blueprints for tempura and Christianity. The former is widely embraced; the latter is eventually banned and its practitioners summarily executed by the powerful ruler Toyotomi Hideyoshi.

1873

Emperor Meiji is seen publicly consuming beef, thus ending a 1,200-year ban on meat consumption (just one of Buddhism's many marks on Japanese cuisine). The rise of Westernized and meat-centric cuisine— yakitori, *tonkatsu*, *yakiniku*, and ramen— soon follows.

1945

Americans begin a seven-year occupation of Japan. They bring with them boatloads of surplus wheat, convincing a starving nation of its nutritional superiority. (In return for cheap wheat, Japan agrees to purchase American arms.) Ramen, udon, and *okonomiyaki* culture flourish.

1975

Akira Okazaki, a Japan Airlines executive, successfully air-delivers bluefin tuna from Nova Scotia to Tokyo, ensuring decades of Japanese sushi superiority but at a steep cost to the world's ocean life. Today's fish markets in Japan are an edible atlas of the twenty-first century.

2011

Bread consumption surpasses rice consumption for the first time in Japanese history. While traditionalists lament the rise of wheat, Japanese cooks continue to one-up the world in the art of pizza, pastry, and baking as the national waistline inches ever so slightly outward.

A Beacon in the Night

THE 8 WONDERS OF THE JAPANESE CONVENIENCE STORE

Located on every block in urban areas (and every other block in rural ones), the Japanese convenience store is much more than a ubiquitous repository of junk food and cheap buzzes. It sells sushi and soba, manga and medicine, single-malt whisky and next-day hangover cures. Many Japanese swear allegiance to one of the Big Three *conbini*—7-Eleven, Lawson, or Family Mart—but all share a common ethos of maximum utility, minimal hassle, and food that's better than it needs to be. There are many things to love about *conbini* (and a few things not to), but these are the most heroic features of the Japanese convenience store.

 01

ONIGIRI

One of Japan's most popular snacks looms large on the shelves of *conbini*—endless triangles of packed rice wrapped in shiny sheaths of crackly seaweed. Try it stuffed with *umeboshi* (pickled plum) or tuna and mayo.

 02

KARAAGE

Fried food has a strong presence in *conbini*, but chicken—spicy nuggets, patties, thighs, and drumsticks—is the standout. Lawson has a deservedly strong reputation for its *karaage*: salty, unreasonably juicy, and as delicious cold as it is hot.

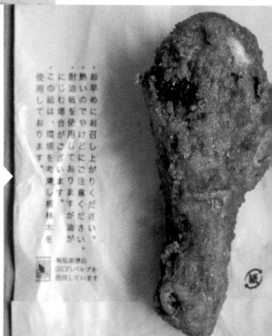

ODEN

Come winter, *oden* dominates the *conbini* landscape: vegetables, meat, tofu, and eggs simmered gently in dashi. The Japanese go crazy for this stuff, and when you feel the chill in your bones, you will too.

YOGASHI

Pillow soft and lightly sweetened, *yogashi* (Western-style desserts) make for a heroic breakfast or late-night binge (try anything made with green tea). Family Mart's line of high-concept pastries is especially impressive.

ICED COFFEE

Nearly as ubiquitous as vending machine coffee, and marginally better. It tends to be super sweet, so best to look for ones with "double" or "espresso" in the name, or custom blend your own hot or cold caffeine fix with the slick coffee machines found at all the big *conbini* these days.

BOOZE

The place to stock up for a street beverage or a hotel stash. Dedicated sake sections, sprawling beer cases, wine, and whisky give the informed drinker a formidable lot to select from. *Chu-his* and pocket Suntory bottles are two standouts.

こだわりたまごのサラダサンド
¥181（税込¥195）

SANDOS

The math doesn't work out—squishy bread, industrial fillings—but what emerges out of those plastic wrappers is glorious. Egg sandwiches from 7-Eleven and Lawson are little miracles of creamy golden yolks and umami-rich kewpie mayonnaise.

EVERYTHING ELSE

The bathrooms are sparkling by U.S. convenience-store standards, the employees are comically cheery, and 7-Elevens remain one of the only places where foreign ATM cards work. You can also pay bills and buy plane and concert tickets while you snack on your egg *sando*.

麺は石臼挽き、つゆには2種の枯節に追い鰹！
新しく生まれ変わった、ざる蕎麦

Agemono

揚げ物

DEEP FRIED

Deep
FRIED

ELEVATING THE ART OF FRYING

The Japanese may boast the longest life spans on earth, but people here love grease as much as the rest of the world. From convenience-store *korokke* to Michelin-starred tempura temples, nobody fries better than the Japanese.

KARAAGE

Chicken thighs marinated in soy, garlic, and ginger, then floured and fried. Also made with shrimp, octopus, and other sea creatures.

KOROKKE

Filled with everything from mashed potatoes and mincemeat to curry and cream of crab. Like a Spanish croquette but executed with Japanese precision.

KUSHIKATSU

Fried meat on a stick eaten elbow to elbow at a bar and washed down with rivers of cold beer: What's not to love? Osaka invented the form, but you'll find it everywhere.

Deep
FRIED

TONKATSU

Panko-breaded pork loins fried to a greaseless crisp, served with hot
mustard, sweet Worcestershire, steamed rice, and shredded cabbage.
The best is made with *kurobuta* (black foot) pork.

TEMPURA

Shokunin dedicate entire lives to tempura, turning battering and frying
into a high art form. For the full experience, go to a tempura-only
restaurant and order the *omakase* — the chef's tasting menu.

THE POWER OF PANKO

Japanese chefs use panko bread crumbs—large, flat flakes that create a shattering, greaseless crust—on *tonkatsu*, *korokke*, and other golden-brown gems.

DEEP-FRIED DEPACHIKA

Japanese department stores (called *depachika*)—wondrous centers of gastronomic greatness—trade in the entire spectrum of fried specialties. A fine place for *korokke*, *katsu*, or tempura. (Be on high alert for free samples of each.)

Chapter Six

HOKKAIDO

——

I wake up on top of the sheets of my cheap hotel bed, fully clothed, smelling of whisky and lamb. Not lamb, actually, but grilled mutton, possibly a few days or weeks past its prime. I struggle to bring the details of last night into focus. If I squint hard enough, I see a pocket bottle of Suntory, an old woman with a pile of raw onions, a smoky bar with karaoke and cheap wine.

But then I find this e-mail, sent to me sometime during the last night's stupor:

Dear Matt,
I have arranged for the complimentary tickets on the SL (Steam Locomotive) Niseko, *which travels from Sapporo to Niseko on the weekends during autumn only. This is designed to let people enjoy the nostalgia of travel from days gone by, enhanced with dramatic scenery and with a variety of different specialty products available in the dining car as you go through the different regions en route to Niseko.*

The e-mail is from Paul Haggart, the sole representative of Niseko Tourism, who insists that I need to come to his tiny mountain community to appreciate the full pastoral majesty of Hokkaido. Paul informs me that the tickets are on hold at the information counter at JR

Sapporo Station, arranged for by one Mr. Yoshitaka Ito from JR Plaza in Tokyo. The train people will be expecting me.

In the harsh glare of the Hokkaido morning light—not to mention the throbbing weight of an all-world hangover—all of this sounds like too much effort. But I have made promises, and nowhere are broken promises more perilous than in Japan, so I roll out of bed, stuff my clothes into my suitcase, and wobble my way toward the station. After days of grilled mutton and bad decisions in Sapporo, maybe a bit of mountain air will do me good.

The SL Niseko is a reptile of a train, muscular and elegant, black as a starless night, spewing thick plumes of smoke from her nose—a seasonal beast ready to slither her way through the jumbled topography of this island. A conductor in a throwback uniform stands guard at the front, his posture so stiff it could slice a soft tomato. All around, people snap photos and film videos and generally lose their shit over the old-world elegance and enduring mechanical mastery of the steam locomotive Niseko.

I fight past the crowds, who look genuinely confused and disappointed that this disheveled gaijin has in his greasy, lamb-stained palm the golden ticket. Inside, the train cars sparkle with the "nostalgia of travel from days gone by." In true Japanese fashion, the interior looks to be lifted directly from 1856, with all the tiny details Hollywood-ready: the polished oak paneling, the meticulous ironwork, the authentically uncomfortable wooden seats.

The train pulls out of Sapporo with a few proud whistles and winds its way southeast along the Sea of Japan. It's barely 8:00 a.m., but my train mates waste little time in breaking out the picnic material. But this isn't standard Japanese picnic fare: not a grain of rice or a pickled plum in sight. Instead, they fill the varnished wooden tables with thick slices of crusty bread, wedges of weeping cheese, batons of hard salamis, and slices of cured ham. To drink, bottles of local white wine, covered in condensation, and high-alcohol microbrews rich in hops and local iconography.

From the coastline we begin our slow, dramatic ascent into the mountains of Hokkaido. The colors bleed from broccoli to banana to butternut to beet as we climb, inching ever closer to the heart of autumn. My neighbors, an increasingly jovial group of thirtysomethings with a few words of English to spare, pass me a glass of wine and a plate of cheese, and I begin to feel the fog dissipate.

We stop at a small train station in the foothills outside of Ginzan, and my entire car suddenly empties. A husband-and-wife team has set up a small stand on the train platform, selling warm apple hand pies made with layers of flaky pastry and apples from their orchard just outside of town. I buy one, take a bite, then immediately buy three more.

Back on the train, young uniformed women flood the cars with samples of Hokkaido ice cream. The group behind me breaks out in song, a ballad, I'm later told, dedicated to the beauty of the season. Everywhere we go, from the golden fields of empty cornstalks to the dense forest thickets to the rushing rivers that carve up this land like the fat of a Wagyu steak, groups of camouflaged photographers lie in wait, tripods and shutter releases ready, hoping to capture the perfect photo of the SL Niseko steaming its way through the hills of Hokkaido.

As I sit there, sipping my wine and snacking on cheese, soaking up the cornucopia of autumn views and the bonhomie of my train mates, one troubling question bounces around in my brain: When did I leave Japan?

米 麺 魚

Hokkaido is roughly the size and shape of Maine, a land of towering mountains, lush valleys, and rugged, lonely coastlines. Imagine Switzerland, if Switzerland were an island in the Sea of Japan instead of a landlocked country in Europe. Separated from Honshu by the Tsugaru Strait, Hokkaido is large and

Locals call Mount Yotei "Hokkaido's Fuji," for obvious reasons.

sparsely populated, making up 25 percent of Japan's landmass but just 5 percent of its population. Host to the 1972 Winter Olympics, the island is known to outsiders primarily as a place to ski, its prodigious snowfall legendary as some of the world's lightest and driest powder.

I did not come to ski. I first came to Hokkaido for two reasons: miso ramen and *uni*, the island's most famous foods and two items on my short list for Last Supper constituents. The only thing they share in common, besides a home, is the intense fits of joy they deliver: the former made from an unholy mix of pork-bone broth, thick miso paste, and wok-crisped pork belly (with the optional addition of a slab of melting Hokkaido butter), the latter arguably the sexiest food on earth, yolk-orange tongues of raw sea urchin roe with a habit-forming blend of fat and umami, sweetness and brine. Fall for *uni* at your own peril; like heroin and high-stakes poker, it's an expensive addiction that's tough to kick.

But my dead-simple plan—to binge on both and catch the first flight back to Tokyo—has been upended by a steam locomotive and Whole Foods foliage, and suddenly Hokkaido seems much bigger than an urchin and a bowl of soup. No one told me about the rolling farmlands, the Fuji-like volcanoes, the stunning national parks, one stacked on top of another. Nobody said there would be wine. And cheese. And bread.

Few understand my sudden itch for exploration better than Ioanna Watanabe. Ioanna came to Niseko in 2004 with plans to spend a few days snowboarding, a few more drinking and eating, before continuing her tour of the Far East. Only she fell in love with the island and its underappreciated virtues, including Hisashi Watanabe, a young Japanese man from Saitama working the ski patrol in the backcountry, and never left.

Today she and Hisashi own one of Hokkaido's hippest cocktail dispensaries, Gyu Bar, a low-lit drinking cave in Hirafu at the foot of the area's biggest ski resort. The two make a formidable team: Ioanna the resident whisky expert, Hisashi the dapper suspender-clad cocktail king. For four months of the year, Gyu Bar and every other establishment within sniffing distance of a ski slope hums with packs of Aussie boarders and Hong Kong powderhounds and the occasional Tokyoite.

But when the snow goes, so do most of the people, which is exactly why I'm here now: to focus on what really counts without the distractions of the winter-clad hordes. I meet Ioanna by chance at a wine shop in Niseko shortly after the locomotive delivers me to the mountains. When she hears about my SL Niseko revelations, she offers to take me around to experience what she calls "the mind-blowing Hokkaido."

Yes, you can come to Sapporo, drink the namesake beer and slurp ramen and enjoy one of Japan's largest and friskiest entertainment districts, take the train to Otaru for a quick *uni* feast, then head back to Honshu, but to truly experience Hokkaido, to understand what this is-land is all about, you'll need to venture out beyond the handful of urban pockets and into the wild. Do that for a few days and you'll realize that, more than anything, Hokkaido is a collection of amazing shit in the middle of nowhere.

This is the kind of place where you buy your eggs on the honor system from a friend's mailbox, where supermarkets sell produce with the face of the farmer on the package so you know exactly who grew your daikon, where your neighbor raises ostriches because he spent his honeymoon in Australia and thought they looked cool and, fuck it, why not?

We spend a week crisscrossing the southern part of Hokkaido in Ioanna's well-worn Honda CRV, eating and drinking in a way that upends my understanding of Japanese food culture. Ioanna is Canadian by birth but deep down as Japanese as fermented soybeans, able to understand and decode both sides of the cultural divide with preternatural ease and grace. I learn many things from Ioanna during our time together: when and how to bow in a variety of social scenarios, the exact combination of sounds to offer up after a delicious meal, the virtues of convenience-store fried chicken.

Ten minutes outside of Hirafu, we find Del Sole, a small cabin tucked into the woods with a world-class pizza operation inside. Kenji Tsugimoto, the owner, built brick by brick the oven that ejects puffy-rimmed, blistered-bottom pies that could rival the finest pizzas of Naples. He serves just five tables at lunch and five more at dinner. "Any more, and I wouldn't be able to make the pizza I want to make."

Signs of Hokkaido's muscular dairy industry tattoo the terrain everywhere: packs of Holsteins chew cud unblinkingly in the sunlight, ice cream shops proffer hyperseason flavors to hungry leaf gazers, and giant silos offer advice to the calcium deficient: "Drink Hokkaido Milk!" Even better than drinking the island's milk is drinking its yogurt, which you can do at Milk Kobo, a converted red barn with cows and tractors and generous views of Mount Yotei, which locals call Ezo Fuji. Kobo sells all manner of dairy products, but you're here for the drinkable yogurt, which has a light current of sweetness and a deep lactic tang, a product so good that the second it hits my lips, I give up water for the week.

The Nikka distillery, one of Japan's oldest and largest whisky makers, rises out of the coastal flats of Yoichi like a high-proof oasis for thirsty island itinerants. Inside, the fires of distillation burn red-hot: like the great SL Niseko, Nikka still runs on coal. Whisky is Ioanna's wheelhouse, and she peppers the self-guided tour with fun facts about the virtues of barrel-aging and the vision of Nikka founder Masataka Taketsuru. In 1918 he traveled to Scotland to learn the secrets of brown liquor from its oldest and wisest practitioners. He returned to Japan two years later with a Scottish wife and a blueprint that would form the basis of Japan's entire whisky industry. He chose Hokkaido as his home base because it was the place that reminded him most of Scotland.

My favorite of these far-flung places, though, is a few miles from the Niseko train station, housed in a steep brown A-frame that looks more like an Austrian ski chalet than a soba shrine. Tatsuru Rai first came to Hokkaido in 1962, when as a high school freshman he rode his bike all the way from Tokyo. He fell in love with the island's rural charms, and four years later, after saving up enough money, he returned, making the thousand-kilometer trip on foot this time. He worked in a hotel at first but wanted to open his own restaurant. There was no soba in the area at the time, despite the abundance of buckwheat grown in Hokkaido, so he rolled up his sleeves and got to work.

Tatsuru built Raku-ichi himself, fashioning a twelve-seat hinoki bar into a quiet viewing area for the performance that unfolds in the kitchen. He makes every order of soba by hand, working in small batches so that by the time you've eaten, you'll have witnessed the extraordinary transformation of grain and water into noodle. It takes him eight minutes from start to finish, a process so lovely and intimate that you blush every time he looks up from his work area.

He starts with 100 percent local buckwheat—a grain stubborn enough that most soba masters cut their dough with wheat flour to make it easier to work with. Once the water is added and the dough shaped into a smooth, seamless ball, he works it with a wooden dowel, using his forearms and his palms to make the mass thinner and thinner. With each pass of the dowel, he pats the dough with his right hand, a quick, seamless motion that acts as a metronome for the elaborate rolling process. The thud of the dowel, the slap of the hand, the rustle of the buckwheat against the board: it starts soft, grows louder and faster, like the building of a great jazz performance. He rolls, slaps, rotates, rolls, slaps, rotates, rolls, slaps, rotates—over and over until the crude circle is shaped into a sharp rectangle. With a twelve-inch soba blade and a

Tatsuru Rai turns buckwheat
and water into performance art.

wooden board to guide him, he transforms the rectangle into thousands of dark brown strands. No wasted motion, no alien movements, not a scrap of dough lost to inexactitude or impatience.

Nobody talks, as if too much breath might break the magical bond of buckwheat and water. (When Tatsuru traveled to Copenhagen to make his noodles in front of a crowd of food-industry luminaries, three hundred of the world's greatest chefs sat slack-jawed in silence as he did nothing more or less than what he does ten times a day in his tiny Hokkaido restaurant.)

The noodles are served by Tatsuru's wife, Midori, a lovely, soft-spoken hostess who wraps herself in gorgeous, expensive kimonos. The soba comes two ways: *seiro*, afloat in a dark, hot dashi spiked with slices of duck breast, or *kake*, cold and naked, to be dipped into a concentrated version of that same broth. Even if it's −50°F outside and you've lost all sensation in your toes, eat these noodles cold, the elegant chew and earthy taste of the buckwheat uncompromised by the heat of the dashi.

"The process is everything," Tatsuru says, in what could be a four-word definition of Japan.

The young man next to me, a spiky-haired pop star from Sapporo, nods his head in agreement. "Once you eat here, it's hard to go back," he says, in what could be a nine-word definition of Hokkaido.

米 麺 魚

The story of Hokkaido is not a lovely one. It is a history of neglect and repression, displacement and discrimination, outcasts and vagabonds. Some have likened Hokkaido to the Wild West, and the parallels are easy enough to draw: the government malfeasance, the band of misfits and clansmen that came here to operate outside of the law, the world of shit forced upon the native population.

For most of its written history, Hokkaido was known as Ezo, an island occupied by the Ainu, believed to be descendants of the ancient Jomon people, with a nomadic streak and a deep dedication to their spirituality. The Ainu had little contact with the Japanese until 1590, when Hideyoshi Toyotomi granted the Matsumae clan, a group of roaming samurai that settled in southern Hokkaido, exclusive trading rights with the "barbarians from the north."

The Ainu had things the rest of Japan wanted—fish, seaweed, furs—and in turn they took what their home couldn't provide: rice, sake, and tools. But the Matsumae clan did more than just trade with the Ainu: they restricted their movements within their own lands, prohibited them from trading with outside groups, and enforced their exclusive relationship with brutal force, gutting the indigenous culture and killing Ainu leaders over minor disputes.

Even with the increased trading between the Ainu and the Japanese, Ezo remained a land apart, one not formally recognized by Japan until the Meiji Restoration was in full swing. In 1869 the new imperial government christened the island Hokkaido and began to actively encourage settlement, primarily as a buffer against Russia, which was quickly encroaching on Japanese territory from the north.

As Hokkaido became more important to the Japanese government, so too did suppressing the Ainu, whose culture they viewed as a threat to Honshu homogeneity. Ainu language was banned, religious practices snuffed out, and the people themselves forcibly assimilated into the Japanese way of life. The Ainu survived in pockets scattered around southern Hokkaido, but their home was no longer theirs alone. (Only in 2008 did the Japanese government formally recognize the Ainu as "an indigenous people with a distinct language, religion and culture." Around 25,000 Ainu live in Hokkaido today, using a mixture of tourism income and government funds to restore many of the traditions and practices they suffered the loss of over the years.)

Like the pack of thieves and scoundrels that protect the Wall in *Game of*

Thrones, the earliest Japanese settlers were people from the margins of society: ex-criminals, forgotten sons, failed families. In the north they saw a chance to trade in their messy pasts for clean canvases. And the new Hokkaido government, for its part, was all too happy to provide them that opportunity.

After World War II, many of the Japanese who had occupied Manchuria repatriated to Hokkaido, adding to the motley mix of new faces looking for a fresh start in Japan's northern reaches. In 1971 the Japanese government decided it was time to finally connect Hokkaido to the rest of the country, and they began construction on an ambitious tunnel project that would reshape the island forever.

The Seikan Tunnel is the world's deepest and longest tunnel, an underwater expanse that takes twenty-two minutes traveling at 140 kilometers an hour to pass through. At the other end of the abyss is Hakodate, the gateway to Hokkaido and, for many years, to the rest of Japan. Hakodate was one of two ports to open to the outside world after Commodore Matthew Perry forced Japan to end its closed-door policy in 1854, a first stop for American and Russian ships winding their way down the country. It was once the most important city in Hokkaido—before the rise of Sapporo, before the Great Hakodate Fire of 1934—and signs of its former greatness still linger around town: the generous port and its polished warehouses, the cable cars that climb past the brick Orthodox churches in the hillside Motomachi district, the five-pointed star of Goryokaku, the European-style fort at the southern end of the city. From atop Mount Hakodate at night, you can take in the sparkle of Hakodate's hourglass body, and the bright lights of the squid boats bobbing in the water below.

The clearest signs of Hakodate's current greatness, though, can be found clustered around its central train station, in the morning market, where blocks and blocks of pristine seafood explode onto the sidewalks like an edible aquarium, showcasing the might of the Japanese fishing industry.

Hokkaido is ground zero for the world's high-end sushi culture. The cold waters off the island have long been home to Japan's A-list of seafood: hairy crab, salmon, scallops, squid, and, of course, *uni*. The word "Hokkaido" attached to any of these creatures commands a premium at market, one that the finest sushi chefs around the world are all too happy to pay.

Most of the Hokkaido haul is shipped off to the Tsukiji market in Tokyo, where it's auctioned and scattered piece by piece around Japan and the big cities of the world. But the island keeps a small portion of the good stuff for itself, most of which seems to be concentrated in a two-hundred-meter stretch in Hakodate.

Everything here glistens with that sparkly sea essence, and nearly everything is meant to be consumed in the moment. Live sea urchins, piled high in hillocks of purple spikes, are split with scissors and scraped out raw with chopsticks. Scallops are blowtorched in their shells until their edges char and their sweet liquor concentrates. Somewhere, surely, a young fishmonger will spoon salmon roe directly into your mouth for the right price.

This is Japan, after all, where freshness cannot be faked because everybody knows the difference between yesterday's scallop and today's. But sometimes, in this quest for deliciousness, lines are crossed. In the center of the morning market sits a giant tank of live squid and a handful of fishing poles. I pay my 500 yen and drop a line in. A group of Chinese tourists surround the tank, cheering me on in Mandarin as I try my best to hook one of the squirmy cephalopods. When I finally pull a squid out of the tank, it blasts a jet stream of water onto the crowd, which drives them wild. The squid is air-dropped immediately onto a cutting board where a man with a long blade and a stern face turns the dancing creature into a plate of sashimi

The many wonders of Hokkaido's waters on
display in Hakodate's morning market

before the muscles have a chance to stop wriggling. The body is sweet and supple, but the legs, still busily in search of their final resting state, don't go down without a fight.

Like so much in Japan, it's equal parts cute, impressive, and unsettling. There's a reason that markets like these aren't frequented by locals; they prefer their squid without a crowd of wealthy Shanghainese urging them on. The real game, as I soon discover, is *donburi*. *Donburi*, often shortened to *don*, means "bowl," and the name encapsulates a vast array of rice bowls topped with delicious stuff: *oyakodon* (chicken and egg), *unadon* (grilled eel), *tendon* (tempura). As nice as meat and tempura and eel can be, the *donburi* of yours and mine and every sensible person's dreams is topped with a rainbow bounty of raw fish. Warm rice, cool fish, a dab of wasabi, a splash of soy—sushi, without the pageantry and without the price tag.

At Kikuyo Shokudo Honten you will find more than three dozen varieties of seafood *don*s, including a kaleidoscopic combination of *uni*, salmon, *ikura* (salmon roe), quail eggs, and avocado. I opt for what I've come to call the Hokkaido Superhero's Special: scallops, salmon roe, hairy crab, and *uni*. It's ridiculous hyperbole to call a simple plate of food life changing, but as the tiny briny eggs pop and the sweet scallops dissolve and the *uni* melts like ocean Velveeta, I feel some tectonic shift taking place just below my surface.

Over the next few days, I eat nothing but *donburi*. At 7:00 a.m., when the sun still sleeps with the fishes. At 2:00 p.m., as the local workforce is mustering up the strength to see the day through. At 11:00 p.m., with the staff looking on nervously, trying to determine if I might finally be full. If I had to travel to just one part of Japan to eat one type of food, it would be seafood *donburi* in Hakodate. Truth.

If *uni* is your objective, you can do no better than Uniya Murakami, a fifth-generation family business with unparalleled dedication to the noble urchin, which it serves in dozens of guises: lightly cured in soy sauce, folded into the soft curds of an omelet, clinging to udon noodles like a Far Eastern carbonara. All of this, of course, is a distraction from what really counts: two dozen tongues of *uni*, an umbrella of orange with a green wasabi top, draped over warm rice, the *donburi* to end all others.

If there is anywhere more famous for *uni* than Hakodate, it's Otaru, a small, postcard-pretty harbor town on the west coast of Hokkaido, thirty minutes by train from Sapporo. They say the waters were once so rich in Otaru that you could catch fish with your bare hands. It was a wealthy town, the wealthiest in all of Hokkaido, built on the back of a gangbuster *nishin* industry—tiny herring fished in abundance and processed into fertilizer. Herring mansions, fancy nineteenth-century processing centers that doubled as residences for their wealthy owners, still dot the hillsides

around Otaru, but it's been many years since they've seen any action.

A picturesque canal cuts through the center of town, and on either side you'll find dozens of sprawling sushi venues offering more or less the same set 2,000-yen menu to the packs of day-trippers. But beyond the rows of restaurants, past the covered shopping arcade, down a back alley of tiny wooden huts, Sushiya Ko-Dai stands as a firm rebuke to the cookie-cutter sushi culture that dominates so much of Japan.

Technically it's a *yatai*, a street stall, but it could be mistaken for a closet or a can of sardines. People stand at the bar, pressed against each other, pointing through the glass of the most jumbled fish case you'll ever find in Japan. Presiding over this lovely mess is twenty-eight-year-old Sanada Kodai, a warm, talkative host with a perma-smile and a penchant for self-deprecation.

"I always wanted to be a hairstylist," says Kodai, running his hand over his cue-ball scalp and laughing. "But then

I thought, which job would be cooler when I'm older? I figured cutting fish would be cooler than cutting hair, so here I am."

As he slices and sculpts and passes each piece across the case to a customer, the chatter never stops. "I wanted to open a fun place, an alternative to conveyor sushi for young people. The best for me is when the counter is full of doctors and a high school student walks in and starts ordering."

Just then a group of three young Tokyoites open the sliding glass door and pull back the curtain.

"We tried to reserve," one of them says, seeing the tight space.

"We don't do reservations," says Kodai.

"Well, we're here now."

"Great, but you'll have to wait."

The place may be tiny and the mood relaxed, but the sushi itself is serious stuff. I put myself in Kodai's hands and he walks me, piece by piece, through the greatest of Hokkaido's bounty: mackerel, marinated in soy for twenty min- utes ("In Tokyo they have to marinate their *saba* for three hours"); salmon, streaked with huge deposits of fat, better for keeping the fish warm in these cold waters; a slice of scallop so tender that it seems to vanish before I have time to chew; and a generous pile of hairy crab crowning a warm, loose mound of rice, the kind of genre-defining bite that follows you places.

The Tokyo crew, who finally find a space at the counter, are visibly moved by the experience. "I wish we had a place like this back home," one of them tells me. Kodai beams like a lighthouse.

We finish with a fat piece of *uni* that trembles like flan, so soft and sweet it could double as dessert. It's a powerful ending to one of the best sushi experiences I've had in Japan, and it cost a fifth of what the big places in Tokyo run.

"Look, I have no staff and I work in this tiny space. That's why I can afford to use the best products."

"So is most of this fish from Otaru?" I ask.

"No. Not exactly. Things are complicated here."

I press him on the complicated part.

"Tomorrow I'll take you to see the fishermen. You'll see."

Today's fishermen live in considerably more humble settings than the herring hunters of Otaru past. Most are clustered in a series of huts and small wooden houses just north of the town center. I meet Kodai there at dawn, and we knock gently on the door of what looks like someone's garage.

An imposing figure in a dark V-neck sweater answers the door. "What do you want? Don't you know I'm famous?"

I struggle to find an appropriate response. "Why are you famous?"

"Because I'm crazy."

"What do you mean crazy? Crazy at night?"

"No, at night I'm a gentleman. I'm crazy on the water—the craziest guy on the water. Today's the only day I won't go out. I sent my sons instead."

Masao-san looks like a villain from a Jean-Claude Van Damme movie: brickhouse build, facial scars, handsome in a slightly menacing way. He is the unofficial leader of the fishermen of Otaru, a pack of seventy-five or so men whose families have worked these waters for generations. Masao's place, a messy shed with a few motorboats parked out back, feels more like a safe house than a fish shack, a place where he and his posse of bandits can lie low while the heat dies down.

Masao moves slowly, except when he's smoking, which is always. "I'm sorry I don't have much to offer you," he says. He reaches into a freezer and pulls out a shrink-wrapped octopus tentacle the size of a small human arm. He tears it open and cuts the tentacle into thick coins with a pocketknife, smears a wad of wasabi on a small plate, pours soy sauce onto another one, and puts it all over a stack of old newspapers.

"Breakfast is served."

Behind Masao sits a giant cooler, which I assume is stuffed full of fish, but when he opens it the only thing inside

Hokkaido's seafood remains the finest in Japan, but overfishing threatens its future.

is Boss coffee—hundreds of tiny black cans emblazoned with the pipe-smoking Boss man (played by Tommy Lee Jones in real life).

As we sit chewing on frozen octopus and sipping canned coffee and bathing in cigarette smoke, Masao explains that this is the most important hour of the day, when the fishermen come back to base with their catch. Historically, Otaru has yielded a rich and diverse catch that evolves throughout the year—salmon in the summer, herring in the fall, octopus and *uni* in the spring—but in recent years, they've been lucky to catch enough to live on.

"Every year there's less coming out. Even when I was young the herring supply was way down. This year we're seeing a third of what we had last year."

While we eat, a neighbor fisherman—short, with long hair and a rubber apron—walks in. "Zero. Zero, zero," he says, opening the cooler and grabbing a Boss. "I got enough for dinner, but that's it."

"The summers are hotter, and it's im-pacted our fish supplies," says Masao. "There aren't enough good bacteria. Less kombu, less places for fish to lay eggs. The balance is off."

There are many things to admire about Japanese food culture, but resource management isn't one of them. It's no secret that the Japanese are voracious consumers of life aquatic, eating fifty-five kilograms for every man, woman, and child—more than three times the global average. In the wake of World War II, with protein sources scarce, it was a matter of national policy to catch as much fish as possible, which has left fishermen with little to catch these days.

Cries from conservationists looking to impose some level of sustainability on Japan's fish habits have largely been ignored by all, including consumers. At the heart of these complicated issues—the whale hunting, the tuna desolation, the systematic emptying of the seas—is a simple argument that stops all other arguments in their tracks: it's our tradition. It's true, Japan for millennia has been a nation that survives largely off seafood, but a dense population combined with the rise of convenience-store and conveyor sushi has stretched its dining habits to the limits.

It's a loaded debate, a cultural minefield for a foreigner, but one can't help but get the sense that if the Japanese preserved ecosystems as carefully as they preserve tradition, the future of the fishing industry might not look so grim. Masao seems stranded somewhere between the two sides: he respects the tradition and is desperate to make a living, but he sees the need to adapt to the limitations of today.

Another fisherman enters and dramatically drops two live shrimp on the table. "Today's catch, your majesty." Masao lights another cigarette.

"We overfished. We should have made changes earlier. The older people would just take whatever they could take. The ones without sons were the worst. And now we're paying for it."

On cue, Masao's younger son walks in empty-handed. "I had one, it was right there, but it got away." He grabs a Boss and lights a cigarette.

Finally Masao's older son—heavyset, with dark red hair and a patchy beard—enters through the back door. He's carrying a plastic sack, which he opens and shakes in front of us. An orange octopus with two-foot-long tentacles drops to the floor and slithers its way across the cement.

"I was afraid of what Dad might do if I came back empty-handed." He gives the octopus a good kick, then looks up and notices me for the first time. "Who brought the gaijin here?" We all have a good laugh.

Soon the entire room is smoking and eating octopus and drinking cans of Boss coffee.

"Are there fishermen in America?" the older brother asks.

"Yeah," the younger one responds. "They look really cool."

A discussion about king crab ensues,

and I explain that my brother used to work on the Alaskan crab boats and made some really good coin doing it. Suddenly the fishermen are ready for a relocation.

"If we're all going to America, I'm coming too," says the younger brother.

"You should all get insurance," says Masao, lighting another cigarette. "I'll stay here and collect when you die."

米　麵　魚

In the early years of the Meiji Restoration, the new imperial government of Japan implemented a series of measures that would forever change the country and its culture. Closed off to the outside world for 180 years, the leaders of new Japan looked to modernize the country overnight, and to do so called upon foreign experts to help bring the country up to speed.

And so it was that William S. Clark, a Massachusetts-born son of a country doctor, found himself in Sapporo, charged with establishing Hokkaido's first agricultural college. Clark was a powerful academic, with a doctorate in mineralogy from Germany and a high-ranking post at Amherst as a professor of chemistry, zoology, and botany. A vigorous supporter of the Union cause, he took a leave from his teaching to lead a regiment in the Civil War. His bravery earned him accolades and a legion of loyal troops; in one immortalized moment during the Battle of New Bern, he mounted a Confederate canon like a metal steed, allowing his men to advance and overtake the enemy battery. Between the war heroics, the deep education, and a prodigious growth of facial hair, Clark would have made a strong candidate for Most Interesting Man of the Nineteenth Century.

He landed in Hokkaido in the spring of 1876 and got down to business, building out the Sapporo Agricultural College in a month flat. He introduced new crops to Hokkaido, along with lessons on Western agricultural techniques, animal husbandry, and Christianity. He became a trusted adviser to Hokkaido governor Kuroda Kiyotaka, offering counsel on everything from fisheries management to architecture to the textiles industry.

Clark was called back to the States after just eight months in Hokkaido, and a pack of his students rode with him to the outskirts of Sapporo to see him off. In a good-bye that was destined to inspire generations of Japanese, he turned back to the pack of young Hokkaidoans and offered his final words: "Boys, be ambitious!"

Today statues of Clark can be found all around Hokkaido, and his parting words, emblazoned on government buildings and appropriated by makers of manga and J-pop, maintain an outsize place in Japanese culture.

The message wasn't lost on the people of Hokkaido. Since the days of Clark's dramatic send-off, they've worked to prove that Hokkaido is as much an idea as it is an island. It's the idea of a Japan apart, the world beyond Honshu, Kanto, and Kyushu, the island that operates on

its own time, plays by its own rules. Even after hundreds of years of gentle growth, Hokkaido remains uncharted territory, the place you come to start new, to reinvent yourself and make a footprint in a way that would be impossible down below, where conformity is the unwritten rule that governs so much of society. For those who need to breathe deeply, to live beyond the white noise of the urban experiment; for those with a few jagged skeletons stuffed in their closets; for those who won't be tethered to the totems of history and tradition that cast impossible shadows across the rest of Japan, there will always be Hokkaido: once and forever the new frontier.

Takahiko Soga knows the frontier spirit better than most. He was born in the mountains around Nagano, son to a first-generation winemaker. He inherited the family winery, along with his brother, but quickly realized he needed his own space to make the wine he wanted. "The first thing that I learned was having a winery with your brother isn't a good idea. We needed some distance between us, so I came to Hokkaido."

Domaine Takahiko is a ten-acre winery situated on the rolling hills outside of Yoichi, about three miles from the coast. At the crest of the hill, Hokkaido flags flap in the gentle breeze that sweeps in off the sea.

Japanese wine consumption has shot up since the 1980s, when a growing appetite for foreign culture and the blossoming of expense accounts introduced the country to the virtues of French burgundies and Italian Barolos. The domestic wine industry took off around the same time, centered around Yamanashi Prefecture, close to where Soga was born, and spreading from the northern reaches to the bottom of Kyushu. Hokkaido is proving one of the country's most promising regions for wine production, not just because of the terrain and the weather but because producers have the space—physical, psychic—to experiment with their fruit.

Not everyone is playing the right way, though, according to Soga. He says that too many Japanese wineries blindly imitate California and France without considering the soil, the conditions, or the type of food that will be served with their wines. "We should be making wines to pair with Japanese food, and umami and dark, intense wines don't pair well."

Instead, Soga has embraced natural wines, a lighter, more esoteric style better suited to Japanese terrain and Japanese palates. He experiments with up to a hundred different types of wild yeasts, prefers long periods of fermentation, and above all wants his wines to express the earth they come from. "I want you to be able to taste Hokkaido in every bottle," he says.

As we sit talking and tasting in his bodega, taking in the damp funk of deep fermentation, it's easy to see what he means. Soga, like most of the serious terroir evangelists, thinks of wine as more art than science, a craft that requires soul and touch and deep-seated dedication. His mind is filled with big ideas about wine, and he reaches constantly for metaphors and analogies to drive his points home. In the first hour we meet, he likens wine to burgers, pickles, seaweed, miso, onion rings, bowls of ramen. "If you use the best seaweed in your *tonkotsu* broth, you'll never taste it because *tonkotsu* is so intense. But with *shio* ramen, you taste every ingredient. I like my wine like *shio* ramen."

He wants to be sure I understand that Domaine Takahiko is not a company and he is not a businessman. I take the bait and ask him how many people he employs. Soga brings his two hands together to make a large zero.

"If I was going to do it, I wanted to be a part of every step of the process." He tends to the wines, picks the grapes, smashes, inoculates, ferments, ages, and bottles them. He even designs the labels for everything he produces. It's hard to imagine Soga gets a lot of shut-eye, but this level of dedication is not without its

rewards: everything he makes sells out months before it's ready to drink, making him the island's cult winemaker of choice.

"If you're a *shokunin*, Hokkaido is a good place to be."

Saito Narumitsu would probably agree. He dedicates his life to making small batches of high-quality cheeses, which he sells out of a small wooden stand on the side of a two-lane highway between Niseko and Otaru. He learned the craft during a five-year apprenticeship at Kyodo Gakusha, one of Hokkaido's most famous cheese producers, which operates as an incubator for the island's rapidly expanding cheese culture.

In 2007 he opened Tokari Ranch, a business he runs with his wife, whom he met studying cheese at Kyodo, and his brother, who raises the cows.

Like many of Hokkaido's young entrepreneurs, Saito isn't from the island; he moved from Niigata a dozen years ago, when life stalled on Honshu and he saw an opportunity to try something new.

"In Honshu, a hundred years is nothing. But here we have a much shorter history, so instead of tradition, we have room to develop our own culture."

There is one Hokkaido tradition, though, that he does follow. "This was Ainu land a thousand years ago, and we wanted to respect that." He honors the Ainu roots in the names of his creations. Retara, which means "white" in Ainu, is a soft, fresh cheese similar to a ricotta or a fromage blanc. Another—a firm, nutty cheese with a grassy finish—has a name that means "waking of the springtime."

My Ainu is rusty, so I can't help but refer to each cheese by its apparent European inspiration—Gruyère, Camembert, scamorza—much to Saito's (understandable) consternation.

"Sure, there are strong French, Italian, and American influences, but the ingredients are from Hokkaido and we are from Hokkaido, so this is Hokkaido cheese. It's not world-class, not yet, but our cheese is getting better every year. With time, we will get there."

Which makes his choice of names for his farm all the more fitting: Takara is Ainu for "growing your dream."

If Hokkaido's cheese and wine industries are still fermenting, its bread culture is fully baked.

Aigues Vives sits on a cliff perched above Otaru with generous views of the Sea of Japan. The owner, Tanno Takoyashi, converted part of his home into a country bakery, with a set of stone steps that leads you through the trees and to the front door.

Tanno invites me back to see his oven, a wood-burning beauty brought over from France. It's 10:00 a.m., time for the second round of baking of the day. After feeding the fire with chunks of maple, he loads the bread and pastries according to cooking time: first the fat country rounds, then long, skinny loaves dense with nuts and dried fruit, and finally a dozen purple crescent moons: raspberry croissants pocked with chunks of white chocolate.

He and his wife traveled to France fifteen years ago and fell in love with the bread culture. For six months he watched the best bakers he could find, living off carbohydrates and the scent of a dream slowly proofing. He took notes; he took pictures. Later he returned and began to re-create the work he'd witnessed in the West. "I made a lot of bread. A lot of bad bread."

In certain corners of the Japanese food world, chefs and farmers and even politicians see guys like Tanno as the enemy. In their eyes he is aiding and abetting an unsettling shift in the Japanese diet—the continuing move from a rice- to a wheat-based diet. In 2011, for the first time ever, Japanese families spent more money on bread than they did on rice. This overtake has been a long time coming, put into motion by the U.S. and Japanese governments in the wake of World War II, but it has suddenly set off alarms in certain corners of the food world—chefs, producers, and politicians who see it as not just a domestic dietary issue but an affront to the national identity as a whole.

Tanno, for his part, doesn't see what

the fuss is about; you wouldn't either if you put in the time and the heart this guy puts into his breads. "Why should we have to choose between rice and bread when we can have both?"

He isn't referring to the soft, spongy industrial stuff most Japanese eat. He is referring to the heroic loaves and pastries that he pulls from his oven every morning, bread that wears a thick, crisp crust, a soft, faintly sour crumb, and a dedication to an ideal that borders on obsession.

It's not just the French oven and the French technique. The flour (at least part of it) and the starter are French. The cars parked on the gravel outside are French. As I walk from the oven in the back to the counter, I pass the kitchen and can't help but take a long look: Le Creuset enameled pans, a cast-iron stove, jars filled with preserves—it looks like a museum piece from the future, showcasing the French country kitchen of the twentieth century.

"We didn't just want a bakery. We wanted to create an environment, that's

Tanno Takoyashi lines up loaves to feed into his
wood-fired oven at Aigues Vives.

why we came here. For so many years people never thought about Hokkaido as a place for food. But that's changing."

It's baffling enough to find one place like this in the middle of nowhere, but the Takoyashis aren't the only ones wood-firing their own ovens in the neighborhood.

At Boulangerie Jin, you'll find another country house with maple wood in the front, a blazing oven in the back, and a shiny Peugeot on the side. Inside, husband and wife team up to make crisp-edged baguettes and one of the finest croissants I've eaten anywhere. Over the years, offers have come in to sell their products all over Niseko with heavy markups for the carb-craving snowboarders, but they don't want more money, they don't want some stranger selling their creations, and they don't want more exposure. (When the wife sees me take out a notebook, she immediately shuts down.)

Sokesyu Bread, just a few hundred yards down the road from Takara Ranch, is pretty much as crazy as the other two.

French house, French oven, French car. But Yusuke Konno, tall and skinny, with round glasses and a bandanna wrapped tight around his head, makes his bread with 100 percent Hokkaido flour. "Of course."

He makes superb versions of all the French classics—pain de campagne; baguettes; golden, flaky croissants—but he has a few funky new projects in the works, too. "We can experiment because Hokkaido culture isn't as deep as Tokyo's or Kyoto's." He's been talking about making the switch to dense, German-style brown breads. "Now maybe I'll need an Audi."

Let's consider the evidence: three separate, unrelated bakeries, all of whose owners drive French-made automobiles, have hand-built European wood-fired ovens, and dress like Provençal marmalade makers. All of this in one of the least-densely populated areas in all of Japan? The odds must be infinitesimal.

But these aren't just bakeries; these are affirmations of a much larger idea. Every detail matters. The source of your heat, the type of flour, the age of your starter—of course these form the fundamental base for the flavor of our daily bread. But somewhere, in the deep recesses of taste and perception, it matters that he drives a Peugeot. It matters that she wears a French country wife's blouse. It matters that the kitchen doesn't just *look* French.

It matters that they're all the way up here, in Hokkaido, where the air is green and the skies are wide and everything feels just a little more possible.

It matters.

米 麺 魚

Even if you travel to Hokkaido to get lost in the wilderness, it feels good to come back to a city of Sapporo's caliber— familiar for its sprawling entertainment district, covered shopping arcades, and preponderance of noodle shops and *sushi-ya*s, but with a collection of wide avenues, green spaces, and Western architecture like nothing you've ever seen in urban Japan.

Few cities eat better than Sapporo. The morning markets teem with *donburi* dreams. Sophisticated yakitori and tempura and haute cuisine restaurants serving only Hokkaido ingredients dot the downtown area. At Ramen Yokocho, a dark, narrow alley that claims to be the birthplace of miso ramen, a dozen tiny bars serve up steaming bowls of the rich noodle soup.

But I don't want ramen or raw fish or cabernet and Camembert. At midnight on my last night on the island, I am on the hunt for Genghis Khan, or, as he's known in these parts, Jingisukan—an unlikely fixture of Sapporo's dining scene. The name refers to a style of mutton grilled over convex metal domes thought to resemble the helmets worn by Mongol armies. Supposedly Hokkaidoans, once flush with sheep used for clothing the Japanese military, based the cooking on the belief that Mongol armies cooked lamb on their shields and helmets. Today dozens of Jingisukan joints cover Hokkaido's capital.

Jingisukan, Hokkaido's unlikely
mutton conqueror

Daruma Honten is a fifteen-person bar down a tiny alley in Susukino, Sapporo's pulsing pleasure district, the largest you will find north of Tokyo. Diners sit at a countertop while stoic women in bandannas fill their helmet grills with burning charcoal, then baste the iron surface with cubes of melting mutton fat. Thin slices of meat marinated in soy and ginger tent the smoking black domes, with onions positioned on the rim to absorb the tide of drippings that flows down their surface. The ladies leave me with the tongs but eye me with suspicion as I let the lamb build up a char deep enough to make a Mongol warrior proud.

The man next to me, a Wagyu farmer from upper Tohoku, comes to Hokkaido every few months to wrangle up more cattle—"The best in Japan," he says. While he's in town, he likes to drink Nikka whisky and eat sheep. "Sometimes I wonder why I don't live here."

While the mutton sizzles, I drink icy mugs of Sapporo, Japan's oldest beer, created by a German-trained Hokkaidoan at the dawn of the Meiji era. The Beach Boys play over the speakers, just audible over the protein chorus. When the meat is ready, I pluck it directly from the helmet, pinched between chopsticks with a soft petal of onion or two, and dip it into soy sauce spiked with garlic and chili.

It makes for fine late-night dining, to be sure, but the whole scene has me chewing on a few important questions as I eat. How, in a country where I've never seen lamb before, did Jingisukan conquer Sapporo? Why are there only women cooking this most manly of meats? And what takes the stink of mutton out of cotton and denim?

But as the night inches forward, as the smell soaks into my clothes and the beer into my blood, the barnyard funk of mutton stinging my eyes, the questions slowly disappear. Japanese diners, American music, Mongol myth. There's only one answer that makes sense: it's a Hokkaido thing.

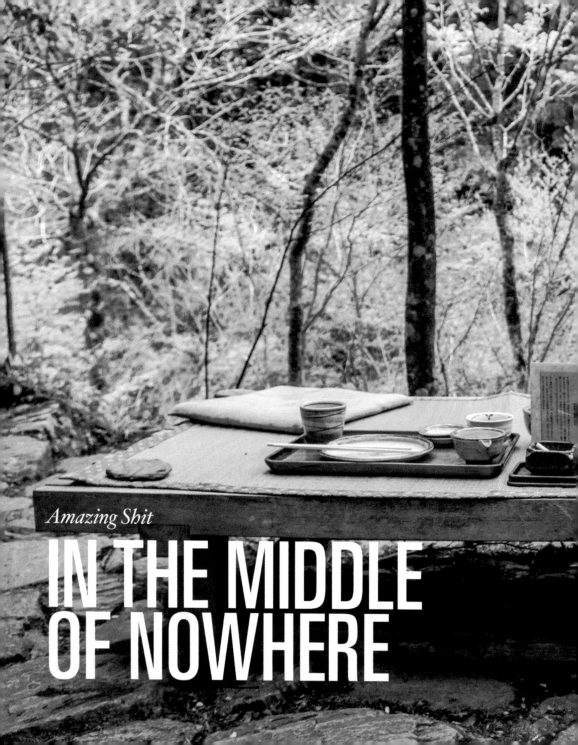

Amazing Shit

IN THE MIDDLE
OF NOWHERE

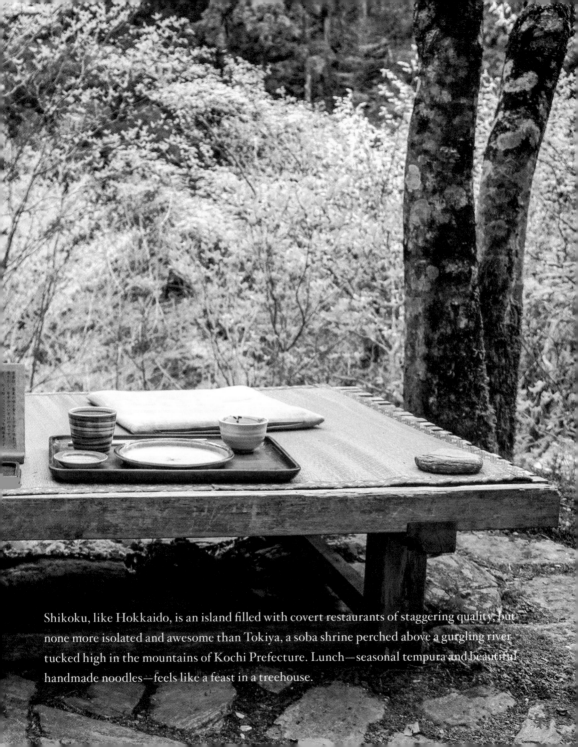

Shikoku, like Hokkaido, is an island filled with covert restaurants of staggering quality, but none more isolated and awesome than Tokiya, a soba shrine perched above a gurgling river tucked high in the mountains of Kochi Prefecture. Lunch—seasonal tempura and beautiful handmade noodles—feels like a feast in a treehouse.

Noto Peninsula

ジェラート
RICE-PADDY GELATO

A wooden stand found in a rice field deep on the Noto Peninsula in Ishikawa Prefecture, the family-run Malga Gelato stand specializes in flavors from the immediate surroundings: sea salt produced fron Noto's coastal waters, persimmon from a nearby orchard, and sake lees, the rice pressings used to make Japan's beverage of choice, from a small producer down the road. The most radical flavor, *ishiri*, based on Noto's famed fish sauce, may take the concept of local a step too far, but bless Malga for trying.

Hokkaido

パン
VOLCANO BAKERY

Niseko in the rural reaches of Hokkaido makes for an unlikely breadbasket, but the area teems with bakeries that would challenge the best in Paris. None more unlikely than Boulangerie Jin—so deeply removed from this already far-flung community that you will feel lost until the moment you stumble onto this country home and see the wisps of smoke rising from the wood-burning oven out back. The husband-and-wife team learned the art of bread in Paris and now produce flaky layered pastries; dark, dense, crusty brown breads; and a baguette so yeasty and complex that you may hope to stay forever.

Sado Island

和牛
ONE-TABLE TASTING MENU

Restaurant Seisuke, located on Sado Island off the northwestern coast of Japan, is run by Kuniaki Osaki, who channeled his Michelin-starred restaurant experience into one of Japan's tiniest and most isolated eateries. Located up a winding mountain road and boasting only one table, Seisuke is really an extension of Kuniaki's home, with his wife at his side and his kids peeking out from behind the kitchen. The food is a seamless mix of East and West: blowtorched yellowtail with yuzu chili paste, roasted whitefish with local mushrooms, and a plate of ripe cheeses served with a selection of esoteric European wines.

Shigaraki

懐石
COVERT KAISEKI

After training at Kyoto's top kaiseki temples, Furatani Tadamitsu opened Obana an hour from the fray of the old city in the quiet town of Shigaraki. At a beautiful cedar countertop, he serves fresh figs bathed in a thick sesame sauce, a first-rate tempura of tilefish and seasonal vegetables, and a stunning rendition of roast salmon marinated in sake, soy, and mirin. He may only have a few customers a day at times, but that's the whole point. "Beauty operates on a different level out here."

Naoshima

うどん
ISLAND UDON

Naoshima is best known for its esoteric art, the small island in the Seto Inland Sea transformed into a living, breathing exhibition. But beyond the Tadao Ando–designed museums, giant glass pumpkins, and funky village installations, you'll find a superlative bowl of noodles at Udon Yamamoto. Specializing in Sanuki-style udon from nearby Takamatsu, Yamamoto-san uses both hands and feet to knead the noodles, then massages them in ice water right after cooking to deliver an al dente chew that eludes all but the best udon *shokunin*—an art form in its own right.

One Night with the

SALARYMEN

OPEN THINGS UP

By the third drink, social norms dissolve. Ask the questions you could never get away with in daylight.

WARM UP SLOWLY

The initial moments will be tense as the suits shed the stress of the day. Be patient.

5pm   6pm   7pm   8pm

STOMACH THE TESTS

The chicken hearts and cow stomach are a form of initiation. Grab your chopsticks and dive in.

KNOW WHO'S THE BOSS

In the early hours, hierarchy still matters. Let the boss order food and drinks.

LAST CALL

The last trains depart at midnight, leaving thirty minutes for a final bite. Make it ramen, *yakisoba*, or anything with carbs and fat.

MAKE IT SUNTORY TIME

Pack a pocket bottle of whisky for when the evening heats up. Your companions will thank you.

9pm   10pm   11pm   12am

ROLL WITH IT

Boorish drunken behavior is accepted in the late hours. Be prepared for things to get weird.

BELT IT OUT

If karaoke comes up, be prepared with a crowd-pleaser. Billy Joel or Phil Collins will do.

Yakitori

焼き鳥
ON A
STICK

THE BEAUTY OF THE BIRD
Yakitori at its best is an elegant exploration
of the totality of one animal. For the full
chicken experience, work your way past the
white meat and into the wondrous tastes and
textures of parts unknown.

せぎも
SEGIMO (sweetbreads)

肝
KIMO (liver)

揚げ物
CHOCHIN (uterus)

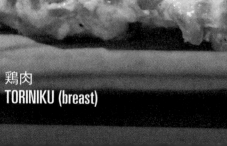

鶏肉
TORINIKU (breast)

はつ
HATSU (heart)

卵
UZURA TAMAGO (quail egg)

ぼんじり
BONJIRI (tail)

つくね
TSUKUNE (meatball)

Chapter Seven

NOTO

—

For the better part of thirty years, Toshihiro and Tomiko Funashita were the king and queen of fermentation in Noto. And since Noto is often regarded as the Kingdom of Fermentation throughout Japan, it could be argued that their skills held dominion across the country. Of course, they would never say it themselves, but Toshiro was recognized by the governor for his smooth, umami-rich fish sauce, and Tomiko was widely accepted as Noto's chief authority on all manners of preserved flora and fauna.

Noto is a peninsula on the coast of western Honshu, a craggy appendage of Ishikawa Prefecture that juts thirty kilometers out into the Sea of Japan. It is a place defined not just by the harshness of its seasons but by the generosity of its geography: rivers and mountains, ocean and valleys, one flowing into the next to create an extraordinary tapestry of ecosystems.

In some ways Noto is a perfect reflection of life in rural Japan: a quiet, self-sufficient tableau of Shinto and Buddhist traditions, where the rhythm of life is so directly tied to the rhythm of the seasons that calendars are beside the point. In other ways Noto remains a place like no other, a beautiful, lonely seascape, a world of distinct environments condensed into a tiny space, where everything is filtered through the lens of food, and the culture of fermentation runs so deep that nearly every meal has been transformed by time and bacteria.

The Jomon, the original settlers of Japan, first came to Noto over two thousand years ago, establishing a hunter-gatherer subsistence and ushering in a culture of food preservation that carries on today. They built large earthen-ware pots—believed to be among the first use of pottery ever by humans—and began to harvest salt. Together they had the tools to ferment fish, vegetables, rice—whatever they needed to survive the long cold months when the land produces little.

Today's Noto looks scarcely different from the Noto of the Jomon. Rice paddies climb the hillsides in wet, verdant staircases, dense woodlands trade space with geometric farmscapes, tiny Shinto shrines sprout like mushrooms in Noto forests. Villages seem to materialize from nowhere—wedged into valleys, perched atop hills, finessed into coastal corners. Pull over, climb out of your car, breathe deep for a taste of the finest air that will ever enter your lungs: green as a high mountain, salty and sweet, with just a whisper of decay in the finish.

Noto gained its reputation as the Kingdom of Fermentation because of this air. For most of its history, Noto was cut off from the rest of Japan, forced into a subsistence model that in many ways endures today. That was possible not only because of the bounty of Noto's fertile environment of trees, grasslands, fresh water, and sea, but because the air is rich with humidity that encourages the growth of healthy bacteria, the building blocks of fermentation.

Toshihiro Funashita's family lived in the interior of Noto, his father a forester, his mother a homemaker and a cook of wide reputation, the one responsible for organizing the elaborate feasts behind their community's most important social events—the highest charge in the local cooking communities of rural Japan.

Like any great and good country, Japan has a culture of gathering—weddings, holidays, seasonal celebrations—with food at the core. In the fall, harvest celebrations mark the changing of the guard with roasted chestnuts, sweet potatoes, and skewers of grilled ginkgo nuts. As the cherry blossoms bloom, festive picnics called *hanami* usher in the spring with elaborate spreads of miso salmon, mountain vegetables, colorful bento, and fresh mochi turned pink with *sakura* petals.

Funerals, in particular, are a time to eat in Noto, and the preparations that surround the passing of a loved one may involve days of work and dozens of participants. As a Shinto ceremony, funerals in Noto are vegetarian affairs, prompting local women to bring to the table the best of the products from their respective gardens and pantries. Toshihiro's mother, as respected in the kitchen as she was in the community, was in charge of overseeing the cooking at funerals in her town, which meant deciding the best way to make use of the gathered ingredients and organizing the women into teams to turn out elaborate spreads of boiled and fried vegetables, tofu dishes, and vinegar pickles.

When mudslides forced Toshihiro's family off their property, they relocated to the Noto coast and eventually opened an inn on 249, the two-lane highway that winds its way around the perimeter of the peninsula. Sannami was a *ryokan*, a traditional Japanese guesthouse, complete with tatami-floored rooms, a wood-fired bath, and full dinner and breakfast service for guests.

During those years, Toshihiro met and eventually married Tomiko Futamata, a young woman from the town of Notocho. He was an electrician who would go on to be a programmer in the infant days of the Japanese computer industry. Tomiko was a librarian, guardian of Noto knowledge, a voracious reader with a busy mind. She lost her mother at

The dining room in Flatt's Inn, with a
generous view of Toyama Bay

an early age, but she spent hours in the kitchen with her mother-in-law, learning how to transform a momentary surplus into a year's worth of good eating.

For most of Noto history, men weren't allowed in the kitchen. The kitchen was considered a sacred place for women, and having a man enter was tantamount to an invasion of privacy. But Toshihiro was different from most Noto men: he was deeply curious about food, about the tastes of Noto that defined his childhood, and as he watched his parents feed travelers from around Japan, he began to imagine what he would do differently.

米 麺 魚

Fermentation is the art of controlled decay. In fermentation's most basic form, enzymes produced by molds, yeasts, and bacteria break down organic matter, converting macronutrients like sugar to alcohol and proteins to amino acids. But there is a fine line between fermentation and decomposition: initiate and control microbial activity carefully, and you've extended an ingredient's life indefinitely; take it too far, and you've lost it forever.

There are many forms of fermentation, but the two most common in the food world are lactic acid fermentation, produced by fungi and bacteria and used to produce most varieties of pickles and fermented condiments, and alcoholic fermentation, induced with yeast, and used to produce the world's supply of adult beverages.

Fermentation is one of man's earliest culinary innovations, stretching back nine thousand years to the Neolithic period, when civilizations in modern-day China turned rice and fruit into alcohol. Since then, you'd be hard-pressed to find a single successful civilization that didn't have fermentation as a core component of its food culture.

Without it ever crossing our minds, most of us consume fermented foods at various points throughout the day: coffee and yogurt for breakfast, wine and cheese for dinner, chocolate for dessert. No small number of man's greatest achievements—from the hams of Spain to the beers of Belgium to the dark, bitter chocolates of Venezuela—are the byproduct of carefully controlled enzymatic breakdown.

The natural coalition of fermentation-loving cultures forms a strange Venn diagram: Russians and northern Europeans use salt to stretch vegetables long into the winter; West Africans ferment cassava root as a means of neutralizing its natural cyanides; southern Asians build entire cuisines around the flavors produced by dead fish; and Bolivians in the high Andes employ the enzymes in human saliva to transform chewed corn into fermented beer.

Most of these cultures have a handful of fermented products in their pantry, but in Japan the entire cuisine turns around lactic acid and alcoholic fermentation. The grocery list of fermented staples runs long and strong: soy sauce, miso, sake, mirin, *yuzukosho, katsuobushi, natto,* rice vinegar, *tsukemono*: without fermentation, the Japanese kitchen would be a lonely place. It's no coincidence that Japanese food places such a premium on umami, since umami is one of the primary byproducts of the fermentation process.

Beyond the basic advantage of preservation, fermentation offers a host of other benefits to consumers: a surge in B vitamins, the introduction of friendly gut bacteria into our systems, and of course the deepening of flavor and aroma in everyday ingredients.

In recent years, in certain corners of the food world, fermentation has become the fascination of chefs, hipsters, and DIYers, but what goes down in Noto has nothing to do with a young chef geeking out over a lacto-fermented heirloom carrot or a crunchy commune denizen making kombucha in the bathtub; this is a lifestyle necessity emblazoned in the DNA of this peninsula.

米 麺 魚

Toshihiro's parents retired in 1982, and Toshihiro and his wife took over running Sannami. They were ready for this moment: Tomiko's career as a librarian gave her ample time to digest every last piece of text dedicated to the topic of Noto food, and Toshihiro's limber mind and unwavering drive made him the perfect person to refine some of the more challenging culinary practices at hand. Soon after assuming ownership of Sannami, they began to slowly transform the inn into a living encyclopedia of Noto food traditions.

The *shokeba* is the most important room in the Noto home. As small as a closet or as large as a bedroom, this is where a family stores their stock of fermented goods: purple jars of *umeboshi*, pots of mocha-colored miso, barrels holding batches of homemade soy sauce. Like most local families, Toshihiro's parents kept a well-stocked *shokeba*, but the basic staples of the Noto kitchen were reserved for family consumption. At the hotel, they focused their efforts on serving a broader menu of Japanese food. To serve Noto food, products of necessity and distinct local character, to their guests would have been an embarrassment.

But Toshihiro and Tomiko had a different vision. Tomiko made it her business to put every piece of knowledge she had into practice, quickly turning the *shokeba* into an edible calendar of the Noto bounty. In the summer she harvested seaweed, picked plums, turned a rich garden harvest into a rainbow of preserved produce. In the winter she dried persimmons, pickled fish beneath the weight of stone slabs, fermented soybeans into dark batches of miso.

Toshihiro put his efforts into realizing the vision he'd shaped during years of watching his mother at work. His idea was driven by the tastes of his childhood, tastes that he feared Noto was losing, tastes that he felt he and his wife could restore and carry forward. He shaped himself into an expert on seafood, turning out beautiful, precise plates of sashimi and local fish dishes for his guests. Above all, he dedicated himself to *ishiri*, Noto's ancient fish sauce.

The history of fish sauce is the history of the world's greatest powers: the Byzantines, the Greeks, and the Romans all produced *garum*, made by salting and sun-drying fish blood and guts and extracting and filtering the resulting liquid. Civilizations across the Asian continent developed different takes on salt-fermented fish sauce, from Vietnam's nuoc mam to Korea's *aekjeot*. Even English Worcestershire sauce, based on a formula of fermented anchovies, is a form of fish sauce. Whether all of these cultures understood the science of umami is doubtful, but it's clear humans have known the simple secret of fish sauce for thousands of years: it's nature's greatest force multiplier, a few drops enough to intensify the flavor of anything it touches.

In Noto, fish sauce goes back to the eighth century, predating soy sauce on the peninsula by hundreds of years. Though shoyu became the predominant umami-enhancing condiment of Japan, *ishiri* remains a linchpin of true Noto cuisine. The region produces two types of fish sauce, depending on which side of the peninsula you live on. On the west coast, where anchovies and mackerel are abundant, they produce the cheaper, somewhat harsher *ishiru*. On the east coast, where some of Japan's finest squid spend time in the channel between Noto and Toyama, *ishiri* is king.

To make *ishiri*, Toshihiro would salt hundreds of pounds of squid guts at a time, leaving them to ferment for two, three, sometimes up to five years (the longer the ferment, the deeper the umami flavor). He would then press the guts to extract the liquid, bottle it, and store it for use at the inn. At the end, you have a liquid as dark as night and as fragrant as a laundry basket of old socks, but with a sweet, dense concentration of amino acids perfect for stews and sauces and, of course, for fermenting other products. In the totem pole of global fish sauces, *ishiri* sits squarely at the top.

Soon Toshihiro became celebrated for his *ishiri*. Customers, most raised on soy sauce and who had never tasted Japanese fish sauce, fell in love with the flavor. The governor of Ishikawa designated Toshihiro with the prefecture's only Takumi award, a distinction reserved for the top class of Japanese artisans. Meanwhile, Tomiko's reputation as a guardian of Noto's culinary heritage grew (she would go on to be one of ten women from guesthouses across Japan recognized for passing on local traditions to the next generation), and the inn became famous for its dedication to a way of eating that some in the area thought was lost and many in Japan never knew existed in the first place.

Normally, a son would inherit this world created by Mom and Dad and be expected to carry on the family reputation through the business they built. Toshihiro and Tomiko never had a son, though, so the duty fell instead to their eldest daughter, Chikako.

From a young age, Chikako was an independent girl. She played sports, which allowed her to travel around the region and later to other parts of Japan—Kanazawa, Tokyo, Akita. When she was twelve, her table tennis team received an invite to play in a tournament in Fukui, 250 kilometers south of Noto, but no parents or chaperones could make the trip. Instead, Chikako organized everything—the train tickets, the hotel, the tournament details—and took her eight teammates on a weekend road trip to play Ping-Pong.

Chikako went to university in Kyoto and studied to be a teacher, but dedicated most of those years living outside Noto to a mixture of work and partying. She took a job at a hotel, serving breakfast for four hours before school, then dinner for six hours after class let out. On the weekends, she worked weddings—massive, elaborate banquets where she learned the ins and outs of service. She studied full-time and still earned $3,000 a month, establishing a rhythm of hard work and quiet deter-

"RIVERS AND MOUNTAINS, OCEAN AND VALLEYS, ONE FLOWING INTO THE NEXT."

mination that would follow her back to Noto and beyond.

As the oldest daughter, Chikako had two primary responsibilities: to inherit the inn her parents owned and to assume the onus of the family name. The former is standard practice in family-based businesses across Japan but the latter is an old Noto tradition that comes with a host of loaded social responsibilities: pitching in with seasonal events, gifting money at weddings and funerals, and generally maintaining a strong, continuous presence for the family in the local community. Chikako accepted her fate, considered it an unwritten contract between parents and daughter, but before she settled down in Noto for the long haul, she wanted to see more of the world. She asked her parents if she could go to Australia, and they said no. The next year she bought a plane ticket, secured a passport, and organized a visa. A week before her flight, she told her parents she was off to Australia, with or without their blessing. Before she left,

they made her promise that she'd be back in a year.

In Australia, she kept up the kind of lifestyle she'd started in her college years in Kyoto, working multiple jobs, studying English, sleeping on occasion. She organized a homestay with a family just outside Sydney, and even when she moved out a few months later, they continued to invite her to barbecues and family events, where she practiced English, watched rugby, and slowly became acquainted with the family's twenty-five-year-old son.

Ben Flatt grew up in Sofala, a gold-mining town two hundred kilometers northwest of Sydney. Ben's first job was cooking at his parents' restaurant, a French-Italian café with a blackboard menu where most of the ingredients came from the family's backyard. He learned from an early age never to name the animals, because one day his mom or dad would ask him to step out back and take its life. His dad was an eccentric type—he would go on to a career as a writer under the pen name Captain Chaos—but his parents were good cooks and hard workers, and Ben picked up the passion at an early age. His parents eventually sold their restaurant, and Ben took off for Sydney to pursue his own culinary career. He spent the next few years cooking at trattoria around the city, slowly falling in love with rustic Italian food.

Pasta wasn't his only muse at the time, though. He and Chikako started dating a few months after she arrived in Australia, spending what little free time both of them had with each other. When her year was up, Chikako made good on her promise to her parents and prepared to return to Noto. She felt strongly for Ben, but she also knew that she couldn't back away from her duty to the family. When Ben said he would go with her, she hesitated. "I don't think you understand the world I'm going back to."

Ben wasn't fazed. He had traveled and worked around Asia, lived on his own for years, and in his own way was every bit as independent and determined as the woman he was pursuing. Shortly after Chikako left, he packed up his life in Australia and set coordinates for Noto, arriving on the doorstep of her parents' inn with most of his life in tow. Toshihiro and Tomiko liked the young man from Australia, but were surprised to find out that he was dating their daughter. A few weeks after arriving, with Chikako translating for him, Ben asked Toshihiro for his daughter's hand in marriage. Dad said no: Ben was not Japanese, was not from Noto, and couldn't possibly understand the life that Chikako had in front of her. Chikako was inheriting not just an inn but an entire life circumscribed by the rhythms and rituals of a land Ben knew nothing about. It would be too hard for everyone, he said.

But Ben was undeterred. He told Chikako and her parents that he could live anywhere, that he wasn't afraid of Japan or Noto or the culture the rest of the family was working to preserve. To prove it, he stayed. He studied Japanese and helped around the inn, especially in the kitchen. Three months after Ben arrived, Toshihiro presented him with a Japanese chef's knife, a peace offering in a struggle he knew he couldn't win.

A few months later Chikako and Ben were married in Kenroken in Kanazawa, one of Japan's most beautiful gardens. The reception was held in the old shogun's summer residence, with a menu handwritten by Chikako. Japanese tradition has it that the bride shouldn't be seen laughing or drinking or generally enjoying herself on her wedding day, but a photo from the afternoon shows Toshihiro pouring Chikako a glass of sake, the bride smiling widely.

米 麺 魚

Flatt's Inn sits on a bluff in Noto-cho overlooking an inlet on the Sea of Japan, a two-story home fronted by a dense forest and surrounded in the back by a large, active garden with yuzu and *sudachi* lime and persimmon trees, rows of leeks and cabbage, beans and daikon, and a large cherry tree that hangs over a tiny wooden bench, where, on a clear morning like the ones after it's been raining for a week and everything around Noto has that brave new sparkle, you can see across the channel to the outline of mountains that loom over Toyama.

You enter Flatt's through a corridor of stone steps and lush foliage. Inside, you'll find four traditional ten-tatami-sized rooms (the mats also serve as measurements) with squat rectangular tables, wooden-backed chairs that sit directly on the tatami, and no other decoration of note besides a dispenser for hot tea and cups for sipping. The restaurant, used by both guests and day visitors, has four tables that sit low to the ground, where diners eat on the floor; an *irori*, a charcoal fireplace used for cooking; long strings of produce—persimmons, radishes, chilies—in various stages of drying that dangle from the ceiling like garden necklaces; and large bay windows with generous views of the back-yard and the sea in the distance. There are two main baths at Flatt's, an outdoor wooden tub with a sprawling sea view and an indoor stone bath for when snow covers the ground and bathing outdoors is too difficult.

The *ryokan* stay is designed to be a fully immersive experience. Upon arrival, you trade your shoes and street clothes for slippers and a robe (called a *yukata*), your smartphone for a cup of sencha, your worries for a long, contemplative cleanse in the tub. Sip, soak, think, breathe: this is all that is required of you during your stay.

This being Japan, food is at the center of the *ryokan* experience. Dinner is normally an elaborate multicourse meal, often with a structure and progression borrowed from kaiseki. After strolling the gardens, after reading a chapter or two, after soaking your bones in simmering water, you sit down to a three-hour dinner heavy with signs of the season and tastes of the local terroir.

While you eat, someone is back in your room, silently laying out a thick base of comforters and blankets on the tatami, which will embrace your warm, distended body as soon as you finish chewing. You will sleep like the dead, and when you wake up, there will be another elaborate multicourse feast set for you in the dining area, waiting to push your appetite to the limit. By the time you check out, the worries of the world long since evaporated, you will exhale deeply and turn to your partner. "We should do this more often."

Flatt's Inn is like nearly every other traditional Japanese guesthouse you'll find in the rural corners of this country, except for one primary difference: the large Australian man with a bushy mustache working the stoves in the kitchen.

In many ways, Ben Flatt is the last person you would expect to fit into this world. He's twice the size of most of the customers he's serving, with the mouth of a marine and a tendency to wear his emotions like the kitchen scars that cover his arms. He plays the guitar, rides a motorcycle on his days off, starts his morning with Vegemite spread thick on toast. In Noto, where people from Tokyo or Kyoto can appear like foreign invaders, Ben might as well be from another galaxy.

For many years, Chikako and Ben ran Flatt's just down the road in the space once occupied by Sannami. Chikako's parents were still working full-time back then, but in 1996 they built a new home for the inn, in the same lovely garden space where Flatt's is now. After getting married, Ben and Chikako didn't want to wait for her parents to retire before starting their own place, especially when it looked like Toshihiro and Tomiko could go on forever, so in 1997 they took over the old four-room *ryokan* and began to assert their own vision on the business. The food incorporated the flavors and ingredients of Noto, the same ones Chikako's parents were working so hard to produce, but through the filter of Ben's Italian cooking. Soon enough,

both inns had obtained a measure of recognition for their respective cuisines. People would come for a weekend, stay one night at Sannami and one night at Flatt's, tasting the same ingredients in two very different expressions.

Toshihiro and Tomiko finally retired in 2011, and Ben and Chikako moved Flatt's up the road to the former Sannami space—inheriting its active gardens, its dozens of fruit trees, and its robust pickle shed. Chikako runs the front of the house with the help of a part-time assistant, while Ben helms the kitchen mostly on his own. For dinner, he serves dishes such as raw local fish accented with touches like fresh basil and balsamic vinegar; roasted pumpkin soup laced with *ishiri*; fat, chewy handmade spaghetti with tender rings of squid on a puddle of ink enhanced with another few drops of fish sauce. It's what Italian food would be if Italy were a windswept peninsula in the Far East.

If dinner is Ben's personal take on Noto ingredients, breakfast still belongs to his in-laws. It's an elaborate a.m. feast, fierce in flavor, rich in history, dense with centuries of knowledge passed from one generation to the next: soft tofu dressed with homemade soy and yuzu chili paste; soup made with homemade miso and simmered fish bones; shiso leaves fermented kimchi-style, with chilies and *ishiri*; *kaibe*, rice mixed with *ishiri* and fresh squid, pressed into patties and grilled slowly over a charcoal fire; yellowtail fermented for six months, called the blue cheese of the sea for its lactic funk. The mix of plates will change from one morning to the next but will invariably include a small chunk of *konka saba*, mackerel fermented for up to five years, depending on the day you visit. Even when it's broken into tiny pieces and sprinkled over rice, the years of fermentation will pulse through your body like an electric current.

In total, half a dozen different expressions of Noto fermentation, a breakfast that took more than a decade of molecular breakdown to bring to the table. And all of it virtually unchanged since the days when Chikako's parents ran the inn.

The first time I eat Flatt's breakfast, I feel like I went to bed in 2014 and woke up a few centuries earlier. The flavors are timeless, the textures all-encompassing, a meal so dense with umami and history that you wonder if your taste buds will ever recover. At first it feels like an act of aggression, like floating a stick of dynamite in your coffee, but the more I eat this meal, the more I realize that my concept of breakfast will never be the same.

To Chikako, breakfast at Flatt's is more than just a collection of taste and textures; it's the legacy she inherited from her mom and dad condensed into a single spread. This—the drizzle of homemade soy, the swipe of yuzu chili paste, the hunk of hyperfermented fish—is what her parents worked so hard to create, and it's what Chikako signed on for when she moved back to Noto and assumed the Funashita name. Ben can push the cuisine in new and interesting directions at night, so long as Chikako keeps the table filled with the fruits of fermentation in the morning.

This is no small responsibility. This isn't like inheriting your mom's cookie skills or carrying on your dad's reputation at the grill. To make Noto cuisine is an act of patience and sacrifice, one that forgoes the ease of modern conveniences like supermarkets and industrial ingredients for a deeper commitment to land and legacy. It means adapting your life to fit the fickle behavior of the seasons. It means understanding tidal rhythms and weather patterns by how they translate to the table. It means *mottainai*, "nothing goes to waste," a philosophy that resonates through every facet of Japanese food culture. It's an ethos born not simply out of necessity or industriousness but out of the Shinto belief that objects have souls and should be honored accordingly.

To understand how seriously the peo-ple of Noto take the concept of waste, consider the fugu dilemma. Japanese blowfish, best known for its high toxicity, has been a staple of Noto cuisine for hundreds of years. During the late Meiji and early Edo periods, local cooks in Noto began to address a growing concern with fugu fabrication; namely, how to make use of the fish's deadly ovaries. Pregnant with enough poison to kill up to twenty people, the ovaries—like the toxic liver—had always been disposed of, but the cooks of Noto finally had enough of the waste and set out to crack the code of the toxic reproductive organs. Thus ensued a long, perilous period of experimentation. Locals rubbed ovaries in salt, then in *nukamiso*, a paste made from rice bran, and left them to ferment. Taste-testing the not-quite-detoxified fugu ovary was a lethal but necessary part of the process, and many years and many lives later, they arrived at a recipe that transformed the ovaries from a deadly disposable into an intensely flavored staple. Today pickled

The star of the breakfast table: a piece of
mackerel fermented for four years

fugu ovaries remain one of Noto's most treasured delicacies.

Chikako doesn't pickle fugu ovaries at Flatt's—one of the few ingredients spared fermentation at the inn—but to dedicate yourself to Noto cuisine is to see every ingredient through the same prism: how to extract every last bit of life from what nature provides.

Once you accept *mottainai* as a starting point, your life must be organized accordingly. Those persimmons don't stop ripening just because you wanted to go to Kanazawa today; that fish won't dry properly unless you gut it and salt it before the sun goes down. Chikako never stops moving, her day like a seamless sixteen-hour tutorial on how to carry the traditions of Noto forward: serve breakfast, scale some tiny fish, talk with guests, peel and juice a hundred mandarins, draw a bath, fill a bucket with plums and purple shiso leaves.

"In twenty-seven years, my parents never took a day off," says Chikako. "My dad would say, 'Day off? What would I do with a day off? You can't take a day off from your life.'"

More than just hard work and organization, these practices require an immense body of knowledge. Which mushrooms are safe for pickling and which will kill you? Is this type of fish best preserved in rice bran or in salt? What can I do with this tiny piece of the fruit that always ends up in the compost pile?

"The other day my mom got really upset that I was throwing away the stems on the persimmons we pick," Chikako tells me one morning. "We pickle the peels, we dry the flesh of the fruit, but apparently the stems can be used to make tea."

Persimmon-stem tea isn't a recipe you'll find online; it's not an idea you'd stumble onto when you buy a bag of persimmons at the store. It strikes you only after enough dirt has found its way under your fingernails.

Chikako and Ben's lives are inexorably linked to an ever-expanding list of seasonal tasks. In summer, they work through the garden bounty, drying and pickling the fruits and vegetables at peak ripeness. Fall brings chestnuts to pick, chili paste to make, mushrooms to hunt. Come winter, Noto's seas are flush with the finest sea creatures, which means pickling fish for *hinezushi* and salting squid guts for *ishiri*. In the spring, after picking mountain vegetables and harvesting seaweed, they plant the garden and begin again the cycle that will feed them, their family, and their guests in the year ahead.

When things go well in the wild, Noto tradition has it that you should share with your neighbors. If generous rain brings you a bumper crop of mandarins, you give the families living around you a surprise taste of the season. In turn, when their cherry trees explode or their sweet potatoes sprout, they'll return the favor. It's a carryover from the barter economy that existed on this peninsula for most of its history, well into the twentieth century. In a country known best for its overwhelming urban sprawl, these flashes of rural ritual take on a very special importance.

"We might not wear kimonos every day," says Chikako (who just so happens to be trained in the intricate art of kimono dress), "but it's amazing the traditional way still survives."

One morning, after days of politely ignoring my request, Chikako takes me down to the *shokeba*. This is the most important room in the house, the nerve center of Noto cuisine, and I've been eager to take it all in. At first I think Chikako's hesitance is because the room might be messy, or because she fears I might try to reveal the family recipes, but the more time I spend in Noto and the more I speak with Chikako and Ben, the more I realize that to invite someone into your *shokeba* is like sitting them down with a family album—an intimate experience that requires a level of trust and familiarity.

The *shokeba* at Flatt's is housed in a basement below the kitchen. It looks exactly like you'd imagine a pickle shed to look: dark, crowded, shelves and cement floor cluttered with plastic bottles, glass jars, large yellow buckets with contents unknown. In total Chikako and Ben have nearly two hundred different projects in the works down here, a motley collection of floating fruit, shrinking vegetables, and degrading protein. There are vinegars made from persimmon and plum, kimchi made with cabbage and daikon, liquors infused with anything that grows: yuzu, quince, grape, wild strawberry.

Like a bodega, the pickle shed is filled with living, evolving products that capture a particular moment in time: the great rains of '88, the dry spell of '91, the near-perfection of 2002. The beauty of the *shokeba* is that right now, at this very moment, it all tastes incrementally different from how it tasted yesterday and how it will taste tomorrow. Today is today, and no other day will ever be the same.

Chikako opens a few buckets to show me what she has working. In one, she grabs a fistful of tiny plums stained half purple with shiso leaves, *umeboshi* midway through its cure. Another contains soybeans well on their way to becoming miso.

The room is thick with the smell of transformation, a powerful stench that recalls a dark corner of an old library, emanating a mysterious and meaningful musk. Chikako squats down and lifts the lid on a short, wide yellow trash can, and the room explodes with another dimension of funk. "This is our *konka saba*," she says, wiping off a muddy layer of rice husk. Below is buried a heap of mackerel rubbed in salt and chilies. "Some people bring it up after half a year, which isn't even fermented. These here have been fermenting for nearly fifteen years." I try to do the math but can come up only with this: when the fish went into this bucket, the world was a very different place.

米　麵　魚

Wednesday is the traditional day of rest in Japan's service industry, and

Flatt's closes accordingly. But little rest ever goes down around this inn; Ben and Chikako use the time mostly to catch up on the various projects they have in the works.

One Wednesday morning, Ben wakes me up at dawn, and we head to the Suzu fish market, where the local fish auction takes place every day at 7:00 a.m. As the first rays of sun bounce off the sea and fill the market with a warm, speckled light, a mix of chefs, distributors, and fishermen survey the day's catch: buckets of tiny baitfish, giant squid oozing puddles of black ink below them, cod pregnant with the season's first roe ("Those will go for a lot today—the Japanese are willing to pay for the first taste of just about anything"). On the edge of the market, a shark, two meters long with a swollen belly streaked with blood, attracts a small group of fishermen who smoke cigarettes and ponder its demise.

Buri, Japanese yellowtail rich with fat stored to combat the cold winter waters, have just come in, and most of the morning's energy hovers around the three hundred midsize fish lined up on the wet cement floor. The auctioneer, an old man with a walking stick he uses as a pointer, works his way quickly through the catch, balancing himself on the edges of the plastic boxes that hold the fish. He's not as animated as the tuna auctioneers of Tokyo's Tsukiji market, but he doesn't need to be; everyone here knows exactly what they want and how much they're willing to pay for it. The actual bidding comes out in thick Noto dialect, thickened further by the fact that these are fishermen—a lifetime at sea turning their tongues into mysterious instruments. Within fifteen minutes, it's over, and Ben has a bucket of sardines to add to the day's chores.

Another morning, we drive over to a grassy riverbank down the road from the inn to look for mountain vegetables, a rite of passage to the Japanese spring. "People take this shit seriously," says Ben, explaining how different families

"TO MAKE NOTO CUISINE IS AN ACT OF PATIENCE AND SACRIFICE."

work different tracts of land, which are closely guarded and kept within the family for generations. We return to the kitchen with three plastic bags full of long-stemmed fiddlehead ferns. Some will go in a pasta dish later tonight for dinner service but most will be preserved in *ishiri*, and served as breakfast pickles later in the year, when spring is only a distant memory.

To watch Ben navigate the thickets of Noto's physical and social landscape, I can think only of all the acrobatics he's performed over the years to get a foothold on this culture. Even today, two decades later, he remains a perplexing character for certain locals. "I'll be in the supermarket and people will come up to me and literally go through my basket and ask me what I'm planning to do with certain ingredients."

It's tough for a foreigner to penetrate any area of Japanese culture, but to come to Noto, try to marry a local woman, be denied by her parents, marry her anyway, and then proceed to dedicate your life to

the daily preservation of her culture—one so dense and pregnant with mystery and vagaries that it's widely unknown to the citizens of Noto themselves—to do that takes a strong mind, an iron will, and rock-hard stones in equal measure. But Ben sees it differently. "It's been incredibly humbling to learn from this family. To be in the same kitchen, to understand the mentality," he says. "It's more than just a lifestyle; it's our life."

No small part of that life means picking fruits and vegetables at just the right moment. When the yuzu are so swollen with juice that they begin to drop from the tree, Ben and I head out with a ladder and trash bags, wrapped in a swaddling layer of puffy pants and jackets and thick gloves to protect us from the bastard spikes of the yuzu tree. The harvest isn't quite what Ben expected this season, and he knows his father-in-law will have a few words of pointed advice for him when he finds out.

Life after death for a yuzu is an arduous journey toward reincarnation. At

Flatt's, the juice is preserved with salt and kept throughout the year for vinaigrettes and sauces. The pith becomes marmalade. Even the seeds are salvaged, slowly dried, then mixed with shochu to use as a natural moisturizer.

The star of the yuzu anatomy, though, is the peel, which Ben and Chikako combine with dried chilies and salt and lacto-ferment for two years. The mass is then pureed into *yunamba*, a powerful combination of umami, heat, and a bright citrus uppercut—the kind of insane condiment that, once you taste it, you wonder if you'll ever be able to live without it. The bright red paste finds its way onto tofu at breakfast and sashimi at dinner and into my suitcase to hold me over between trips to Japan.

All told, four products created over the course of two years, a seed-to-skin transformation that yields vital components of the Flatt's pantry. *Mottainai, mottainai.*

When there are no fruit to pick, no vegetables to forage, no fish to gut,

we load into the Flatts' van and stake out around the peninsula. Even then, fermentation follows us everywhere around Noto. One day we visit the salt flats of Okunoto on the northwest coast of Noto, the longest-running producer on a peninsula long dependent on salt to fuel fermentation. Hiroshi Kikutaro, a sixth-generation salt farmer, still starts with seawater and cooks it down in large wooden buckets. It takes him a week of shoveling and boiling in a small hut where temperatures hover around 130°F to make a single batch of salt.

At a market in Wajima, a town on the west coast of the peninsula best known for production of some of Japan's shiniest lacquerware, we run into an autumn food festival. Two men in karate outfits with bandannas tied around their heads trade off pounding cooked rice with a massive wooden mallet, working the grain into a fine warm paste that they stuff with sweetened adzuki beans to form mochi, one of Japan's favorite festival foods (every year about a dozen people die from choking on warm mochi, but the Japanese chew on, undeterred). A food market displays the best of Noto's fermentation muscle, from smoked and sun-dried clams to squid tossed with fermented rice and yuzu peel to those harbingers of a deadly serious food culture, pickled fugu ovaries.

Another day, we travel to Nanao at the base of the peninsula for a beautiful sushi lunch at Kozushi, Ben and Chikako's favorite place to eat on their day off. Walking the street after the feast, we come upon a soy sauce shop in an old merchant home. When we walk in, the smell hits us, and we realize the shop isn't just a shop, but the factory as well. The owner takes us to the back, shows us the soybeans, which have been slowly fermenting in massive wooden barrels since the end of the Meiji period. We all agree that the resulting potion, more sweet and savory than salty, is among the best we've tasted. Chikako buys three liters to take back to the inn.

Closer to home, just a few miles from Flatt's, we find Japan's arguably most important form of fermentation at work: sake. The rice wine production at Tanizumi Sake remains a steadfastly analog operation, best suited to Midori Tsuruno, its sixty-two-year-old owner.

"Even if I make a seven-hundred-kilogram batch, I wash the rice ten kilograms at a time," she says, showing us the washbasin where the sake process begins.

She still uses old wooden buckets for steaming the rice, leaving the steel tanks she bought years ago in a moment of weakness to idle in the corner. "I don't get consistent results with the metal."

After the rice steams for fifty minutes, it is spread on tables and left to sit for two or three days, which allows for the formation of *koji* bacteria, the invisible hand behind so many of Japan's most important fermented goods: soy sauce, miso, shochu.

The rice is then moved upstairs to the attic for two weeks, where more stable

Chikako and Ben in the kitchen at Flatt's Inn

and better bacteria will allow for even fermentation. Eventually the cooked rice is combined with water and more *koji*, stored in a bag, and the whole package is placed in a press and squeezed. It rests overnight before undergoing another squeezing. The resulting liquid, fermented for anywhere from twenty-five to forty days, is one of the world's oldest and greatest alcoholic beverages.

"I don't like to filter my sake. It takes away the umami flavor." No doubt: a glass of her milky white potion has just an edge of floral sweetness, with an intense savory kick that leaves your mouth watering. "I'm a small producer, I don't need my sake to always taste the same. I want you to taste the difference from one year to the next."

One night, with no customers booked for lunch the following day, Ben and Chikako take me to Buranka's, a bar dense with cigarette smoke and karaoke tunes and whisky-soaked barflies. Mama runs the bar on her own, pouring drinks, lighting cigarettes, warming up planks of dried squid over little electric grills that she passes across the bar to her regulars. She has a Marlboro voice box, thick and raspy, but when she takes a break to bless the microphone, everything sounds like sunshine.

Japanese karaoke isn't the twisted spectacle you find in bars in the West. You don't get drunk sorority girls belting out Madonna wildly out of key or packs of Jäger-charged bros imploring you to *don't stop believing*. Instead, participants, mostly older men and women, wait patiently to sing any number of long, crooning ballads with intensity and purpose.

Ben, still an Aussie at heart, tries to open things up with a stirring rendition of "Bohemian Rhapsody," but the locals are unmoved. (They are even less moved by my bare-all version of "La Bamba.") When Chikako's turn comes up, she chooses a long, slow, moody Japanese song—the type that comes accompanied by a video of two lovers walking over bridges and canoodling on park benches.

She starts slowly but warms up after the first verse, hits the choruses with grace and beauty, and by time the song comes to its dramatic close, the entire bar is staring at her. Though I've understood none of it, I find myself blinking back tears in the thick, squid-scented air of the Noto watering hole.

米　麵　魚

"Excuse me, I must go check on my orange peels, they've been in the oven too long," says Chikako's mother. We watch as she disappears off the screen. She keeps talking off camera—something about dehydrating techniques that we can't quite make out—and a few minutes later she comes back with a glass jar and a beaming smile. "Would you like to see my marmalade?"

Chikako and Tomiko talk on Skype at least once a week. "I'll call her on the phone with a question and she'll say, 'Let's get on Skype!' And we'll be there until midnight in the kitchen talking until I tell her I have to go." These conversations typically take place in the kitchen, often with both women in the midst of a seasonal project. Chikako sets her iPad up on the counter, and the two go to work.

As they talk today, Chikako cleans her way through a bucket of *haka haka*, tiny silver fish Ben brought back from the morning market, removing the heads and guts from a thousand little fish in preparation for another long ferment. They talk about life, about Tomo and Emily, Ben and Chikako's kids, but mostly they talk about food—the new experiments, the bottles in the basement, the tiny pieces that hold this whole world together.

You won't find many women in the professional kitchens of Japan. The traditional structure for a family-owned restaurant involves the father running the kitchen, the mother controlling service, and son and daughter—if involved—divided along the same lines. Deep-rooted domestic roles and the odd backward belief arguably make the gender division here worse than you'd find

The entrance to Flatt's Inn

in other parts of the world; some be-lieve, for instance, that women shouldn't make sushi because fluctuations in their body temperature would compromise the fish. There are, of course, women working hard to dissolve these divisions in restaurant kitchens across the coun-try, but it's mostly men you find slicing fugu, boiling soba, battering vegetables, and working the grills, griddles, and stovetops of Japan.

But behind closed doors, women are the ones who feed this country. More than domestic cooks, they are the guard-ians of secrets, keepers of the culinary flame, the ones who work silently to safeguard Japan's remarkable food cul-ture. At the heart of this preservation is the mother-daughter relationship.

When Chikako tells me her first batch of marmalade was a mess, her mother is quick to explain why. "That's because you didn't use enough pectin," says Tomiko.

"She's right, so I turned it into miso instead."

Mom is never far away. Tomiko and Toshihiro still spend plenty of time at their old inn, and when they come, Chikako and Ben know that their prog-ress will be tested. Mom and Dad lift the lids, probe the fish, squeeze the dai-kon, smell the *ishiri*, test the vinegar, taste the *yunamba*, inspect the garden. "It's intense. They run us ragged," says Chikako. They always find problems—room for improvement, let's say—and they try their best to provide guidance without outstaying their welcome.

Tomiko and Toshihiro are quick to point out how grateful they are that Chikako and Ben have made every ef-fort to keep their vision alive. Beyond the bounty in the basement, they orga-nize springtime picnics and an annual autumn beer garden, they gather with other local inn owners to trade recipes and industry tales, they help govern-ment officials promote the area. This is a fragile moment for the cuisine of Noto, and the couple does everything they can to share a way of life with people who may not have benefited from parents as exacting as Tomiko and Toshihiro.

Running the business and helping in the community would be more than enough for even a highly functioning couple to handle alone, but the real work takes place outside, around the garden, on the docks, in the forest—all around them. There are ferns growing down by the river: they must be picked. Seaweed has started to wash up along the shore below the bluff: time to lay it out for drying. Mushrooms cling to logs, begging to be plucked and dried: it's time. The squid needs salting, the fruit needs fermenting. The moment is now.

There is a subtle sense of urgency to these tasks, because when Mom passes, so too does the great store of knowledge she has accumulated over the years. There is no book, no repository of culinary know-how; no recipe would ever suffice. There are only the seasons, and those who have lived through them.

"We don't have that much outside exposure in Noto," says Tomiko. "You learn about food from your mom, and if Mom's not a good cook, you probably won't be either."

"My father knew that the flavors that he was tasting weren't the same as the childhood flavors," says Chikako, "and he wanted to return to those."

"We didn't want to lose those old flavors," says Tomiko. "We never went to the store. We weren't just making dashi, we were making the ingredients for dashi. We dried the kombu, we made the *katsuobushi* ourselves."

"For my mom and my grandma, it was never about saving certain techniques, it was just what they did," Chikako says. "But now we really are losing these traditions. To keep it alive means producing it yourself."

"Nature is very generous here, so there is much to do," says Tomiko. "But only people who know about this through experience know what to do with these products."

"You have to work so hard these days to get the perfect ingredients," says Chikako, nearing the end of her pile of fish. "You have to grow everything yourself, pick everything yourself."

"Noto food is the perfect cipher," says Tomiko, "because it can only exist in Noto."

"I'll stand right next to my mom in the kitchen and make the same recipe with the same ingredients using the same technique, and mine will turn out different every time."

"It's a training with your body," says Tomiko. "It's like a sushi chef, it's an exact routine that your body just knows. An instinct more than something you can explain."

"There is knowledge I just don't have," says daughter, down to her last few fish, her cutting board dark with blood and guts. "I know less than half. I know that much."

"There's a season cycle," says mother, "and Chikako is following the season cycle, and the more she knows, the more she will need to learn each season."

"I don't know enough about picking mushrooms," says daughter. "I don't know wild game."

"You must be patient," says mother.

"I should know more about mountain vegetables," says daughter.

"I never learned the mountain pig," says mother. "That is one of my regrets."

"I don't know what I don't know," says daughter, her hands purple with the fish departed. "That's what bothers me most."

"You're doing it right," says mother. "You're almost there. Almost."

One Night with the
GEISHA

PREPARE FOR THE NIGHT

While you warm up with dinner and drinks, geisha undergo a thorough transformation.

EAT UP

Snacks are there for a reason: to build a base for the rivers of sake to follow.

8pm 9pm 10pm

HONOR YOUR HOST

Taro Nakamura is a ninth-generation sake maker with a long history with this geisha house.

KNOW YOUR HISTORY

After Kyoto, Kanazawa has Japan's largest geisha district. These teahouses date back to the seventeenth century.

STUMBLE ON

The geisha decide when the night is over. No touching, no funny stuff, not ever. Be happy to be one of the few gaijin to enter this house.

ENJOY THE SHOW

Geisha are the ultimate entertainers: dancers, singers, musicians, and world-class conversationalists. Soak it up.

11pm   12am   1am

KEEP IT FLOWING

Nakamura sake is some of Japan's finest *nihonshu*, and geisha pour as fast as you can drink. *Kanpai!*

SHARPEN YOUR SKILLS

Drinking games push the night to the brink. Stay focused, but know that the ladies rarely lose.

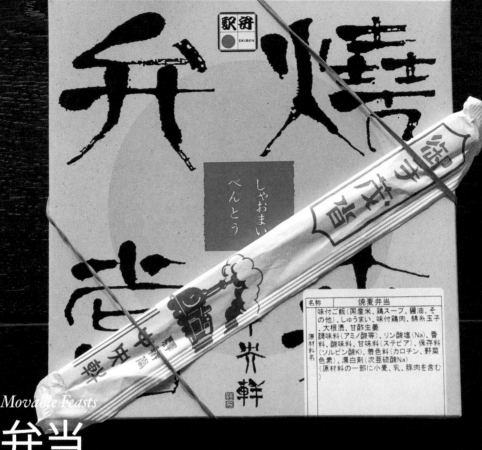

Movable Feasts

弁当

THE BEAUTY
OF BENTO

Japan is a country made for train travel. It's not just the sleek Shinkansen that snake silently through the countryside; it's an entire culture of train cuisine developed around Japan's preferred method of transportation. That means cold beer, hot tea, salty snacks, and a steady supply of *ekiben*, first-class bento boxes based on regional specialties and sold exclusively in train stations.

The first *ekiben* was created in 1885. Since then, more than two thousand local bento have been developed, mostly by small, family-run operations, giving you a chance to taste a town—the grilled beef tongue of Sendai! the buckwheat buns of Nagano!— without ever leaving the train platform. Of course, your goal should be to hunt down the *ekiben* at their source, but if you need to cheat, you can head to Matsuri in Tokyo Station, which offers 170 *ekiben* from around the country.

After ten thousand kilometers and over a hundred train meals, these *ekiben* have emerged as the finest movable feasts in Japan.

UNI, IKURA, TAMAGO
Hakodate Station

The best eggs in Hokkaido combined in one beautiful bowl: creamy curls of sea urchin, briny orbs of salmon roe, and soft, sweet deposits of chicken eggs, with the vinegar twang of pickled vegetables to tie it all together. Best when washed down with one of Hokkaido's many microbrews.

TOHGE-NO-KANEMESHI
Yokokawa Station

A treasure trove stuffed full of Yokokawa's most famous flavors: tender soy-marinated chicken thigh, fat caps of shiitake, bamboo shoots, sweet chestnut, and a single boiled quail's egg. All served in *mashiko ware*, a clay pot perfect to take home.

...A MESHI
...tion

...the most famous of the hundreds of chicken-based *ekiben*—for a reason.
...ived marinated chicken, the shreds of fried egg, and the rice cooked in a
...cken stock hit all the right notes: sweet, savory, umami-rich, and perfectly
...e. (The side of juicy shumai dumplings doesn't hurt, either.)

MASU-NO SUSHI
Toyama Station

A peerless example of Japanese pressed sushi: thin slices of rosy river trout spackled with a thin layer of Kewpie mayo and draped over a flotilla of pressed rice like a savory cake for adults. Unchanged since 1912 and so good that Japanese go to great lengths to buy it and bring it to friends and family around the country

ANAGO MESHI
Miyajima Station

One of the oldest and greatest *ekiben* in all of Japan. The same family has been making this beauty since 1901, roasting the saltwater eel over charcoal, glazing the meat with soy, simmering the rice in eel stock. It's best in the restaurant when the eel comes directly off the grill, but the *ekiben* (also available in Hiroshima Station) makes for all-world road food.

ACKNOWLEDGMENTS

It takes a village to publish a book, but it takes a nation to publish one about Japan—at least it does when you are as clueless as I was when I first touched down in Tokyo years ago. My primary debt is to the people of Japan, whose extraordinary generosity turned an incomprehensible country into a place of abiding beauty.

This book would not be possible without the help of the following people, in particular:

Ioanna Morelli showed incredible grace and skill in being my interpreter—of language, culture, behavior, everything—through most of the book's research. I owe much of what I know and love about this country to her; her husband, Hisashi; and their friends.

Ken Yokoyama, a *shokunin* in the art of hospitality, performed minor miracles to help me better understand and appreciate Kyoto. He did so with the selflessness and precision that represents the very best of his country and his people.

I spent many an Osaka night in the expert hands of Yuko Suzuki, eating and drinking and learning things that would be inconceivable without her generous gift of time, talent, and spirit.

Hisaichiro Yanagihara (a wise and generous master of the food scene in Fukuoka).

Robbie Swinnerton should have laughed me out of his adopted country when I first told him about the idea for this book. Instead, he selflessly shared the expertise that makes him one of the great translators of Japanese culinary culture for the English-speaking world.

And the dozens of people who welcomed me into their restaurants, homes, inns, and lives: the Matsuno family of Arashiyama, Ben and Chikako Flatt, Fernando and Makiko Lopez, Kamimura Toshiyuki, Robert Yellin, Yoshiteru Ikegawa, Shinji Nohara, Brian MacDuckston, Gen Yamamoto, Nick Szasz and the ace staff of Fukuoka Now, Eric Eto, Sojiki Nakahigashi, Toshiro Ogata, Mick Nippard, Sanada Kodai, Sander Jackson Siswojo, and Miriam Goldberg.

Special thanks to Lauren Scharf and the Art of Travel crew in Kanazawa for showing me that Ishikawa Prefecture is deserving of a book itself. And to the fine folks at the JNTO offices in New York and Tokyo for supporting this project back when it was nothing more than a naive idea.

Closer to home, I owe pretty much everything I write to Nathan Thornburgh, my partner at Roads & Kingdoms, who has been the creative force behind this project since its genesis. You are the finest editor I know, and yet, somehow, an even better friend and collaborator.

Douglas Hughmanick, an alchemist of the highest order, could turn a few scribbles and a stack of Polaroids into a work of art. You've once again broken new ground with the design of this book. Thanks for always making us look good.

A huge thanks to Michael Magers, an endless source of positive energy, photographic excellence, and *conbini* love: your images say all the things that my words can't.

Tony Bourdain blew the doors off the food-writing world many years ago and continues to expand its boundaries to parts unknown. Anyone who writes about food and travel is in your debt—me more than anyone. Thanks for believing in Roads & Kingdoms and everything that we do.

Kim Witherspoon knows how to navigate the turbulent waters of the New York publishing world with preternatural ease and precision. Thanks for steering this ship safely into port.

To Karen Rinaldi, for believing that there was life after *Eat This, Not That!*, and for providing all the support and creative freedom to bring it to fruition. Her team at Harper Wave—including Hannah Robinson, Leah Carlson-Stanisic, and John Jusino—have helped us shape this book with incredible skill and patience.

And, above all, to my wife, Laura, my not-so-secret weapon, whose grace and beauty is the skeleton key to a world of closed doors.

PHOTO CREDITS

Matt Goulding is a cofounder of Roads & Kingdoms and the coauthor of the *New York Times* bestselling series *Eat This, Not That!*, a series with more than 10 million books in print. He divides his time between the tapas bars of Barcelona and the barbecue joints of North Carolina.

Nathan Thornburgh is a cofounder of Roads & Kingdoms, where he puts all his previous careers—as a musician, a foreign correspondent for *Time* magazine, and an accomplished drinker—to good daily use.

Douglas Hughmanick is the head of the Roads & Kingdoms design department. He also founded and operates ANML, a digital design studio in the San Francisco Bay Area.

Roads & Kingdoms is a digital media company at the intersection of food, travel, politics, and culture. Its partners have included Tumblr, *Sports Illustrated*, *Time*, and the voracious curiosity of Anthony Bourdain. Check out more of our work at roadsandkingdoms.com.

NOW THAT YOU HAVE THE INSPIRATION, GET THE INFORMATION.

Find intel on the best places to eat, drink, and sleep across the seven regions covered in this book, all available in the palm of your hand. For more information, go to roadsandkingdoms.com/japan.

R&K

THE KNOWLEDGE
Where to eat, drink and sleep in Tokyo

1   Butagumi

2   Cerulean Tower Tokyu Hotel

3   Rokurinsha Tokyo Tokyo Ramen Street

4   Gen Yamamoto

5   Tori-Shiki

6   Golden Gai

7   Cafe de L'Ambre

8   Ippudo Ebisu

9   Omotesando Koffee

TORI-SHIKI

Tokyo's most elegant yaktori restaurant, where a 20-course tasting menu will have you rethinking your entire notion of chicken."

2-14-12 Kamiosaki, Shinagawa, Tokyo 141-0021, Japan

4.1 ★★★★★